THE NOVELS OF FIELDING

HENRY FIELDING.

THE NOVELS
OF
FIELDING

BY

AURELIEN DIGEON

NEW YORK
RUSSELL & RUSSELL · INC
1962

FIRST PUBLISHED IN 1925
REISSUED, 1962, BT RUSSELL & RUSSELL, INC.
L. C. CATALOG CARD NO: 62—20320

PRINTED IN THE UNITED STATES OF AMERICA

TO THE MEMORY
OF MY FATHER AND MOTHER

FOREWORD TO THE ENGLISH EDITION

ONE of Fielding's most striking qualities is the thorough " Englishness " of his humour and characters. Dickens alone can compare to him in this. Yet although one cannot say that he is neglected by English readers to-day, he does not seem to enjoy his full share of glory. I should like to think that my little study might persuade a few more of his countrymen to turn again to one of the greatest writers ever produced by their race.

The title of my book defines its character and limits.

It is possible to treat Fielding's novels as a separate whole. They are complete in themselves and distinct from the rest of his work ; it is in them, and not in his other works, that we find the immortal Fielding. His comedies, polemical tracts, translations and journals were seldom anything more to him than " pot-boilers ". He produced them just as César Franck gave music lessons, to earn a living. His novels, on the contrary, were written for eternity.

As my desire was to study the novels alone, I have been led to give only a brief account of what I may call Fielding's daily life. This does not, however, imply that I could dispense with a knowledge of it. I had, on the contrary, examined it as minutely as possible, for my own sake, at a time when the books of Austin Dobson and Miss Godden were the only modern works on the subject. During the course of this preparation, I even made several of those small discoveries which are so comforting to a scholar. The war supervened and I was kept from my task for so long that, in 1918, Mr Cross was able to make public a number of the little discoveries which I had hoped to reveal in 1916. He said much else that was useful, and I gladly acknowledge the debt of gratitude which I owe him for the valuable help which I have derived from his book.

Yet even after Mr Cross's three compact and well-documented volumes, I have no hesitation in publishing my book, because it is of a different order. While Mr Cross has written a detailed biography, I have only taken from Fielding's life those details which would help my readers to understand the development of his literary genius.

While setting biographical anecdote aside I have also tried to prevent my study from drifting into pure history. One cannot, of course, speak of Fielding without having studied the type of novel which preceded and followed his ; one cannot, in particular, speak of his *Jonathan Wild* without being familiar with the genesis of the Picaresque novel. After having worked on these lines for one's own personal benefit, the temptation is strong to impart one's knowledge to others. I have nevertheless deemed it necessary to restrain myself from such erudite idling.

It seemed to me that I should be doing a greater service to those who are interested in such matters, by tracing my own furrow as deep as I could, without any deviation into other paths. I hope that I have omitted nothing which has materially contributed to the formation of Fielding's personality as a novelist. All that has no direct bearing on the subject has been voluntarily excluded.

FOREWORD

Finally, I should be wanting in gratitude should I fail to express my thanks to my masters, Professors Legouis and Cazamian, whose example, encouragement and advice have been invaluable in helping me to carry out my work. My thanks are also due to my translators, who have done a difficult task with the most faithful and intelligent attention. Nowhere have I found my intention betrayed or my meaning obscured in their version of my book

A. D.

Paris, June, 1924.

CONTENTS

xi

THE NOVELS OF FIELDING

CONTENTS

CONTENTS

The evolution of Fielding as it appears in his four novels ; transition from reason to sentiment ; Fielding as representative of his age and nation ; England's transition from reason to sentiment ; growth of sentimentality in the middle of the century, in politics, religion, morality ; and literature ; Fielding and the novel ; the prose epic ; the building up of the plot ; Fielding's sources ; his selection ; and themes ; his psychological realism ; the spirit of comedy ; relationship of Fielding and Molière ; impression left by Fielding on the English novel ; his tone impressed upon it.

THE NOVELS OF FIELDING

CHAPTER I

BRIEF ACCOUNT OF FIELDING'S LIFE

> " But I must submit to bear that character
> which my worthy contemporaries have been
> pleased to give me ; and indeed if those who
> know me only by their writings, have not a bad
> opinion of my morals, they must be strangely
> incredulous or extremely candid."
>
> (H. Fielding, *The Covent Garden Journal*, November 25th, 1752)

Henry Fielding[1] was born on April 22nd, 1707. His father, Edmund Fielding, was the son of an archdeacon of Dorset and had, the year before, married possibly after an elopement Sarah Gould, the daughter of a magistrate. The actual birthplace of the child has never been definitely determined. It may have been Sharpham Park, near Glastonbury, the residence of the Gould family, or more doubtfully, as tradition has it, Capel Street, Dublin, where, about this time,

---

[1] The principal source of Fielding's biography is Murphy's introduction to the edition of his works which appeared in 1763. It was, however, full of errors. Hardly any of Fielding's letters are extant. His correspondence was doubtless destroyed with the papers of his half-brother, John Fielding, during the Gordon Riots of 1780. (cf. Paul de Castro, in *Notes and Queries*, September 12th, 1914). In writing Fielding's biography it is extremely difficult to rid one's mind of the numerous legends which have gathered round his name or which were spread abroad by his enemies. The great critical survey by Dobson, which appeared in 1883, was the first biography worthy of the name. Dobson has since then published many excellent articles on the subject. Miss Godden, in her book published in 1910, brought to light many new facts, connected in particular with Fielding's childhood and life as a magistrate. For fifteen years many research-workers have been

the major must have been stationed with his regiment [1].

Fielding was, therefore, of good family on both sides. The Fieldings were closely related to the Earls of Denbigh, and a tradition, since disproved but not before it had given rise to one of Gibbon's famous epigrams, claimed that they traced their descent from the Hapsburgs [2].

Fielding's earliest childhood was passed in Sharpham Park and later in East Stour, a village in Dorset, where Colonel Edmund Fielding, who was placed on half-pay about 1710, had settled in order to try the life of a gentleman-farmer. He was not quite cut out for success in such a venture. Perhaps this soldier-farmer was too fond of London life, for Miss Godden has discovered that he once (in 1716) lost there £780 at faro.

Henry, the eldest of five children, was rather less than eleven years of age when his mother died in April, 1718. This was the beginning of a somewhat ugly family quarrel. The Colonel soon went away to London, leaving his children in the care of a sister of Lady Gould, his mother-in-law. After a year he married again and returned to East Stour with his second wife. She was said to be an Italian and a Roman Catholic, which would make her new family doubly suspicious of her. The result was a lengthy law-suit between Lady Gould and her son-in-law, each of whom claimed the custody of the

busy with the life of Fielding. We may make special mention of Messrs J. E. Wells and F. S. Dickson of U.S.A. ; and Mr Paul de Castro of England, whose discoveries have been exceptionally fortunate. In 1918, Mr W. L. Cross published a monumental biography of Fielding. My own research, conducted for ten years and interrupted by the War, has with two or three exceptions led me to form the same conclusions as he. His book is rich in well-established facts, and the only complaint I can make is that he too often takes the tone of a panegyrist.

[1] cf. Paul de Castro, *Notes and Queries*, November, 1917, p. 468.

[2] cf. J. H. Round, ' Our English Hapsburgs ' in *The Genealogis* 1894, New Series X, 193. The passage by Gibbon which Thackeray quotes in his *English Humourists*, ends with the following sentence : " The successors of Charles V may disdain their humble brethren of England, but the romance of *Tom Jones*, that exquisite picture of human manners, will outlive the palace of the Escurial, and the Imperial Eagle of the House of Austria."

children. The grandmother at last obtained permission to place the girls in a boarding-school at Salisbury, while Henry was sent to Eton in October, 1719. After a series of incidents, dilatory manoeuvres, and at least one attempt made by the Colonel to kidnap the children, the Lord High Chancellor s final decision, given on May 28th, 1722, granted Lady Gould the entire custody of her grandchildren and the administration of their mother's fortune and estate [1].

Edmund Fielding, whose new family increased rapidly, died a lieutenant general in 1741, having served brilliantly in the wars against France [2].

Several features of Fielding's earliest years must be noted at once. He was a ' gentleman ', the only boy and later the only man, among women who doubtless pampered and spoilt him. Painful disputes formed his youthful character very early, perhaps too early. At the age of twelve he already took part in the quarrel, and seems to have ranged himself on his grandmother's side. It may be that she incited him, or perhaps the little fellow rebelled on his own account against a papist step mother. Whatever the truth may be, the fact remains that in one of the documents included in the lawsuit, the Colonel complained that his children were badly brought up, " headstrong and undutiful ", particularly, added the governess, " the eldest son ", Henry. Nor did the matter rest there ; one fine day (April 7th, 1721) the fourteen year old boy ran away from Eton, took the road, and joined his grandmother in Salisbury. Whether she sent for him in order to prevent his being kidnapped or whether he went of his own accord, the escapade shows signs of a character which was already finely tempered, and a soul which feared no adventure.

Again, let us note here the country surroundings in which Fielding spent his early childhood ; he was steeped in them, and their influence is apparent throughout his work. He

[1] The history of this lawsuit was discovered and related in full by Miss Godden.

[2] One of the children of this second marriage, John, who was blind, became his half-brother Henry's constant companion.

3

will be more shocked than a town-bred man by the corruption of the big cities. His comparisons between town and country life will never be the mechanical repetitions of the commonplaces to be found in every Latin poet. Like Rousseau, he will always retain in the depths of his heart, a secret longing, a lingering nostalgia, and a prejudice for the village as the home of ' natural ' virtue.

Of the five or six years which he probably spent at Eton we know very little, except that Pitt and George Lyttleton were his school-fellows, and remained his friends and patrons in after life. He must have studied to some purpose, for his works show a profound knowledge of Latin poetry. He knew French very well, and Italian too if we may believe him. As for Greek :

Tuscan and French are in my head
Latin I write, and Greek I—read.

All his life he adored Lucian and made him his chief model.

There may be some doubt as to why he did not pursue the conventional course of going straight from Eton to the University. His most recent biographer, Mr Cross, thinks that he obtained permission from his grandmother to travel for a year or two in the West of England. This hypothesis is as good as any other ; we again find Henry Fielding in 1725 with his valet, Joseph Lewis, in the little Dorsetshire village of Lyme Regis, where he becomes the hero of a somewhat strange adventure. He was courting, at eighteen, a girl of fifteen, Miss Sarah Andrew, a pretty and rich relation of Lady Gould. Unfortunately, the young lady's uncle and guardian had destined her for his own son and kept a close watch upon her. An attempted elopement failed, whereupon Henry Fielding went so far as to threaten this unmanageable guardian with violence. The authorities could not allow such a breach of public peace and private plans. The village Agnes had never read *L'Ecole des Femmes*; neither had her suitor : eventually the guardian had the best of it. Fielding avenged his discomfiture by translating Juvenal's sixth satire, in which women are treated with scant gallantry [1].

Apart from this tragi-comic episode, which throws a clear light on one aspect of our hero's temperament, we know nothing up to the present of those years which immediately followed his school-days. They may have brought the young man other and similar experiences which increased his knowledge of life, but did not yet indicate his future.

Then came a crisis. In July, 1727, we find Lady Mary Wortley Montagu writing to her sister, the Countess of Mar : " Our poor cousins, the Fieldings, are grown yet poorer by the loss of all the money they had which, in their infinite wisdom, they put into the hands of a roguish broker, who has fairly walked off with it [2]." It is, perhaps, to this reverse of fortune that we owe Fielding's decision to earn his living with his pen. Writing of his youth, he afterwards said that he had the alternative of becoming " either a hackney-writer or a hackney-coachman."

In January 1728, Fielding was back in London, where he published his first poem, *The Masquerade*, which deserves hardly more than a mention. He also prepared his first play, *Love in Several Masques*. At the time drama was already the most lucrative of all branches of literature, and it was natural that Fielding, who wanted to make money, should profit by the introductions which he could obtain to the theatre and should make a first trial of his skill in this direction. Lady Mary recommended him, was present at two performances of his play, and consented to accept the dedication.

---

[1] Miss Godden (*Henry Fielding*, p. 24) reprints from Mr Dobson's quotation from the *Register Book* of Lyme Regis—(date November 14th, 1725). " . . . Andrew Tucker, gent., one of the corporation, caused Henry Fielding, gent. and his servant or companion, Joseph Lewis, both now for some time past residing in the borough—to be bound over to keep the peace, as he was in fear of his life or some bodily hurt to be done or to be procured to be done to him by H. Fielding and his man. Mr Tucker feared that the man would beat, maim, or kill him."

[2] None of Fielding's biographers quote this letter or seem to have any knowledge of this great reverse of fortune. It is, however, very important, because at the same moment we find Fielding leaving the easy life of a ' gentleman ' and taking to work. Henceforth the need of money was to become one of the chief factors in his life.

THE NOVELS OF FIELDING

The first performance took place on February 16th, 1728, at Drury Lane, and the play succeeded quite creditably although it had to squeeze itself between Congreve's comedy *The Provoked Husband*, which had preceded it on the bills, and the enormously successful *The Beggar's Opera* [1].

His theatrical début was on the whole encouraging. Yet less than a month later (March 16th), we find Fielding's name in the list of foreign students entered at Leyden University. This sudden departure has puzzled his biographers. Mr Cross seems to think he went there to enrich his know· ledge of life which had just proved inadequate. This would imply a well-defined plan of action which is hardly to be expected of a young man of twenty-one or twenty-two. I should be more ready to believe that there is some unknown motive, which might supply a very obvious explanation could we but discover it. Let us rather avoid conjectures which cannot be tested and merely accept the fact until chance may bring some explanation to light.

The University of Leyden was famous. For two years

[1] *Love in Several Masques* is an intelligent and witty application of Congreve's formula. It frequently makes use of Molière, for example in the character of Wisemore, an English Alceste, and in the artifice which brings about the *dénouement*, inspired by *Les Femmes Savantes*. Wisemore, a bucolic misanthrope, is in love with Lady Matchless, a coquettish widow ; she receives a false letter saying she is ruined. All her lovers then leave her with the exception of the faithful Wisemore. There are also two other couples, Merital and Helena, Malvil and Vermilia, engaged in a complicated love-intrigue. Some of the scenes go with a most amusing swing, such as that in which Malvil disguised as a clergyman comes to carry Helena off, or when the prudish old Lady Positive Trap, takes advantage of the night to receive kisses destined for another. The following is a humorous declaration of love made by Sir Apish, who thinks he has found favour in Lady Matchless's eyes :
Sir Apish : " Ah l'amour ! a perfect declaration ! She is in love with me, mordie ! Ah Madam, if I durst declare it, there is a certain person in the world who, in a certain person's eye, is a more agreeable person than any person, amongst all the persons whom persons think agreeable persons."
Lady Matchless : " Whoever that person is she certainly is a very happy person."
Sir Apish : " Ah Madam ! my eyes sufficiently and evidently declare that that person is no other person than your ladyship's own person."
(Act III, sc. X) There is a textual reminiscence of this jingle in Mrs Slipslop (*Joseph Andrews*).

6

Fielding was entered in the faculty of letters (he did not go there to study law, as was long supposed), and doubtless his Latin scholarship and his knowledge of French gained from his sojourn there. Holland was the home of free, vigorous, and active thinkers. It was also, at this time, famous for its caricaturists. Fielding may have sharpened and cultivated his sense of comedy by looking at their cartoons.

As soon as he returned to London he began to follow his profession as a man of letters. One of his earliest works, probably his first, was not unnaturally a poem in which he begged Walpole to make him a grant ! Then his second play, *The Temple Beau* was performed on January 26th, 1730, at the theatre in Goodman's Fields. It is the story of a young law-student who poses to his father, a rich country squire, as a hard worker. He has huge bills for books. Here is a bill which rejoices the heart of old Wilding : " For law books, 50l., *Item*, for paper, pens, ink, sand, pencils, penknives, 10l. For fire and candles, 8l. Paid a woman to brush books, 8l., etc. (Sc. IV). One day however the old man happens to go into his son's room during his absence, and is visited there by all the young roisterer's creditors. Add to this theme the complicated intrigues of three pairs of lovers and the character of a studious young man, own brother to Molière's Thomas Diafoirus. The play was amusing enough and was preceded by a clever prologue[1] which drew attention to the need for reforming and purifying the stage, where farce

[1] " . . . Only Farce and show will now go down—
And Harlequin's the darling of the town .. . .
But if the gay, the courtly world disdain
To hear the muses and their sons complain,
Each injured Bard shall to this refuge fly,
And find that comfort which the great deny,
Shall frequently employ this infant stage,
And boldly aim to wake a dreaming age."
Then, addressing the patrons of the new theatre in Goodman's Fields the author adds :
" Convince that town, which boasts its better breeding,
That riches—are not all that you exceed in."
The author of this prologue was Ralph, who was to become associate with many of Fielding's journalistic ventures.

reigned supreme; and it urged the rich London merchants to support the efforts of young authors. The public gave *The Temple Beau* a fairly good reception.

Two months later Fielding presented a new play at the Little Theatre, Haymarket. *The Author's Farce, and the Pleasures of the Town*, (March 30th, 1730) was made up of two parts. The first gave an amusing picture of the literary Bohemians of the time, in the person of a young author, reading his play to the critics and theatrical managers. The second contained a humorous satire on the chief absurdities of the day and was spiced with a number of personal allusions, which have now lost much of their savour.

This farce was far more successful than the play which had preceded it. Naturally enough, Fielding who was writing plays in order to earn his living, was induced to cater for the general public and produce other works of the same nature. Less than a month after the *Author's Farce* (April 24th), *Tom Thumb, a tragedy* was performed. It was a spirited and sometimes truculent parody of the pomposity of heroic drama.

After manifold absurd adventures, from which the hero, Tom Thumb the Great [1], always emerges with honour, all the nine characters in the play either commit suicide or are murdered in the course of the last scene. In his preface, Fielding pretends he has discovered an Elizabethan tragedy, and asserts that the verses from contemporary plays with which his farce is crammed, were borrowed by modern authors from this ancient work. *Tom Thumb the Great* gives the first signs of Fielding's marvellous gift of parody.

Finally, on June 23rd of this same year, 1730, *Rape upon Rape* was performed. The name of this play was then altered to *The Justice caught in his own trap*, or *The Coffee-House Politician*. It has in common with all Fielding's plays, the elements of a modern Vaudeville with just the right touch of satire on contemporary manners to give reality to the plot.

[1] This may be the first allusion to Walpole, the " great man ".

Some of the characters, although rather vaguely drawn, are amusing. Among them is Mr Politic, a monomaniac, who thinks of nothing but the Eastern question and foreign politics as seen through the eyes of his coffee-house friends, and whose mind is deep in the fate of Budapest, while his daughter is being abducted under his very nose [1]. But above all here is one Judge Squeezum, Fielding's first sketch, rather mechanically drawn as yet, of a type which we shall find later in his novels, the finest example being Judge Thrasher in *Amelia* [2].

Four plays in six months! Fielding's first season had been busy and fruitful. His second was less of a success. On March 20th, 1731, a new version of *Tom Thumb* appeared. It was longer and accompanied by a comedy called *The Letter-Writers* or *A New Way to Keep a Wife at Home*. The play concerns the useless precautions taken by two husbands, who try to keep their wives at home by writing them threatening letters. The subject was thin. After a month, Fielding had to replace this little piece by *The Welsh Opera* (April 2nd, 1731). Still running after fortune, he had taken for his

---

[1] This character is developed and enriched in Aunt Western (*Tom Jones*).

[2] Already here and there, the dialogue discusses everything with open-eyed frankness :

Cloris : I had a rogue of a husband that robbed me of all I had, and kept a mistress under my nose, but I was even with him ; for it has ever been my opinion, that a husband like a courtier, who is above doing the duties of his office, should keep a deputy.

Hilaret : But suppose you had been in love with your husband ?

Cloris : Why so I was, Madam, so long as he deserved it ; but love like fire, naturally goes out when it has nothing to feed on. (I, i)

The following are some of Judge Squeezum's tirades—amusing in themselves, but are they in character ?

Squeezum : The laws are turnpikes, only made to stop people who walk on foot, and not to interrupt those who drive through them in their coaches. The laws are like a game at loo, where a blaze of court cards is always secure, and the knaves are the safest cards in the pack. (II, ii)

"Come, come child, you had better take the oath, though you are not altogether so sure. Justice should be rigorous. It is better for the public that ten innocent people should suffer, than that one guilty should escape." (II v,) His irony is obviously still a little heavy and untrained.

model *The Beggar's Opera*, which was perhaps the greatest success of the century. *The Welsh Opera* was composed of dialogue interspersed with songs, one of which ' The Roast Beef of Old England ' still retains its popularity. It was supposed to portray a family of Welsh rustics, but its interest lay in the many satirical allusions to Walpole and even to the royal family. These allusions became still more pointed and definite in a new version of the play called *The Grub-Street Opera*, which may never have been performed in public. The attacks from the Little Theatre in the Haymarket at last wore out the patience of the Government [1]. Mr Cross conjectures, with much probability, that some sort of intervention, more or less discreet, put an end to them ; and the Little Theatre once more returned to innocuous entertainments made up of dancing, music, and acrobatic feats.

So Fielding came back to Drury Lane, and in January, 1732, presented *The Lottery*, a mild satire on lotteries [2]. *The Modern Husband* which followed on February 14th, is one of his most interesting dramatic efforts. It is a biting indictment of fashionable corruption. The central point of the situation is a husband who is prepared to sell his wife to a dissolute lord. Our author portrays this without evasion or attenuation of any kind. We have here the first clear example of that daring and sometimes brutal realism which was

[1] The following is a song by *Robin*, the head servant, and it is a good example of the satirical tone in Fielding's play :

" Great courtiers palaces contain,
While small ones fear the gaol,
Great parsons riot in champagne,
Small parsons sot on ale ;
Great whores in coaches gang
  Smaller misses
  For their kisses
Are in Bridewell bang'd :
  While in vogue
Lives the great rogue,
Small rogues are by the dozen hang'd."

[2] The play centres in the marriage of a young lord with a girl, whom he supposes the possessor of a fortune of £10,000. All her wealth, however, lies in the golden hopes of a lottery ticket, and when she loses he abandons her. Her faithful lover then returns and marries her.

always so dear to his soul. Not that his interest therein was
unhealthy, but he had already made up his mind that no
good could come of hiding or covering a social evil, and that
it was necessary first to open up the wound before seeking
to cure it.

This was the first vibration of a note which sounded,
time and again, in Fielding's novels. Side by side with Mr
and Mrs Modern, another couple is portrayed, and in these
Bellamants, of whom the husband is very much in love with
his wife and yet deceives her through pure sensual weakness,
are foreshadowed the conjugal relations which will be described in *Amelia*. Fielding worked and re-worked at his
Modern Husband. As early as September, 1730, it had been
announced under that title by *The Craftsman* [1]. The prologue [2] gives one the impression that he wanted to try a new
type of comedy, and at all events to abandon farce in which
the taste of the public had imprisoned him. He considered
his talent to lie rather in a drama of moral and social criticism.
But for this new kind of comedy the stage offered no scope.
The traditions of the English stage hampered him, and he was
destined to escape them only in the novel.

[1] cf. Cross, *op. cit.* I, p.95 : " We hear that the town will shortly
be diverted by a comedy of Mr. Fielding's, call'd the Modern Husband,
which is said to bear a great reputation."

[2] The play, in book-form, was dedicated to Walpole. This seems
a little strange unless one of the two following explanations be accepted ;
either the compliments paid to Walpole were ironical (which is quite
possible) ; or, if they were sincere or supposed to be so, Fielding was
attempting a reconciliation.

The following are some interesting verses from the prologue :
" In early youth our author first begun
To combat with the follies of the town :
His want of art his unskilled muse bewailed,
And where his fancy pleas'd, his judgment fail'd . . .
At length, repenting frolic flights of youth,
Once more he flies to nature and to truth :
In virtue's just defence aspires to fame,
And courts applause without the applauder's shame."
He finally asks his audience to help him to :
" Restore the sinking honour of the stage,
The stage which was not for low farce designed
But to divert, instruct, and mend mankind."

THE NOVELS OF FIELDING

The public received *The Modern Husband* coldly not to say inimicably, and Fielding's enemies, who were already numerous and noisy, made merry at his expense in the *Grub-Street Journal*. Their hostility was soon destined to find a further outlet. In *The Old Debauchees, or the Jesuit Caught*, Fielding put upon the stage an episode which had actually taken place, the year before, in France at Aix, where Father Girard, a Jesuit, had seduced one of his penitents, Mlle Cadière. The affair had caused a terrible scandal [1]. Fielding worked the whole incident into a rather gross and virulently anti-papist drama [2]. He followed it by a burlesque-tragedy in which the scene of action was a well-known house of ill-fame, the proprietress of which appeared as one of the characters in the play. This *Covent Garden Tragedy* was in many places extremely amusing [3]. But the subject was altogether too coarse and the public could hardly sit through the first performance of June 1st, 1732.

Fielding, taken aback, hastened to replace his farce by an adaptation of *Le Médecin malgré lui* called *The Mock-Doctor* or *The Dumb Lady Cured*, a translation of Molière's work, turned into a sort of English musical comedy, and filled with allusions to Dr Misaubin, a contemporary physician.

[1] For particulars of this scandal, cf. Michelet, *Histoire de France*, vol. 18, p.105, *seqq.*

[2] A Jesuit attempts to seduce a young girl and is helped by her father who trusts him blindly. The girl pretends not to understand what the Jesuit wants, meets him at the appointed place, and outwits him. Here the influence of Molière's *Tartuffe* is obvious. As an example of burlesque (used again in *Joseph Andrews*) one may quote the form of exorcism pronounced by the Jesuit : " *Exorciso te, exorciso te, Satan, ton dapamibominos prosephe podas ocus Achilleus.*" (II, 5).

[3] Quoted at the beginning of the volume are *Prolegomena*, which contain the following definition of tragedy : " Tragedy is a thing of five acts written dialogue-wise, consisting of several fine similes, metaphors, and moral phrases, with here and there a speech upon liberty." The following is an example of parody :

> " Oh, if you love Stormandra, come with me,
> Skin off your flesh, and bite away your eyes,
> Lug out your heart and dry it in your hands ;
> Grind it to powder, make it into pills,
> And take it down your throat . . . (Sc. XII).

Encouraged by the success of this, his first adaptation, and full of admiration for Molière—an admiration which he frequently expressed[1], Fielding now tackled a more important piece of work. His version of *L'Avare, The Miser,* is still a classic in England ; and Voltaire, who knew it, thought that Fielding had added to the original ' beauties of dialogue peculiar to his nation '[2]. When we discuss the novels we shall have occasion to point out how much Fielding's artistry is indebted to Molière [3]. The modifications which he has carried

[1] He writes in his preface to *The Mock-Doctor :* " One pleasure I enjoy from the success of this piece is a prospect of transplanting successfully some others of Molière of great value."

[2] " M. Fielding, meilleur poète [que Shadwell] et plus modeste, a traduit *l'Avare,* et l'a fait jouer à Londres en 1733. Il y a ajouté réellement quelques beautés de dialogue particulières à sa nation, et sa pièce a eu près de trente représentations ; succès très rare à Londres, où les pièces qui ont le plus de cours ne sont jouées tout au plus que quinze fois." Voltaire. *Vie de Molière, avec de petits sommaires de ses pièces,* 1739.

[Mr Fielding who is a better and more modest poet (than Shadwell) has made a translation of *L'Avare* which has been acted in London in 1733. He has added to it some real beauties of dialogue peculiar to his nation and his play has been performed nearly thirty times. Such success is rare in London, where the plays which have the longest runs seldom exceed fifteen performances.]

[3] The preface of *The Mock-Doctor* invited the reader to examine and compare the literal translation of Molière's works, which was being published in eight volumes by John Watts, who also published Fielding's plays. Mr Cross thinks that Fielding must have been one of the translators. This seems highly probable. He certainly had a profound and familiar knowledge of the great French dramatist's works.

On the other hand, the unknown author of the Prologue to *The Mock-Doctor* speaks of English comedy and Molière in the following terms. Since the days of Ben Jonson he says there has been no great comedy.

" No characters from Nature now we trace . . .
Our modern bards who to assemblies stray,
Frequent the park, the visit, or the play,
Regard not what fools do, but what wits say . . .
Thus without characters from Nature got,
Without a moral, and without a plot,
A due collection of insipid jokes . . .
We call high comedy and seem content. . .
To-night our author treats you with Molière.
Molière, who Nature's inmost secrets knew
Whose justest pen, like Kneller's pencil, drew,
In whose strong scenes all characters are shown,
Not by low jests, but actions of their own."

out in *L'Avare* are already very interesting and the two plays are well worth a detailed comparison. Here we can only note the essentials. Fielding has done rather more than add mere ' beauties of dialogue '. His principal changes bear on the plot, which is indeed the weak spot in Molière's comedy. In Fielding's play Marianne has been changed into a coquette, who obtains from Lovegold (Harpagon) a promise of marriage in default of which he must pay a large fine. No sooner is the contract signed than she becomes so extravagant a spendthrift that Lovegold is terrified, breaks off the engagement and pays the fine. New scenes are added to portray the coquetry of Marianne, who becomes one of the chief characters, and to show the serving-maid Lappet (Frosine) manoeuvring to carry out her intrigues. The plot turns then on another axle : no longer, as in the French play, have we the picture of a central vice which breaks up a regular family circle ; here the essential thing becomes the intrigue to rob a miser of his fortune. No doubt this is a gain in dramatic verisimilitude ; but has it not often been pointed out that the very unlikeliness of Molière's *dénouements* proves that they are brought from the outside, that all may end well ; they destroy the pitilessly logical trend of the rest of the play —and of life itself—which would lead to the triumph of rogues.

Let us carry our analysis a stage further. This ' improvement ' on Molière's *dénouements* is not so much due to Fielding as to the tradition of English comedy. In his novels he will do what Molière did in his plays. *Joseph Andrews, Tom Jones, Amelia*—and *Jonathan Wild* too—could and should terminate in the triumph of villains, did not ' Providence ' intervene in the end, as with Molière. Why, then, does Fielding correct in his plays what he will not correct in his novels ? Because in his novels, he will be himself, while in his plays the tradition of a too deft school of drama dictates its tricks, its stage-machinery, and its characters. And so we get the full value of Voltaire's expression ' beauties of dialogue peculiar to his nation.' There existed in England not only a dramatic method but a dramatic dialogue built up by tradition, a form from which there was no salvation, ' patches ' which the public expected and demanded.

Observe, for instance, how La Flèche's answer, " *C'est de tous les humains l'humain le moins humain* " becomes in Fielding's version a collection of trite witticisms : " sooner than to extract gold from him, I would engage to extract religion from a hypocrite, honesty from a lawyer, health from a physician, sincerity from a courtier, or modesty from a poet." (II, 5).

Elsewhere he thinks it necessary to explain an attitude[1] or amplify a joke[2] which his public might not understand. For his English public is always in his mind ; coquette, *soubrette*, foppish lord, and ingenuous lovers, intrigues and puns, even Molière must fit into the traditional mould. With more reverence and without the slightest indecency *L'Avare* is seasoned to the taste of English palates, even as *le Misanthrope* had been turned into *The Plain Dealer* and *L'Ecole des Femmes* into *The Country Wife*.

The public gave Fielding's *Miser* a very good reception. The following year (January 15th, 1734) he once more sought inspiration from the French theatre and founded his *Intriguing Chambermaid* on Regnard's *Retour Imprévu*. He also staged again for the same occasion his *Author's Farce*, adapting it to the taste of the day by adding sundry allusions to the

---

[1] In a well-known scene in *L'Avare*, Cléante who is about to interview his moneylender, suddenly finds himself confronted with Harpagon. A violent tirade from the father is met with an equally violent reply from the son. Fielding here deems it necessary to explain the son's attitude :

Lovegold : " How, rascal, is it you that abandon yourself to these intolerable extravagances ?
Fred : (aside) : I must even stand buff and outface him. And is it you, father, etc." (II, 2)
The *aside* is added by Fielding.

[2] cf., for example, the witticism in the inscription ' in letters of gold ' proposed by Harpagon. Fielding thinks it necessary to emphasize the irony by adding the words (which follow in italics) : " I'm resolved to have 'em done in letters of gold, *or black and white rather,* over my hall chimney." (III, 3).

violent quarrels of various actors which were at that time amusing the public. Finally, he presented in April, what seems to have been his first attempt at comedy, *Don Quixote in England* begun, he tells us, at Leyden in 1728. " I soon discovered . . . that my too small experience in, and little knowledge of the world, had led me into an error. I soon found it infinitely more difficult than I imagined to vary the scene, and give my knight an opportunity of displaying himself in a different manner from that wherein he appears in the romance. Human nature is everywhere the same : and the modes and habits of peculiar nations do not change it enough, sufficiently to distinguish a Quixote in England from a Quixote in Spain ". This confession is interesting. Even at this stage it is clear that if Fielding reads Cervantes, Lucian, and Molière with profit, it is only that he may extract from each those things which are universal and eternal, and which show forth human nature, ' everywhere the same '. Here he spices his ' human nature ' with a touch of contemporary politics in the form of burlesque election scenes. A certain Badger also appears, the uncouth and boorish country squire of the traditional Restoration comedy. He is particularly alive and already seems to announce the great humorous creation of Squire Western, in *Tom Jones* [1].

Fielding's reputation as a dramatist was now well enough established. At the age of twenty-seven he was already the

---

[1] *Sancho :* " Sir, your true English Squire and his hounds are as inseparable as the Spaniard and his Toledo. He eats with his hounds, drinks with his hounds and lies with his hounds ; your true arrant English Squire is but the first dog-boy in his house."

Squire Badger comes drunk into the presence of the girl whom it is desired that he should marry, and brutally tries to kiss her :

Dorothea : " I hate and despise you.

Badger : Do you ? Then you may kiss—'sbud, I can hate as well as you." (III, 13). This is the same expression which Western always uses.

Mr. Brief, a lawyer, uses the jargon of his profession. " Pshaw, the man is no more mad than I am. I should be finely off if he could be proved *non compos mentis* ! 'tis an easy thing for a man to pretend madness, *ex post facto*." (III, 15). Here, again, are elements of caricature which are reproduced in the novels.

author of sixteen plays, several of which had been undeniably successful while a few had been revived several times. He then married Miss Charlotte Cradock, who was thought one of the beauties of Salisbury. He had known her for several years, as in 1730 he dedicated some verses to her, which were afterwards to be reprinted in his *Miscellanies*. The Salisbury registers were for a long time ransacked in vain for the actual date of his marriage, and it was only in 1906 that the following inscription was discovered in the register of St Mary's, a little church in the village of Charlcomb about a mile and a half north of Bath : " November ye 28th, 1734, Henry Fielding of St James in Bath, Esquire, and Charlotte Cradock of ye same parish, spinster, were married by virtue of a licence from ye Court of Wells [1]." The fact that their marriage took place at such a distance makes the hypothesis of an elopement seem probable. In any case the bride's mother bore Fielding no ill-will, for when she died in 1735, she left her entire fortune to Charlotte and disinherited her younger daughter [2].

Fielding returned to London with his wife and settled in Buckingham Street. On January 17th, 1735, he presented his farce *An Old man Taught Wisdom, or the Virgin Unmasked*, which was to enjoy a long popularity. It is the story of a young girl, brought up in complete ignorance of the world, who despises all her suitors and finally marries a footman. A month later (February 10th) a play in five acts called *The Universal Gallant or the Different Husbands* was violently hissed [3]. In his preface Fielding complains of an audience

[1] cf. *Notes and Queries*, July 21st, 1906.

[2] Possibly this family history was in part reproduced in *Amelia* where there is a ' bad sister ' and an elopement ; but Amelia's sister is painted in such black colours that one hesitates to believe it is a family portrait.

[3] The two different husbands are Mr Ruffler and Sir Simon Ruffler ; the first is indulgent on principle and the second morbidly jealous, also on principle. The first does not think he is being deceived, when he is—abundantly ; and the second imagines he is being deceived when he is not. Numerous misunderstandings complicate the plot and often make it very difficult to follow.

which can light-heartedly condemn a play, often without realizing that the author's pen is his means of livelihood.

Mrs Cradock's legacy doubtless relieved the young couple for some time, of money difficulties. After staying at East Stour for a while, Fielding returned to London where his eldest daughter was born (April 27th, 1736). He became manager of the Little Theatre in the Haymarket, and formed the actors into the ' Great Mogul's Company of Comedians '. At the same time he renewed his friendship with Pitt and Lyttleton who had been made Members of Parliament at the by-elections of 1735 ; and through the medium of his theatre, launched against the Minister a campaign of opposition which increased in violence every day. From March to May, 1736, *Pasquin, a Dramatic Satire on the Times*, was an enormous success, comparable to *The Beggar's Opera*, and had a run of over sixty performances. Here Fielding made use of a formula which he had tried before. He shows two rehearsals, one of a comedy and the other of a tragedy. The first is the comedy, satirically treated, of an election with all its Government corruption, bribery of the mayor and electors, etc. The second, a burlesque tragedy, brings on the stage the Queen of Common Sense and the Queen of Ignorance and ends, very naturally, with the triumph of the latter. Full of wit, ranging from the grossest to the most delicate, stuffed with jokes at the expense of the Government, society, and the stage, *Pasquin* was soon reinforced by yet another fantastic piece, *Tumble-down Dick* [1], in which Fielding introduced behind the footlights one Rich, the Manager of the Covent Garden Theatre.

---

[1] *Tumble-Down Dick or Phaeton in the suds.* First performance April 29th, 1736. *Pasquin* contained numerous stinging attacks on the pantomines and variety shows which Rich presented at the Covent Garden Theatre. Rich replied by a *Marforio* (which was never printed) in which the Great Mogul (evidently Fielding) appeared and was reproached with borrowing his best ideas from Rich. *Marforio* was only performed once. Fielding's play is a parody on the *Fall of Phaeton* which was then being acted at Covent Garden. Mr Cross has collected and carefully classified, a quantity of new material regarding this theatrical rivalry and Fielding's activities as a dramatist. The story had never before been told. (cf. for *Pasquin*, Cross *op. cit.*, 1, 8).

During this time he also staged a number of other plays, notably *Fatal Curiosity* by his friend George Lillo, author of that *London Merchant* which is still considered the type of bourgeois drama [1].

Fielding was now the happy manager of a prosperous theatre, and after the failure of a farce, *Eurydice* [2], he presented at the beginning of April 1737, a new play *The Historical Register for the year* 1736. The play is not a review of historical events as the title might seem to suggest, but rather a satire of the same type as *Pasquin*. The same subterfuge is employed of a mock rehearsal. It was no more a masterpiece than any of his former plays, but *Pasquin* had brought him a great deal of money ; so he repeated *Pasquin*. I cannot help thinking that Fielding never looked upon play writing as anything more than a trade.

But his trade was going to fail him. The *Historical Register* contained scenes of extremely violent satire wherein Walpole was furiously attacked, and electoral corruption painted in colours which often remind one of Aristophanes .[3]

[1] *Fatal Curiosity*, May 27th, 1736.

[2] He took his defeat with good grace and printed the play described as *Eurydice, a farce ; as it was d-mnd at the Theatre Royal, Drury Lane*, then, under the title *Eurydice hissed*, he added to his *Historical Register* a humorous commentary on his failure.

[3] cf., in Act I, the *Politicians'* scene :
5th Politician : " Hang foreign affairs, let us apply ourselves to money.
Omnes : Ay, ay, ay.
2nd Polit. : All we have to consider relating to money is how we shall get it. Suppose we put a tax upon learning.
3rd Polit. : Learning, it is true, is a senseless commodity, but I think we had better lay it on Ignorance ; for Learning being the property but of a very few, and those poor ones, too, I am afraid we can get little among them : whereas Ignorance will take in most of the great fortunes in the kingdom."
The politicians depart, Sourwit asks what has become of them and Medley replies : "They are gone, Sir, they're gone ; they have finish'd the business they met about, which was to agree on a tax ; that being done they are gone to raise it ; and this, Sir, is the full account of the whole history of Europe, as far as we know of it, compris'd in one scene."
cf. in particular the sale by auction in Act II, where a conscience, which has belonged successively to a judge and a bishop, is, after much persuasion, knocked down to a bidder for one shilling.

It has so great a *succès de scandale* that the Government, which felt that opposition was increasing, grew nervous and decided to take strong measures. Sheltering behind the usual pretext of safeguarding public morality, it succeeded in obtaining a vote in favour of a censorship, and on June 6th, 1737, the *Licensing Act* passed its third reading in the House of Lords, having given Lord Chesterfield occasion for a speech which is still famous. On June 24th, the three theatres which had no licences were closed, and one of these was the Little Theatre in the Haymarket.

Fielding submitted. As this trade had failed him, he set about looking for another. Did he really regret the first ? " I left off writing for the stage ", he said later, " when I ought to have begun." Indeed, all these plays which interested his contemporaries, because they borrowed an ephemeral life from contemporary events, had never really interested their author as works of art [1]. Hardly more than once or twice do we see him taking special pains over a play. Most of the time he writes with lightning speed, and in *Eurydice Hiss'd* he represents himself as composing nine scenes in one day [2]. He never attempts to refute the reputation he had of being careless [3]. His characters are seldom really *observed*.

[1] He shows that he recognized the artificiality of these productions when he makes his characters say :
2nd Player : " What subjects wouldst thou write on ?
1st Player : Why, no subject at all, Sir ; but I would have a humming deal of satire, and I would repeat in every page that courtiers are cheats and don't pay their debts, that lawyers are rogues, physicians blockheads, soldiers cowards, and Ministers. . .
2nd Plyer : What, what, Sir ?
1st Player : Nay, I'll only name them, that's enough to set the audience a-hooting." (*The Historicl Register for* 1736, *I*, i).

[2] Pillage speaks to his muse :
" Not more I felt thy power, nor fiercer burnt
My vig'rous fancy, when thy blushing charms
First yielded trembling, and inspired my pen
To write nine scenes with spirit in one day. . ."
Eurydice Hiss'd.

[3] There are numerous allusions to this negligence in contemporary lampoons. The following, for example, appeared in 1734, and is quoted by Mr Dobson : " *Item,* I give and bequeath to my very negligent

They are the traditional, stereotyped heroes of Restoration drama. Their names are like so many labels attached to their persons and allow the author to dispense with psychology. They are Lord Pride, Lord Puff or Colonel Bluff, unless they be Trapwit an author, Sneerwell a critic, Squire Tankard, Mrs Useful or Mrs Plotwell; fops, cynical and rakish lords, scheming coquettes, and as a contrast to these, a few pale *ingénues* and harmless young lovers. I must confess that all these plays mostly interest me by reason of the signature affixed to them [1].

Fielding thus gave up the theatre and decided to go on reading for the bar. In November, 1737, he was admitted to the Middle Temple. But he still had to live and so he undertook a variety of odd jobs, and ' pot boilers ' for publishers. One of these efforts has recently been brought to light—a

friend, Henry Drama, Esq., all my Industry. And whereas the world may think this an unnecessary legacy, forasmuch as the said Henry Drama, Esq., brings on the stage four pieces every season ; yet as such pieces are always wrote with uncommon rapidity, and during such fatal intervals only as the stocks have been on the fall, this legacy will be of use to him to revise and correct his works. Furthermore, for fear the said Henry Drama should make an ill use of the said Industry, and expend it all on a ballad farce, it's my will the said legacy should be paid him by equal portions, and as his necessities may require."

(Dobson, *Fielding*, p. 26).

Pope in his *Epistle to Arbuthnot* which serves as a *Prologue* to the *Satires*, and, if we are to believe Mr Courthope, the first hundred and fifty verses of which date from 1734, spoke in the following terms of a poet who could have been none other than Fielding, who was at that time Manager of Drury Lane :

" I sit with sad civility, I read
With honest anguish, and an aching head,
And drop at last but in unwilling ears,
This saving counsel : ' Keep your piece nine years.'
' Nine years ', cries he, who high in Drury Lane
Lulled by soft zephyrs through the broken pane
Rhymes ere he wakes, and prints before Term ends,
Obliged by hunger and request of friends :
' The piece, you think, is incorrect ? Why take it ;
I'm all submission ; what you'd have it, make it '."

(Verses 40-47).

[1] After some strange vicissitudes a lost play, *The Fathers or the Good-Natured Man*, was found by Garrick and played by him, with moderate success, for the benefit of Fielding's family, (November, 1776).

THE NOVELS OF FIELDING

History of Charles XII[1] by Adlerfeld which he translated from the French. It was doubtless for the same reason—*Rabelais' " faute d'argent, c'est douleur non pareille "*[2]—that he became editor-in-chief of a paper called *The Champion, or British Mercury*[3], in which he took the pseudonym of Captain Hercules Vinegar and threatened with his great club all the enemies of common sense, the public weal, and the British language, whom he arraigned before his tribunal. The first number of *The Champion* appeared on November 12th, 1739, and Fielding only retired from the editorial chair in March, 1741. There are some beautiful pages in *The Champion*. Fielding was here practising a form of art infinitely nearer than the theatre had ever been to his conception of the novel. Many of the articles already foreshadow the literary and moral developments of certain chapters in *Joseph Andrews* or *Tom Jones*. A notable example is the series of four articles on the good *Clergyman*, whose principal virtues should be charity, forgiveness, and above all poverty, who should spend his life among his parishioners, especially among those who most need his help, the poor and the unhappy. Here we have, as it were, a proof before the letter, a sketch, still in its initial stages, of Parson Adams[4]. Elsewhere the authors of strange travellers' tales are parodied in Mr Job Vinegar's description of a journey to the land of the Ptfghsiumgski[5]. This same subject will again be taken up in *Jonathan Wild*, when Mrs

[1] cf. Chapt. on *Jonathan Wild*, p. 102 n. 1. The title of the work is *The Military History of Charles XII, King of Sweden, written by the express order of His Majesty, by Mr Gustavus Adlerfeld, Chamberlain to the King*, 1740.

[2] How grievous a pain it is to lack money.

[3] *The Champion, or British Mercury*, by Capt. Hercules Vinegar, of Hockley in the Hole. It was published three times a week. All the numbers prior to No. 64 (April 10th, 1740) have been lost; but the articles which appeared from November, 1739, to June 19th, 1740 were published in London in 1741, 1743, and 1766. (cf. *Cross, op. cit.* bibliography, III, p. 302).

[4] March 29th, April 5th, 12th, and 19th, 1740.

[5] March 20th, 1739-40; cf. Chapter on *Jonathan Wild*.

Heartfree's extraordinary journey is described. A number of 'visions' are related and one of them, which shows us the infernal regions with all the stage properties and actors to be found in them, from Mercury to the barque of Charon, gives us a foretaste of *The Journey from this World to the Next* [1].

But *The Champion* was, above all, a fighting paper. The 'Captain' had two great enemies. One of these was Colley Cibber whom he accused, among other crimes, of writing badly. Three articles of scorching wit are consecrated to the most pitiless examination of his style, with the conclusion that the language is probably English, since it cannot be anything else, but that no one would have recognized it [2]. The second was a greater enemy, for it was Walpole himself, who is held up to fierce and scathing ridicule. He is Robin Hood, and his partisans are 'the Roberdsmen', a name (it is explained) which is given to "any set of thieves or rascals." He is accused of having profited by his position shamelessly to enrich himself and his family. Horace Walpole was never to forget that Fielding had spoken in such cruel terms of his father—and of himself—nor was he ever to lose an opportunity of slandering him [3].

For those who know Fielding's novels well, *The Champion* makes interesting reading, for here in their earliest form, still young and modest, are ideas which he expressed later with a conviction fortified by experience ; this, for example, which was the basis of his moral philosophy : " Virtue is

---

[1] May 24th, 1740. See also (December 29th, 1739) a description of the Palace of Wealth and the Cave of Poverty.

[2] April 22nd and 29th, May 17th ; see chapter on *Joseph Andrews*.

[3] A comic trial of Walpole ends : " How the Defendant, from owing more than he was worth in the world, should in the space of twenty years, out of an employment of five thousand pounds a year, etc. ." June 14th, 1740. Further on, he adds : " The Right Honourable Sir Robert Walpole, being Chancellor of the Exchequer, the Right Honourable Lord Walpole, Auditor, and Edward Walpole, Esq., Clerk of the Pells ; it is presumed the Teller's place lately vacated by Lord Onslow, will be given to Horatio Walpole, Esq., Jun., that the Virtues, not the Iniquities of the father, may be rewarded in the children to the third and fourth generation."

a delight in doing good." [1] And does not this panegyric of Hogarth also give a portrait of our novelist, the confirmed painter of 'vulgar' realities in contrast to Richardson, the moralist of 'distinction'?

" I shall venture to assert that we are much better and easier taught by the examples of what we are to shun, than by those which would instruct us what to pursue ; which opinion, if not new, I do not remember to have seen accounted for, tho' the reason is perhaps obvious enough, and may be that we are more inclined to detest and loathe what is odious in others, than to admire what is laudable. . . On which account I esteem the ingenious Mr Hogarth as one of the most useful satyrists any age hath produced. In his excellent works you see the delusive scene exposed with all the force of humour, and, on casting your eyes on another picture, you behold the dreadful and fatal consequence. I almost dare affirm that those two works of his, which he calls *The Rake's* and *The Harlot's Progress*, are calculated more to serve the cause of virtue, and for the preservation of mankind, than all the folios of morality which have been ever written : and a sober family should be no more without them, than without *The Whole Duty of Man* in their house [2]."

I have spent some little time on this attempt at journalism, because it helps us to understand the ideas which were in Fielding's mind on the eve of his first novel, and because it forms a sort of transition from the dramatist to the novelist. We must, however, still add to the catalogue of his works an

[1] " I do not know a better general definition of virtue, than that it is a delight in going good " . . . (January 3rd, 1739-40). " Good nature is a delight in the happiness of mankind, and a concern at their misery, with a desire as much as possible to procure the former and avert the latter ; and this with a constant regard to desert." (March 27th, 1740). Here again is a very characteristic opinion on a hypocrite : " . . . He is all the while deceiving himself : he may be well assured . . . that he would be much happier, was he really as good as he has hitherto appeared to the world." (December 11th, 1739). All this reminds one of the ethics of *Tom Jones*. Many allusions are made to *Jonathan Wild*, particularly on March 4th, 1740.

[2] June 10th, 1740. This remark on Hogarth was often to be repeated in the novels.

impassioned appeal to electors, published in April, 1741, under
the title of *The Crisis*[1] ; a poem *On True Greatness*, another
paying homage to Admiral Vernon and entitled *The Vernoniad ;*
and, finally, in December, 1741, after Walpole had been de-
feated in the elections, a pamphlet, headed *The Opposition,
A Vision*, in which he draws a moral for his own party, urging
it not to spoil a great victory.   None of these productions
can add much to his fame.

We have now reached the period of the great novels.
When Fielding began to write them, he was a little over
thirty years of age. His financial position was barely assured.
Though not the Bohemian of legend, he was by no means
wealthy, nor even in what might be called comfortable
circumstances.   He lived partly on his professional earnings
as a lawyer, followed the western circuit of the assizes, studied
law (at his death, his library contained more than three
hundred legal works), and possibly sought appointment as a
magistrate. Yet he continued to ' grind ' for various publishers,
writing a *Vindication of the Duchess of Marlborough*[2] and
planning with his friend the Rev. Dr Young, (who is reported
to have been the original of Parson Adams), a translation of
Aristophanes which never got beyond *Plutus* [3]. He also, at
Garrick's request, staged an old farce, which obtained a certain
amount of success [4], and re-wrote a play, which was practically
a failure [5]. His situation as depicted by the preface to the
Miscellanies[6] was not brilliant. His wife, whom he adored,

---

[1] *The Crisis*, a Sermon . . . by a Lover of his Country. Attributed
to Fielding by Nicholls in his *Literary Anecdotes*. Mr Cross who has
seen a copy has also no hesitation in attributing it to Fielding ; cf. Cross,
op. cit., I, pp. 295-6.
[2] *A full Vindication of the Duchess Dowager of Marlborough*, etc.,
April, 1742.
[3] *Plutus, the God of Riches, a Comedy*, translated from the original
Greek of Aristophanes ; with large notes, explanatory and critical ;
by Henry Fielding, Esq., and the Rev. Mr Young, May 31st, 1742.
[4] *Miss Lucy in Town*, a sequel to *The Virgin Unmasked*. First
performance, May 6th, 1742.
[5] *The Wedding Day, a Comedy*, First performance, February 17th,
1743.
[6] cf. *infra*, p. 95, n. 1.

was often ill and he could not surround her with those comforts which he longed to give her ; creditors dunned him ; his health, which had been vigorous for so long, began to fail as a result of various excesses. Overwork was no doubt to blame, but we must probably add to this the excesses of a gay and careless youth. He had powerful friends, who respected him, colleagues who subscribed handsomely when the *Miscellanies* were announced ; it is also to be inferred that his rich bene-factor, Ralph Allen of Bath, began to help him about this time. Still his shoulders were unceasingly burdened with material cares.

The History of the Adventures of Joseph Andrews and his friend Mr Abraham Adams had been published on February 22nd, 1742. The *Miscellanies* were somewhat slow to appear. The only prospectus extant, which is dated June, 1742, was certainly not the first ; and the three promised volumes were not issued until the beginning of April, 1743.

Mr Cross suggests that after this Fielding decided to give up literature. There is, however, no reason for thinking that the novelist's silence, which followed the *Miscellanies*, was due to a resolution of this kind rather than to the toil and difficulties of a life, which did not leave him enough leisure for his own satisfaction. He had obviously found it very difficult to finish the *Miscellanies*, which were promised to subscribers, and the elements of which were for the most part ready and only needed careful revision ; he had not even been able to finish his *Journey from this World to the Next* [1]. How could he begin a new novel ?

In my view, circumstances were to blame rather than a decision of principle, which nothing would have justified.

Towards the end of 1744, he was overtaken by a great sorrow. His wife, who had been ill for some time, died at Bath [2]. We know, for he often speaks of it, how Fielding had worshipped her and how lovingly he cherished her memory.

[1] cf. *infra*, p. 94, n. 1.
[2] She was buried in London, November 14th, 1744.

She was to be the Sophia of *Tom Jones* and again the original of *Amelia*. Only one daughter, Harriot, was left to him. He kept his servant, Mary Daniel, and probably brought to his house his sister, Sarah Fielding, author of *David Simple*. The brother and sister have left us more than one proof of the bond of sympathy which united them. Sarah played a curious rôle of confidante and ' liaison officer ' between her brother, Fielding, and her friend, Richardson [1].

If Fielding had already—as I believe he had—formed the intention of writing a new novel, circumstances soon postponed it by reawakening in him the dormant journalist. Towards the end of September, 1745, the menace of the invasion of Charles Edward, the Pretender, who had been victorious at Preston Pans, grouped every loyalist element round the Government. Fielding's friends were too numerous and too powerful for him to withhold the help of his pen. He is almost certainly the author of *An Address to the People of Great Britain* [2], which vigorously pleads the cause of the Hanoverian dynasty. Another pamphlet, *A Dialogue between the Pope, the Devil, and the Pretender*, has the same purport but uses grosser weapons, as may be imagined from the title. From November 5th, 1745, his chief occupation was the publication of a weekly paper which was violently anti-Stuart. *The True Patriot* was an *oeuvre de circonstance* written for a special public and has, in my opinion, few passages of more than purely historical interest. Nevertheless, these pages show us one characteristic which Fielding, the pamphleteer,

[1] cf. *Revue Germanique*, July and September, 1920. I have tried there to determine the part played by Sarah who typifies a public which admired two rivals and did not always choose between them.

[2] *A serious address to the people of Great Britain, in which the certain consequences of the present Rebellion are fully demonstrated. Necessary to be perused by every lover of his country, at this juncture*, London, 1745.

A Dialogue between the Pope, the Devil and the Pretender, London, 1745.

In addition to the fact that these two tracts are very much in Fielding's style, they are also attributed to him by his editor, Millar, in a list of his works added to the second edition of *Cleopatra and Octavia*, by Sarah Fielding, 1758 ; cf. Cross, *op. cit.*, Vol. III, pp. 310, 312.

shares with Fielding, the novelist, the habit, which grew upon him, of never attacking save through ridicule and parody [1].

Other productions prove that he continued to work for the publishers : *The Female Husband*, a pamphlet founded on a curious contemporary episode [2] ; a paraphrase of Ovid's *Art of Love* [3]. possibly a History of the Rebellion [4], possibly again, a *Dialogue between a Gentleman of London . . . and an honest Alderman*, and certainly, *A Proper Answer to a Late Scurrilous Libel*, which followed close upon it, all of which were election pamphlets [5]. More important for our purpose is the preface to *Familiar Letters between the principal characters in "David Simple" and some others,* which his sister, Sarah Fielding, had published in April, 1747. Three years earlier Fielding had introduced to the public, the second edition of this same *David Simple*, the authorship of which had been attributed to him. This time he confessed to having written five of the letters, but the chief point of interest in the preface is its condemnation of the epistolary novel—a disdainful condemnation which must have been particularly unpleasant to Richardson [6].

[1] The last number (No. 33) appeared on June 17th, 1746.

[2] *The Female-Husband ; or the surprising history of Mrs Mary, alias Mr George Hamilton, convicted for marrying a young woman of Wells*, London, 1746. There is no existing copy of this pamphlet which Mr Cross attributes to Fielding for the same reasons as the *Address* and the *Dialogue*, cf. Cross, *op. cit.*, vol. III, p. 313.

[3] *Ovid's Art of Love, paraphrased and adapted to the present time*, etc. This work, of which there is no existing copy, was reprinted under the title of *The Lover's Assistant, or New Year's Gift*, etc., by the late ingenious Henry Fielding of facetious memory, London, 1759.

[4] *A compleat and authentick history of the rise, progress, and extinction of the late rebellion and of the proceedings against the principal persons concerned therein*, etc., London, 1747. There is scarcely any reason for presuming this to be Fielding's work and Mr Cross's arguments do not appear to me conclusive. In any case, the pamphlet in question, is simply a piece of hack-work turned out for some publisher.

[5] *A dialogue between a Gentleman of London, Agent for two court candidates and an honest Alderman of the Country Party*, etc., June, 1747. Fielding confesses that he is the author in a note on the following pamphlet : *A proper answer to a late scurrilous libel*, etc. . . by the author of the *Jacobite's Journal*, December, 1747.

[6] cf. *infra*, p. 133, n. 3.

Mr de Castro has recently discovered a document, which is, unfortunately, all too eloquent on the subject of Fielding's financial position during this particular period. It gives extracts from a somewhat involved lawsuit, which ended June 4th, 1747, in Fielding's being condemned to pay the sum of £400 for which he had been surety [1]. It was thus, beset by creditors, toiling for publishers, and filled with anxiety for the morrow, that Fielding began to write *Tom Jones*, that epic of laughter.

To all the blows of fortune which daily beset him, there was soon added yet another. We have seen that after the death of his wife, Mary Daniel the servant, continued to be a member of his household. On November 27th, 1747, Fielding married her. Their eldest son, William, was born February 25th, 1748. The proximity of the two dates is more eloquent than a long commentary. In marrying Mary Daniel, Fielding was not forgetting his first wife, whom he had loved so devotedly. He was making the simple reparation of a man of honour. Why should this be hidden ? It reveals, after all, a fine enough side of Fielding's nature, the true inward nobility which will not be deterred for an instant by the prejudices and opinions of the world. In this, indeed, he lacked skill, for the world he had braved avenged itself and never pardoned Henry Fielding for having despised its conventions.

The Jacobite's Journal, by *John Trottplaid, Esq.*, appeared for nearly a year, from December 5th, 1747, to November, 1748. It was the third paper which Fielding published. In it he heaped ridicule on the Jacobite movement, the ideals of which he parodied with a somewhat heavy hand. He was accused of being in Government pay. This seems probable and natural enough. But the main point for us is that these various tasks enabled him to live and to support his family, while he consecrated to the writing of *Tom Jones* those ' thousands of hours ', of which he has so often spoken.

[1] cf. Paul de Castro, *Notes and Queries*, August, 5th, 1916, pp. 104-6.

THE NOVELS OF FIELDING

The History of Tom Jones, a Foundling was known in part at the end of 1748, but appeared definitely in January, 1749, and almost immediately obtained an enormous success [1]. No doubt Fielding then planned to write another novel soon, which was to be *Amelia* [2]. We do not indeed know this through him. His career as a novelist flows, like an isolated current in the sea of his existence. Comedies, papers, political pamphlets, judicial reforms make up his outer and ' daily ' life, the life which will die with him. But his novels reveal his inner self, they are the life of his soul, which can never die. He seems to have written them without directly consulting or telling anyone, listening only to his will to create, steadily convinced that he has found artistic truth. There are indeed to be found in them, reflections of his daily life, and it will be our business to note them in passing [3], but they are not essential. The Four Novels live of themselves.

Three months before the publication of *Tom Jones*, Fielding had at last received from the Government the reward of his efforts as a loyalist. Lyttleton and the Duke of Bedford had procured for him the office of Justice of the Peace at the Bow Street court, and his jurisdiction was soon to extend to the County of Middlesex. It was well known that this office carried with it an income of some thousand pounds, thanks to all sorts of practices which were not always over scrupulous. The trading justice was a prominent figure in the England of the eighteenth century. Fielding's honesty reduced this ' dirtiest money upon earth ', as he himself called it, to three hundred pounds, a large proportion of which went to his secretary.

As a magistrate Fielding showed the most amazing energy.

---

[1] cf. *infra*, p. 193, n. 1.   [2] cf. *infra*, p. 129, n. 3.

[3] For instance, how profoundly true is the picture of Jones yielding to the charms of a Molly Seagrim at the very moment when his soul is glorying in the memory of Sophia Western (a theme used again in *Amelia*, with Miss Matthews), when one remembers that Fielding, after having loved his wife so tenderly, is unfaithful to her memory and, obliged, soon after, to marry his servant.

LIFE OF FIELDING

His ideas of reform were first expressed in an *Address to the Grand Jury*, delivered at the opening of the sessions of June, 1749 [1]. He painted a black picture of London morals and promised, before taking any other steps, to be vigilant and severe in his repression. Under his direction [2], suspects were rounded up, swindlers arrested, and raids carried out by the police. But Fielding wished to achieve more. In an *Enquiry into the Causes of the late increase of robbers* [3], he tried to put before the public the chief elements of the problem. One year's experience at Bow Street [4] had sufficed to show him that this increase was chiefly due to excessive luxury, and too many amusements, which spread a taste for idleness among the masses ; to the growing consumption of intoxicants, especially

[1] *A charge delivered to the Grand Jury, at the Sessions of the Peace, held for the city and liberty of Westminster*, etc., on Thursday the 29th of June, 1749, *by Henry Fielding, Esq., Chairman of the said Sessions.* Published by order of the Court, and at the unanimous request of the Gentlemen of the Grand Jury.

[2] Here, for example, is what the *Gentleman's Magazine* wrote (February 1st, 1751) : " Justice Fielding having received information of a rendezvous of gamesters in the Strand, procured a strong party of guards, who seized 45 at the table, which they broke to pieces, and carried the gamesters before the justice, who committed 39 to the Gatehouse, and admitted the other 6 to bail. There were three tables broken to pieces, which cost near £60 a piece ; under each of them were observed two iron rollers, and two private springs, which those who were in the secret could touch, etc. . ." For a very complete account of Fielding's activity as a magistrate I recommended the books of Miss Godden and Mr Cross. In 1749, the Strand in particular was the scene of many disorders which Fielding energetically suppressed.

[3] *An Enquiry into the Causes of the late increase of robbers*, etc., *with some proposals for remedying this growing evil. In which the present reigning vices are impartially exposed ; and the laws that relate to the provision for the poor, and to the punishment of felons, are largely and freely examined . . . by Henry Fielding, Esq., Barrister at Law, and one of His Majesty's Justices of the Peace for the County of Middlesex and for the city and liberty of Westminster*, London, January, 1751.

[4] " There is no branch of the law more bulky, more full of confusion and contradiction, I had almost said of absurdity, than the law of evidence as it now stands." The following is what he said regarding public hangings : " If executions, therefore, could be so contrived that few could be present at them, they would be much more shocking and terrible to the crowd without doors than at present, as well as much more dreadful to the criminals themselves, who would thus die only in the presence of their enemies. . ."

31

of gin, the ' devil's liquor ', the sale of which he wished to reserve for chemists ; to the increased number of gaming-houses, where card sharpers assembled and multiplied ; to the scandalous administration of the poor laws ; to insufficient legislation dealing with receivers of stolen goods ; to public hangings which were transformed into a veritable apotheosis of the criminal ; and finally, to the absurd inadequacy of the police force.

Thus, probably with the consent of the Government, he placed the whole matter before the public. Parliament soon followed some of his advice and passed various laws dealing with the principal abuses which he had denounced.

Meanwhile his daily contact with crime made a profound impression on Fielding, who began to experience a spiritual evolution which we shall discuss, when we deal later with *Amelia*. His religious feelings, which he had never really abandoned, began to take definite shape. He discovered the social utility of religion, for the class of people with which his profession brought him into touch. He had such a very definite opinion on this point that on April 13th, 1752, he published his *Examples of the Interposition of Providence in the detection and punishment of murder*[1]. But it was the problem of pauperism which seemed to him to be the foundation of criminality. He tried to solve this too, and published a *Proposal for making an effectual provision for the poor, for amending their morals and for rendering them useful members of society. To which is added a plan of the buildings proposed, etc.* This work which was issued on January 19th, 1753, was dedicated to the Prime Minister, Pelham. Fielding formulated a complete scheme, which was not to be realized for another century ; there were even annexed engravings illustrating the complete plan of a workhouse. The Bill proposed in Parliament was not carried, but three laws were afterwards passed for the suppression of misdemeanours and crimes, which as Mr Cross[2]

[1] cf. *infra.* p. 215, n. 2.   [2] cf. Cross, *op. cit.*, II, p. 280.

points out, were indubitably inspired by Fielding. At the same time, he reorganized the police force (as far as he was able, without completely remodelling it), started a new system of criminal intelligence and, in fact, created a real detective force. This war, waged so energetically and intelligently, had marvellous results. Nocturnal attacks and highway robberies disappeared almost completely [1]. In three years Fielding succeeded in purging those London districts for which he was responsible. His half-brother, John Fielding, who afterwards became a judge, gave him invaluable assistance in his work.

Here, too, must be mentioned two affairs which caused a great sensation at the time. One was the case of Bosavern Penlez whom Fielding hanged for having taken part in the pillaging at a brothel, and the other that of Elizabeth Canning, a young girl who was kidnapped, and whose story is somewhat obscure. In each case there was a violent campaign in the Press, and on each occasion Fielding thought it prudent to justify his attitude in pamphlets, which have been preserved [2].

On December 18th, 1751, Fielding published his last novel, *Amelia*, which had considerable success but did not make such a stir as *Tom Jones*.

The work was hardly out of the printer's hands when Fielding started a new enterprise [3]. The *Covent Garden Journal* is incontestably the best paper which he ever published.

[1] Brown, the author of the celebrated *Estimate*, pays homage to Fielding in the following terms : " Remedies, with proper care, may easily be administered. Thus we have lately seen the salutary effects of a new kind of police, established by a useful magistrate in the City of London : by which the reigning evil of street-robberies hath been almost wholly suppressed." (p. 219).

[2] *A true state of the case of Bosavern Penlez, who suffered on account of the late rise in the Strand, etc.*, published November, 18th, 1749. *A clear state of the case of Elizabeth Canning who hath sworn that she was robbed and almost starved to death by a gang of gypsies and other villains in January last, for which one, Mary Squires, now lies under sentence of death, etc.*, published about March 20th, 1753.

[3] Here, we may mention that Fielding was very closely interested in the *Universal Register Office*, a sort of general information bureau which he had helped to found, and in which he was one of the principal shareholders.

His main object seems to have been to contribute to that deep moral reform, which he thought was becoming increasingly necessary in the England of his day. Besides, as a magistrate he was making a great effort to raise the standard of morality and he wanted to win the favour of and obtain help from the public. Finally we must add that he may also have been moved by that same need for money, in which his other journalistic enterprises had originated [1]. On November 25th, 1752, after some vigorous controversies with enemies unworthy of him, he bade farewell to the public : " I shall here lay down a paper, which I have neither inclination nor leisure to carry on any longer.

" Many of my graver friends have chid me for not dropping it long ago ; indeed, for undertaking it at all. They have been pleased to think it was below my character, and some have been kind enough to tell me that I might employ my pen much more to the honour of myself and to the good of the public.

" How partial such representations have been, I may perhaps be hereafter so unfortunate as to prove : however, I hope I shall be admitted yet to take the advice of my friends " ; and he continues " I solemnly declare that unless in revising my former works, I have at present no intention to hold any further correspondence with the gayer Muses [2]." The tone of these lines reflects his weariness. At this period of his life—he was forty-five—Fielding was an invalid who dragged himself on crutches, and whose superhuman energy

[1] *The Covent Garden Journal*, by Sir Alexander Drawcansir, knt. Censor of Great Britain. Mr G. G. Jensen (Yale University Press) Published in 1915, a perfect edition in two volumes preceded by a copious introduction. He gives a complete account of the " paper-war " waged by Fielding against Dr Hill. As regards Fielding's poverty, one must evidently guard against exaggeration. A note of Mr P. de Castro's (*Notes and Queries*, April 1916) shows that Fielding was regular in his payment of taxes from 1744-8, and that the house which he occupied in Boswell Court was the second largest in the district (rent, £45, later £55). Yet he had never any cash in hand and the first pages of his *Voyage to Lisbon*, where he fears to leave his wife and children in distress, are pathetically sincere and ring true.

[2] *The Covent Garden Journal*, November 25th, 1752.

alone kept him alive. For more than ten years he had been a martyr to gout. He had tried many remedies, including tar-water (beloved of Berkeley), but with very little success. Frequent visits to Bath gave him but momentary relief. During the autumn of 1749, after having overworked at *Tom Jones*, he suffered from a very severe attack. Nevertheless his activity, far from decreasing after this date had, on the contrary, redoubled. His fight against crime left him very little leisure. Yet he found time to revise his novels ; to modify *Jonathan Wild*, a new edition of which, with copious corrections, was published in 1754 ; and to undertake a refutation of Bolingbroke, whose *Essays* had just appeared to the great scandal of all ' believers '.

But Fielding had presumed too far upon his strength. There came a time when even the journey to Bath was no longer possible for him. He thought then to seek health in a milder climate like that of the South of France.

But the journey to Aix over land was too painful for him, and he finally chose Lisbon. He left on June 30th, 1754, and arrived on August 6th. He has given us the most charming and vivid description of his crossing [1].

We know very little of this brief visit to Lisbon [2], for, at the age of forty-seven, Fielding died there (October 8th, 1754). His body remained in Lisbon, and his tombstone,

[1] Dobson has discovered that there were two versions of the *Voyage to Lisbon* : " The *Journal* was first set up and printed directly from Fielding's manuscript : then someone intervened, the first impression was laid aside, and for it was substituted a revised text, which went to the reviewers and, of course, to the general public also. By this interchange the second *printed* edition of the journal became the first *published* edition." Mr Cross, who gives this explanation (III, p. 86) supposes, not without reason, that John Fielding corrected the first edition from motives of prudence, as his brother had spoken somewhat freely of the captain and his vessel and of several people whom he met on the way. The Lisbon earthquake which took place a few months later, encouraged the printer to profit by the circumstance and to re-issue the original version which had been suppressed.

[2] In August, 1911, Dobson published in the *National Review* copious extracts from a long letter written by Fielding from Lisbon. For further extracts, see Mr Paul de Castro's article : *Fielding's Last Letter*, *The Times Literary Supplement*, January 15th, 1920.

which was erected in 1830, in the British cemetery, bears the inscription :

Luget Britannia gremio non dari fovere natum.

As a young man, Fielding had been very strong [1], and it cannot be denied that he enjoyed life to the full. His enemies, who were numerous and whom he made no attempt to placate, slandered him as only the men of that time could slander. His vaunted disregard of what the world said, exposed him to the severe judgment of those who make the opposite their rule of life ; and they are many.

His first biographer was Murphy, a man of letters to whom Millar, Fielding's publisher, gave the task of editing the *Complete Works* (1763). Murphy's volumes (the often careless text of which has been followed in most modern editions) were preceded by a biography. For many years all writers, critics, and historians interested in Fielding made this their fountain-head. Some of them, however, sought to embellish their biographies with fresh details. The least excusable of these inventors was certainly Thackeray, who painted in his *Humourists of the Eighteenth Century*, a drunken, dissolute Fielding, a Bohemian scribbling his works hot from an orgy ; an admirable figure for a novel, whose very truculence gave it, for many years, a semblance of reality. But it was not Fielding. The real Fielding only began to appear with Austin Dobson's biography. Since then further careful research has little by little dissipated the lying legends. And so, receding more and more, and finally fading away, the traditional picture of the *bohème* of letters, the coward in face of pleasure, gradually gives place to the live figure of an untiring fighter. The fact is that Fielding's was a life of

---

[1] His contemporaries make frequent allusions to his height. People often made fun, as he did himself, of the length of his nose and chin. The only portrait which we possess, apart from several caricatures, is a profile which Hogarth was said to have drawn from memory for the 1763 edition.

implacable toil. As soon as he reached manhood, he had to work. He worked that his family might live. He worked to fulfil his duty as a magistrate. He worked to satisfy his literary ideals and to discipline his genius.

Of all these different Fieldings I propose here to study only the last, the novelist :

" *Tel qu'en lui-même enfin l'éternité le change*.* "

---

* Such as into himself Eternity at last changes him. (Mallarmé. *Le Tombeau d'Edgar Poe*).

CHAPTER II

JOSEPH ANDREWS

In February 1742, Millar, a publisher, announced *The History of the adventures of Joseph Andrews and his friend Mr Abraham Adams.* This was the first novel published by Fielding [1] and it was also the last of his polemical works.

The book is, indeed, a polemical work and as such does not entirely escape the traditions of the earlier part of the century. Quarrels had never been so rife in England as they were in this epoch. A rain of libels, pamphlets, and open letters poured down upon the public. They were talked of in the coffee-houses and discussed in the papers. Great men of letters such as Addison, Swift, and Pope, were party-men, and the most important prose-writings of the period had a satirical subject or at least a satirical bias. In those days, one attacked men rather than ideas.

Fielding had done so in his plays, and more freely still in his journals and in the numerous pamphlets of which he was undoubtedly the author. At the same time his plays showed a secret taste for characterization of a more general nature, and this was especially obvious in his choice of *L'Avare*, Molière's most perfect character-comedy. Down to Goldsmith's time, his translation of it was frequently acted. The habits of theatre-goers, however, obliged dramatists to follow the traditions of the Restoration and of the comedy of manners.

---

[1] I say ' published ', because *Jonathan Wild*, as we shall see, was certainly planned and perhaps partly written before *Joseph Andrews*.

Fielding's true comedies of character were to be his novels.

Joseph Andrews, however, is still a pamphlet, and by way of making this perfectly plain, its author warns us that when writing it he had in mind two recent works, namely, the biographies of Mr Colley Cibber[1] and of Miss Pamela. What were Fielding's reasons for attacking these two ?

Against Colley Cibber, Fielding had certainly some personal grudge, which has now been forgotten[2]. This strange personality, actor, theatrical manager, dramatist, and to crown all, poet-laureate, seems to have quarrelled with all his contemporaries. He is best remembered for his squabbles with Pope, who was to spoil his *Dunciad* in order to put him into it. His self-importance, his trenchant tone, and his mediocrity made him especially vulnerable. Fielding[3] attacks him violently, accuses him of writing badly, in *Pasquin* sneers at his odes, and in the *Historical Register* makes fun of his versions of Shakespeare. The two men obviously detested one another, and I dare swear that Fielding was the author of an exceedingly scurrilous pamphlet, the *Apology for the life of Mr T.C.*, in which Theophilus Cibber, his enemy's son, is very cruelly handled. Several pages distinctly bear his mark[4]. Others defend him from Cibber's attacks with a note

---

[1] Published in November 1739, under the title, *An Apology for the Life of Mr Colley Cibber, Comedian*, etc. . . *written by himself*. Cibber is grossly insulting to Fielding, " a broken wit, whom I do not choose to name, unless it could be to his advantage."

[2] They were political adversaries. On the other hand, I note that when Fielding was director of the Haymarket he engaged one of Colley Cibber's daughters who had quarrelled with her father, to play in *Pasquin* (1736). He seems to have given her a place of honour in the company. Perhaps we may find in this the secret reason for Cibber's violent attacks on Fielding's management of the Haymarket. (cf. *A Narrative of the life of Mrs Clarke*, London, 1735, p. 63).

[3] They had begun by being friends and in the preface to *Love in Several Masques*, Fielding thanks him for his " civil and kind behaviour." Also, in 1732, Cibber wrote the epilogue to the translation of *L'Avare*.

[4] This pamphlet appeared in 1740. No doubt Fielding had already written a part of *Jonathan Wild*. It is impossible not to think of the latter when reading the following page in the *Apology for the Life of Mr T.C. :* " I come to that customary and important point in all histories of great men, their birth, parentage, and education. So

so personal and an irony so direct, that one is driven to ask whether they could have been written by any other than Fielding himself. Who else was prepared to defend him with such caustic conviction [1] ?

This virulence decreases in *Joseph Andrews*. Colley Cibber here takes the second place, as befits an already vanquished foe. The whole attack of the book is directed towards another object. Only personal grievances and political disagreement stood between Fielding and Cibber, but from the author of *Pamela* he was separated by a fundamental conflict of ideas and of temperament. Here again we get a valuable characteristic for our portrait of Fielding ; he reserves all the force of his anger for an intellectual adversary.

Who then was this *Pamela* ? The *London Evening News* of November 6th-8th, 1740, contained the following announcement : " This day is published, price bound 6 sh., in two neat pocket-volumes *Pamela*, or *Virtue Rewarded*, etc." The author presented his book as a work of piety, informing his

great a curiosity is there in mankind to be informed of these particulars that almost every revolving moon produces illustrious memoirs of heroes and heroines, whom dire Destiny has allotted to a fatal end." (p. 3). This is the irony of *Jonathan Wild* expressed in almost identical terms.

[1] Theophilus Cibber was a piteous creature, and the author of the pamphlet soon leaves him and attacks his father. He quotes Colley Cibber's reproaches and adds " but that posterity may know this iniquitous son of wit, who has fell under the heavy censure of the Laureate for satirizing the just measures of the present just, all-wise, and all-powerful Minister, I will subscribe the name of H——y F—— —g, Esq., author of . . . etc. ", and he continues with the same emphatic irony : " He drew the mob after him from Grosvenor, Cavendish, Hanover, and all the other fashionable squares, as also from Pall Mall, and the Inns of Court. . . These mobs or multitudes, or concourse, or audiences, call them what you will, resorted nightly to hear these farces, and were dull enough not only to think they contained wit and humour, but truth also. It could not but regret me to see some noble Peers and gentlemen I had entertained a very good opinion of. . ., sitting in the side boxes and seemingly delighted with the performance." He goes on to explain how the Prime Minister, in order to avenge himself and at the same time to suppress the liberty of the stage, sent one Giffard, for an infamous play, entitled *The Golden Rump* and written " by a certain great man's (*i.e.*, Walpole's) own direction and as much scurrility and treason larded in it as possible ". This comedy was used by Walpole as an argument in favour of the *Licensing Act*,(pp. 91-4).

reader of the fact in a voluminous preface. Here was an authentic correspondence, the editor of which had limited his activities to copying the letters. The preface ventured to assert that the book would inculcate " religion and morality in so easy and agreeable manner as shall render them equally delightful and profitable " ; it would not raise " a single idea throughout the whole, that shall excite the exactest purity ". Some admirers who had read the letters in manuscript, praised " the beautiful simplicity of the style and happy propriety and clearness of expression ". " Little book, charming Pamela ", wrote one of them, " face the world and never doubt of finding friends and admirers, not only in thine own country but far from home. . . May every headstrong libertine, whose hand you reach be reclaimed ; and every tempted virgin who reads you, imitate the virtue and meet the reward of the high-meriting though low-descended Pamela." This preface is a prospectus.

Wrapped in these testimonials, and launched by the coterie of women who now began to surround Richardson, the " little book " had a success in fashionable circles. The martyrdom of the servant-girl Pamela is here presented for the sympathy of persons of sensibility. Bequeathed by a dying mistress to the tender mercies of the young lord, her son, Pamela writes to her parents long descriptions of the suggestions which he soon begins to make to her. Her young master is in love with her, as a master can be in love with a poor servant ; he wants to possess her and at first asks her consent ; she refuses, and he replies by increasingly brutal attempts on her virtue. Unhappy Pamela ! She fights desperately for her honour. Happy Pamela ! Her master is at last touched by so much purity and consents to wed her.

The novel ended well. So much virtue menaced by such exquisitely odious violence, provoked terror and pity. The final reward was pleasing ; it improved on nature. The young bully, although something of a simpleton, ended by making amends. The young girl, for all her virtue, knew how to avoid being duped. And English literature at last possessed a real novel.

Pamela had a considerable success. Four editions appeared within a few months. It was imitated, continued, translated, and dramatized [1]. " Have you read *Pamela* ? " was the question of the day, and great ladies, meeting on their walks, held up the two little volumes from a distance to show each other. Horace Walpole spoke of it with enthusiasm. Dr Sherlock recommended it to the pious, from the pulpit. The vogue reached Paris, which soon saw the publication of " the rather bad translation of a curious original ". " One cannot go into any house without finding a *Pamela* ; it is the fashionable furniture [2]." La Chaussée even dramatized it, the play being acted in 1743, and dying so (Voltaire said)" on the very day it was born [3].'

This is not the place to insist upon the literary reasons which made, and may justify, the success of a book which is, on the whole, mediocre. It is both more novel and more useful to show the other side of the picture, and to analyse this great success rather more closely. Approval was far from being as unanimous as tradition would have it.

Were it not that the expression might appear a little ponderous, one might almost say that there was a *Pamela controversy*. Unfortunately only a few fragments thereof have been preserved. The rest are lost or unknown. I should like, however, with the help of those pamphlets that remain, to

---

[1] June, 1741, *Pamela's conduct in high life* ; September, *Pamela's conduct to the time of her death* ; November, *Pamela, a Comedy* by J. Love ; December, *Memoirs of the life of Lady H. . . the celebrated Pamela*. (I give the dates of publication cited by the *Gentleman's Magazine* and *Scot's Magazine*).

[2] *Lettre sur Pamela*, 1742. " l'assez mauvaise traduction d'un original singulier. On n'entre point dans une maison sans y trouver un *Pamela*. C'est le meuble à la mode."

[3] It came to life again in somewhat curious circumstances. In December, 1794, the performance of *Pamela*, was made the pretext for arresting almost the entire company of the *Théâtre Français*.

show the attitude of Pamela's enemies[1]. And I shall be justified in speaking in some detail of this quarrel, if it be really something more than a mere literary by-way, if towards 1740 it really placed in opposition two English mentalities, one of which—that of the old merry England—somewhat careless and slightly cynical, was soon to disappear ; if in short, it set at grips with each other two such considerable adversaries as Richardson and Fielding.

In April, 1741, *The Gentleman's Magazine* announces in a list of new books, *An Apology for the Life of Mrs Shamela Andrews*[2]. It is an amusing and often clear-sighted parody, about sixty pages long, of Richardson's book, and contains some excellent passages.

After a dedication in which the author says that he has modelled his style on that of Euclid, two letters are quoted ; one from ' The Editor to Himself ' (signed John Puff) predicts for the work the greatest possible future : " Believe me, it will go through many Editions, be translated into all Languages read in all Nations and Ages." A note to the reader announces the preparation of " several other commendatory Letters and copies of Verses ", for the second edition.

And this is the story. A certain clergyman, Parson Tickle-text, sends a copy of *Pamela* to his colleague, Parson Oliver, announcing that " The Pulpit, as well as the Coffee-House,

---

[1] Richardson's letters, particularly those addressed to Aaron Hill, which are in the Forster collection at South Kensington, show that Pamela had many enemies and that Richardson was very sensitive to their attacks. The following are the titles of some of the pamphlets, some of which have not been preserved : April, 1741, *Shamela* ; May, *Pamela censured* ; June, *Anti-Pamela or Feigned Innocence detected* ; August, *The Virgin in Eden* ; 1742, *Anti-Pamela*, (in French) ; 1742, *Lettre sur Pamela*.

[2] The complete title is : *An Apology for the Life of Mrs Shamela Andrews, in which the many notorious falsehoods and misrepresentations of a book called Pamela are exposed and refuted, and all the matchless arts of that young politician set in a true and just light. Together with a full account of all that passed between her and Parson Arthur Williams, whose character is represented in a manner somewhat different from that which he bears in Pamela. The whole being exact copies of authentic papers delivered to the editor. Necessary to be had in all families. By Mr Conny Keyber, London, printed for A. Dodd, at the Peacock, 1741.*

hath resounded with its Praise, and it is expected shortly, that his Lordship will recommend it in a Letter to our whole Body." He then maliciously reproduces the exaggerated praises of the introductory letters to *Pamela*, risks some rather coarse jokes such as were enjoyed at that time, on a certain ' Grain of Mustard Seed ' to which Richardson had compared his novel, and concludes by describing the book as " the only education we intend henceforth to give our daughters ". To this silly admirer Parson Oliver returns a somewhat rude reply. He knows, he says, the young woman who was the original of Pamela, " and was in hopes that she would have contented herself with the good fortune she hath attained ; and rather suffered her little arts to have been forgotten than have revived their remembrance ". Her real name was Shamela. Her father had often been in prison and her mother sold oranges in the theatre [1]. There follows a correspondence between the mother and the daughter. And what letters ! They disclose the young woman, forearmed by a first slip with Parson Williams, playing an exceedingly adroit game with the young lord, her master. This is how she describes their first conversation : " Then he took me by the hand, and I pretended to be shy ; Laud, says I, Sir, I hope you don't intend to be rude ; no, says he, my dear, and then he kissed me till he took away my breath, and I pretended to be angry and to get away, and then he kissed me again and breathed very short, and looked very silly." (p. 10). But what is really rather roguish of the parodist, is that these details are mostly borrowed verbatim from Richardson. No better way could have been found of criticizing Pamela's secret perversity, which insists so complacently on the compliments, which B——pays her, on his kisses and the effect which they have upon her. As for B—— he is no longer named by an initial only. He becomes Squire Booby. His language is just as violent as that of Richardson's B—— who needs only a very

---

[1] The detail as to the orange girl is to be found again in *Jonathan Wild*, on which Fielding was working at this time.

45

little exaggeration to appear ridiculous [1]. I will not lay stress upon the parody of the bedroom scene, which is so revolting in Richardson's work. Everything therein is ruthlessly taken up and travestied, from the suspicious ingenuity of Pamela, who in this case, *pretends* to faint, to the stupidity of Booby who does not profit by the swoon. " O what a silly fellow is a bashful young Lover." Thus are Richardson's moral reflections parodied. The satire continues in the same vein until the end. Its value as criticism lies in the fact that it scarcely disfigures the original at all ; it has sufficed to take the incidents of the novel and to give them a different interpretation. For example, Richardson tells us that one day Pamela comes into her master's presence in the simple dress of a country girl. She does not wish, says she, to tempt him with fine clothes. He loved her in her grand dress, perhaps he will love her less in this. Strangely simple in a person, otherwise so prudent ! Strangely artful, interprets the author of *Shamela*, who shows us his heroine whetting her master's appetite by this disguise. " As soon as my master saw her, he immediately threw his arms around her neck and smothered her with kisses (for indeed he has very little to say for himself to a woman)." These characteristics are truly those of Richardson's eroto-maniac, and his Pamela also acts in the same way as Shamela ; the whole difference lies in her intentions. And such indeed is the lesson which the author wishes to teach us ; Pamela who is said to be so pure, who claims to be so sincere, acts in exactly the same way as a hypocrite. She is not ' chaste *avec sobriété* '.[2]—this is not the last time we shall think of Molière when speaking of Fielding—her chastity is aggressive and provocative ; is this not an unavowed coquetry, and is not our ' pure ' Pamela, a sly puss ? " And so ", writes Shamela, " we talked a full Hour and a Half about my Vartue ", " and so we sat down and talked about

---

[1] ' He called me Saucy Chops, Bold Face, Hussy, Slut, etc.' (p. 13).
[2] Molière, *Le Misanthrope*.

my Vartue till Dinner Time ". " and so we talked of honourable Designs until Supper Time ". Beware, the author seems to say, of people who are always talking of virtue. Who knows ? Perhaps the author of *Pamela* merely lacked clear-sightedness. He thought he was telling us a moral story whereas " the instruction which it conveys to servant-maids, is, I think, very plainly this : ' To look out for their masters as sharp as they can. . . The consequences of which will be . . . that if the Master is not a fool they will be debauched by him : and if he is a fool they will marry him '." *Pamela* is a lesson in vice.

In this brief analysis I have not been able to give the often witty *verve*, the clean-cut sobriety, the sure swiftness of this parody. It was generally attributed to Fielding. Richardson, in a letter to Mrs Balfour, says quite definitely : " He abused *Pamela* in his *Shamela*." He must have had some personal motive for this opinion ; and there are other and more objective reasons, which allow us to believe that he was right in accusing Fielding.

First of all, *Shamela* contains a sharp attack on Colley Cibber, who was at that time Fielding's *bête noire ; The Apology for the Life of Mrs Shamela Andrews, by Conny Keyber,* obviously ridicules the *Apology for the Life of Mr Colley Cibber* which had appeared not long before (1740). Fielding may at first have thought that the anonymous author of *Pamela*, was his old enemy [1]. The Booby of *Shamela* reappears in *Joseph Andrews*, Parson Tickletext recalls a certain

---

[1] So it would appear from what he writes in *Shamela* concerning the author of *Pamela* : " Who that is I shall leave you to guess from that Ciceronian eloquence, with which the work abounds ; and that excellent knack of making every character amiable. . ." (p. 6). Further on we find yet another passage, which seems to refer to Cibber, who wrote an epilogue to Fielding's *Miser*, containing the lines :

" Nor would I in that lovely circle raise
One blush to gain a thousand coxcombs' praise."

(1732, when Fielding was twenty-five years of age).

The preface to *Shamela* mentions : " Our Author's professions of modesty which in my youth I have heard at the beginning of an epilogue."

THE NOVELS OF FIELDING

Parson Puzzletext whom Fielding had introduced into his *Grub-Street Opera*, and Parson *Oliver* bears the same name as one of the tutors who educated Fielding when he was a boy. If other resemblances are necessary there is Parson Williams, who plays a very ugly part, and who is a disciple of Whitefield. He preaches a sermon on the text " Be not righteous over-much," and explains that our actions are of no importance when our beliefs are pure. This is the very interpretation of Whitefield's doctrines, given and attacked so vigorously by Parson Adams in *Joseph Andrews* [1]. This same Adams who snaps his fingers on every occasion, reproduces one of Shamela's favourite gestures. And Shamela sobs, as Betty the chamber-maid sobs, at the end of a Chapter in *Joseph Andrews* [2]. Mrs Andrews foreshadows Mrs Slipslop in her *lapsus linguae ;* she says *digression* for *discretion*, *poluteness* for *politeness*, etc Finally, observe the terms in which Parson Oliver describes the duties of a clergyman : " He must content himself with the secure satisfaction of a good conscience, the approbation of the wise and good (which never were or will be the generality of mankind) and the extatic pleasure of contemplating that their ways are agreeable to the Creator of the Universe." The rolling period startles one in *Shamela*. But whoever is familiar with Fielding will recognize the tone and accent of his style and the nobility of the speeches which he more than once puts into the mouth of Parson Adams [3]. Finally, in *Shamela* as in *Joseph Andrews*, we find the same curious mixture of natural and of worldly morality ; natural morality con-demns Pamela for her secret perversity and her calculating conduct ; worldly morality laughs at the ninny who has the

[1] *Joseph Andrews*, I, 17.

[2] " You are jealous if she but looks . . . at a poor Pa-a-a-arson in his Pu-u-ulpit." (*Shamela*, p. 45) ; cf. *Joseph Andrews*, I, 18, " my be-betters are wo-orse than me."

[3] Since this chapter was first written (1914) Mr Paul de Castro has confirmed it in an article in *Notes and Queries* (January 8th, 1916) which contains other striking comparisons between expressions in *Shamela* and similar phrases taken from *Joseph Andrews*, The *Champion* or *Jonathan Wild*.

chance of possessing a woman without marrying her, and does not do it.

What must we conclude from these proofs ? Must we admit that Fielding did not write *Shamela* but that he knew the book and borrowed certain points for his own novel ? If this were so, how was it that his contemporaries and his many enemies did not find it out and accuse him of plagiarism ? *Shamela* was well known [1]. No, his contemporaries, with Richardson at their head, who knew Fielding's ways and his style, were not mistaken [2]. We may share their conviction and attribute this little work to him, with as much certainty as is possible in the absence of a signature or formal acknowledgement.

This will once again help to make clearer our picture of Fielding. [Here is a man, irritated by Colley Cibber and hurling against him and his son the *Apology for the Life of Mr T.C.* He is then exasperated by the author of *Pamela*, whom he probably takes to be Cibber again ; he is revolted (he whom the world accuses of immorality) by its false morality and snivelling sermonizing, and he launches *Shamela* against its author. The second work is far superior to the first. Here is a pamphleteer impatient to write, irritated by the bounds imposed upon him, throwing these two lampoons to the public and perceiving in the very act of writing them, that he is capable of better things.] *Shamela* leads straight to *Joseph Andrews*.

The opposition increased. In August, 1741, a little book appeared, entitled *The Virgin in Eden*. It is dull and mystical and very much like all mediocre works of piety, but it shows us that *Pamela* had enemies among religious people. " Immodest romances, printed in images of virtue ", " profane stories, idle histories destructive to the minds and morals of

---

[1] There are two different editions in the British Museum, one published in London and the other in Dublin.

[2] Thirteen years later, his enemies parodied his *Amelia*, under the title of *Shamelia*.

the age." Such is Richardson's work according to the author of this edifying pamphlet.

The quarrel reached Paris. A *Lettre sur Pamela* also criticizes the story of the little servant and accuses her of being " too little of a novice ", " well-versed in ogling ", " initiated very early ". The writer jeers at her " virtuous vapours ", " her swoons, by the constant repetition of which the author almost makes me suspect that Pamela is ' *ticklish* '. This ticklishness is perhaps the effect of a sensitiveness which cannot bear without convulsions the mere preliminaries of a pleasure which she does not yet know. It makes one tremble. But no more." We too, will stop here. We have read enough to know that when *Joseph Andrews* appeared, a certain number of convinced and obstinate anti-pamelists were in existence [1]. A public was ready for Fielding's book.

What irritates and sometimes exasperates in Richardson's novel is not so much the prudery of Pamela's character, small-minded and fundamentally immoral as it is ; nay, all her little vanities, her naive and complacent admiration for wealth, her indulgent attitude towards B . . ., whose unspeakable coarseness she forgives because he is handsome and rich, her love of dress, even her somewhat morbid erotic sensibilities, all these are exact and drawn from life. If the author's attitude had only been more critical he might have

---

[1] We must also mention here a French anti-Pamelist, Aubert de la Chesnaye-Desbois, author of *Lettres Amusantes et critiques sur les romans en général, anglais et français, tant anciens que modernes* (Paris, 1743.) Two of the letters are devoted to Pamela, who, says the author, has " neither amused nor pleased ". " She loves the compliments that are paid her, delights in telling her parents of them, is exaggerated in her praise, extreme in her invective, curious in her clothes, and is not always annoyed by Milord's attentions, affecting, perhaps, a shy virtue in order the better to attain her ends. . . She gives a lesson indeed, but to whom ? To girls of her own kind whom she teaches to manage the passion which men, in a station above them, may feel for them." " I do not think I am going too far when I say that Pamela, because of some rather too natural expressions will cause her readers to peruse the letters with rather less tranquillity than their editor desires." " The glory of passing for virtuous charms her as much as being virtuous." The author concludes by saying : " I doubt if any novel has ever been more criticized."

made of *Pamela* an admirable and profound psychological study, pitilessly true, the penetrating portrait of a little eighteenth-century waiting-maid, rather mincing, cautiously romantic, and very skilled in making her virtue pay. No, the thing which irritates and sometimes exasperates is not the heroine herself, but the author's devout admiration for her. One feels that his view of the world is the same as hers, narrow and conventional. In painting her he has laid bare the secret of his own soul [1].

Again, what irritates the reader is to find that under the pretence of giving us an edifying and moral novel, the author has presented a salacious tale, the sole interest of which lies in discovering whether a ruffian will finally succeed in seducing a young woman : " Will Pamela be violated or not ? " Such, in a word, is the question which soon becomes the point at issue, such the agonizing problem which has caused so many panting readers feverishly to turn the pages of this book and read without disgust scenes as painful as that in which the author, having cast Pamela and B . . . into the same bed, complacently describes with unmentionable details an attempt at rape.

One feels quite clearly in reading Fielding that he is in revolt against the author's state of mind and his perpetual affectation of virtue, much more than against the novel itself. The preface of *Joseph Andrews* states that " the only source of the true Ridiculous (as it appears to me) is affecta-tion. . . Now affectation proceeds from one of these two causes, vanity or hypocrisy . ." Which of these two springs set the author of *Pamela* in motion ? One was as likely as the other.

[1] This must preclude any comparison with Marivaux, whose Marianne may find herself in a similar situation but is far from posing as virtuous. Her aim is success and she has no hesitation in saying so. She ridicules her old lover and very consciously leads him by the nose. Another great difference lies in the fact that *Marianne* is a story told by a woman of experience who reviews and judges her past. It is a series of memories, very critical, and not as with Richardson, a diary kept from hour to hour.

⌈Joseph Andrews is the brother of the " illustrious Pamela, whose virtue is at present so famous." He admires and desires to imitate her. Sure enough, he will find himself in the same situation as she. In appearance he is personable, he has been fairly well educated, and his voice is so sweet that he cannot be utilized for the usual tasks of country children. Instead of scaring the birds his cries attract them, and the hounds turn from the huntsman and his horn to follow the boy's tuneful notes.⌋ So Joseph is attached to the personal service of Lady Booby, who succumbs to the charms of the handsome boy. On her husband's death her love for the young groom increases. She makes her passion known to him, first by words, then by attitudes, and, finally, by gestures which cannot possibly be misconstrued. Indeed, Joseph does not misunderstand her [1], but as Pamela's brother, he wishes to prove worthy of " the most adorable and most virtuous of sisters ". Like Pamela, he attempts to improve his mind by reading ' good books ' ; he has her manners and borrows her phrases. " I should not care ", he writes to her, " to have folks say I discover what passes in our family ; but if it had not been so great a lady, I should have thought she had had a mind to me. . . " Fielding has not pursued the parody so far as to publish Pamela's reply. Events follow hard upon one another. Joseph resists his mistress and the more definite suggestions of Mrs Slipslop, ' the waiting-gentlewoman '. His chastity triumphs, but mistress and maid, each counselling the other, agree at last in turning him out of doors.

We have now reached the end of Chapter X, and up to this point the parody has followed its model closely enough. ⌈The brother imitates his sister to the point of heroism, and indeed of absurdity.⌋ To-day, this ' Josephism ' (the word

---

[1] This situation obviously recalls that of Jacob (in Marivaux's *Paysan parvenu*) watching his mistress at her toilet, and still more the scene in which Madame de Fécour (Part IV) gives the ' gros Brunet ' to understand that he pleases her. But Jacob has no resemblance to Joseph, and Fielding had no need to seek in Marivaux a situation which is that of the biblical Joseph and Potiphar's wife !

is Fielding's) of a fine lusty fellow might perhaps find defenders, but to Fielding's century it certainly seemed foolish. [The men of those days did not pride themselves upon virtue. The purest contented themselves with not seeking for an opportunity ; but they would have thought it superhuman to flee from one. In their eyes Joseph Andrews was affected, and therefore, ridiculous, for we know that " the only source of the true Ridiculous is affectation"]

But " he is a sagacious reader ", remarks Fielding " who can see two chapters before him." Chapter XI changes all this. We are now given the explanation that Joseph is chaste, not from any absurd sense of modesty, but for the simple reason that he is in love with someone else. Surely then he has ceased to be ridiculous [1] ? What sane man, in love with as exquisite a bride as Fanny, could be moved by the mature beauty of Lady Booby or the hugs of a whiskered Slipslop ? And if Joseph Andrews is no longer ridiculous, what becomes of our parody of Richardson and *Pamela* ? Has Fielding forgotten his original plan ?

This apparent *volte-face* has surprised most critics. Their explanation is that Fielding was carried away by his story, and became so much interested in it that he forgot to parody Richardson. I mistrust an explanation which is founded on a supposed weakness of so great a writer. The truth seems to me simpler. If Fielding ceased to develop the original idea of his book, it was perhaps simply because the idea did not lend itself to further development.

There is indeed a great difference between the situation of Joseph Andrews and that of Pamela. The latter is secretly in love with her seducer, and she is playing her woman's part when she defends herself against him without entirely discouraging him ; her persecutor is young ; he finds in her

---

[1] I am not quite certain whether this would have been Fielding's view. Tom Jones, who was sincerely in love, did not deny himself a little poaching all round. But there are many excuses for Tom Jones, and besides, he is sorry for his faults.

resistance the proof of those moral qualities which make him love her. On the contrary, the same subject as treated by Fielding, necessitates Lady Booby's being a mature woman, who alone can make advances to Joseph. In this case Joseph cannot love her in any real sense of the word. On the other hand his refusals will make him look a fool in her eyes, and there will be an end of the book. Let us borrow from Fielding another reason which he gives with a somewhat brutal frankness ; a lover may hope to possess the woman whom he desires in spite of herself ; thus, a Squire B. can pursue a Pamela for a long while without wearying. [A man's " chastity, however, is always in his own power."] Lady Booby tries and tries again to force the enemy's stronghold ; she finally yields when she finds that the young man is impregnable, and dismisses him.

So now Joseph is cast upon the roads of England. This is just the result which had to be achieved. The whole parody, contained in the first ten chapters, falls suddenly to the ground, slips away from the characters whom it encumbered and whom we now see as they are. It has not, however, disappeared never to return. After having indicated it so firmly at the beginning, the author need not now adhere to it so closely. Just as a ship continues to move after the engines have stopped so is the novel borne forward by the impulse of its first chapters ; and we shall see how artfully Fielding, at the end, will gather together the loose threads of his plot.

Joseph Andrews leaves his master's house, regretted, as was Pamela, by all the servants. A misadventure makes him meet at the inn, his old friend Parson Adams ; from that moment they travel together. On the way they find Fanny and after many adventures and fights, finally reach home. Just as the parody supplied the opening, it now supplies the *dénouement* of the book. In spite of all Lady Booby's plots, Joseph Andrews, loaded with favours by his brother-in-law, graciously received by his sister Pamela, eventually leads his

Fanny to the altar and receives good Parson Adams' blessing.

Thus the parody of Richardson is found at the beginning of the novel, it guides the general movement, and comes in again at the journey's-end. This being so, how can it be said that Fielding forgot it ?

Nevertheless, although he did not forget it, he is now too great to limit himself to parody. [Joseph is more than a mere caricature of his sister Pamela. True, he, also, resists repeated attacks upon his purity. After Lady Booby and Dame Slipslop, he has to eject from his room one Betty, the maid at the inn, whose significant gestures solicit a little love. But Joseph is guilty neither of stupidity nor insensibility. He confesses that he was not insensible to the charms of Lady Booby : " I had once," says he, " almost forgotten every word Parson Adams had ever said to me." Later we see him as an impatient lover, quick to profit by the friendly darkness and talk at closer quarters with his Fanny. Once, indeed, he becomes the shepherd of the Eclogue [1], but for the most part he is nothing more than the amusing figure of a young lover, simple and frank, both morally and physically vigorous.]

His human qualities already seem to foreshadow the great heroes of Fielding's novels. When he is in danger of death, he is quite ready to confess and repent of his faults but he is energetic in his refusal to repent of his love for Fanny, or to forgive the robbers who have wounded him ; ' a good hater ', the expression is as English as the quality it describes. Again, when Pamela, with the airs of an elder sister, is chiding Fanny " for her assurance in aiming at such a match as her brother ", Fanny only weeps, but Joseph, folding her arm in his, leads her away swearing that he will not recognize the enemies of his beloved Fanny, either as relations or as allies ; and his manner is so decided that Mr Booby does not think it " proper to oppose him ".[2] The Joseph who, at the beginning

[1] *Joseph Andrews*, II, 12, p. 181. In our quotations, the first figure (Roman) refers to the book, and the second to the chapter. The page is that of J. P. Browne's edition (London, Bickers & Son, 1903).
[2] Ibid, IV, 11, p. 382.

of the novel, wrote such timid letters to his sister, is far removed from this Joseph, who dares to resist Parson Adams, when his own interest is at stake. The boy of the earlier episodes has become a man. A few weeks of life on the roads have sufficed to develop him.

In Joseph's betrothed, Fanny, Fielding may perhaps have wished to oppose to the false *ingénue*, Pamela, the portrait of a really chaste young woman. At any rate, she will not abandon herself to any epistolary intemperance, for she can neither read nor write. She is a beautiful, plump country girl, who loves her Joseph rather greedily. She is ignorant of Pamela's affectations and vapours about her honour. Compare the description of the first kiss in *Pamela*, lingered upon with such relish, with the frank, simple charm of lines such as these, which describe the first separation of the two lovers : " A thousand sighs heaved the bosom of Joseph, a thousand tears distilled from the lovely eyes of Fanny. Though her modesty would only suffer her to admit his easy kisses, her violent love made her more than passive in his embraces ; and she often pulled him to her breast with a soft pressure." Here the blushful modesty of the words adds to their effect. We are in another world than Richardson's, a world where nerves are calmer and sensibilities less ' heady '. In Coleridge's phrase, " to take him up after Richardson is like emerging from a sick-room, heated by stoves, into an open lawn on a breezy day in May."

As for Pamela, Fielding amuses himself by showing her as a young wife. She preaches and moralizes without end. At one point, a revelation only half made leads to a belief that Joseph and Fanny are brother and sister, and the two lovers are in the depths of despair at finding themselves reduced to brotherly love : Pamela comes in appositely with a lecture. If, she says, Joseph " loves Fanny as he ought, with a pure affection, he has no reason to lament being related to her ". Has she no senses ? Her swoons have proved the contrary. But she will not admit it, and the whole case at issue between Richardson and Fielding is condensed in this opposition.

As we approach the end of the novel, the parody becomes more delicate. The author is now more certain of himself. His blows are less heavy but more penetrating. A person as affected in her humility as Pamela, cannot but affect pride when she in her turn is exalted. That regard for worldly position, which once moved her in her relations to her superiors, she now applies to herself and her inferiors. Someone tells her that Fanny is her " equal, at least ". She purses up her lips and answers " She was my equal. But I am no longer Pamela Andrews ; I am, now, this gentleman's lady [1] and as such, am above her." (IV, 7). The satire is keen and the psychological deduction very just. Elsewhere Fielding indulges in a little fun, as when, for instance, during Joseph's marriage ceremony he makes Parson Adams publicly rebuke Booby and Pamela for laughing in church. Of Booby I can say no more than that he is an insignificant person but withal a gentleman.

Joseph Andrews cannot then be called a parody in the sense in which the word is used of *Virgile Travesti*. Fielding has not followed Richardson's novel, page by page [2]. He has merely borrowed the original scheme. He has, as Richardson himself declared, grafted his novel on to *Pamela* [3]. For the rest parody was too secret a form of art for him to content himself with it for long. The author of a parody wears a mask, and Fielding, at the point which we have now reached, was sufficiently sure of himself to go with uncovered face. He wished to be himself. This is why the actual plot, which springs from the parody, only plays a secondary part. It is

[1] The first edition used the word ' wife '. The second cleverly corrects this to ' lady '.

[2] A few divergencies are noticeable, the chief being that while Richardson, speaking of Pamela's parents says, " They brought up a great family of which I am the youngest, etc. . ." Fielding writes: " Mr Joseph Andrews . . . was esteemed to be the only son of Gaffer and Gammer Andrews. . ." (I, 2).

[3] " A lewd and ungenerous engraftment."

there merely to place the characters into situations wherein their qualities will be displayed. And it is in this respect that Fielding, even at this stage of his career, distinguishes himself from the picaresque novelists. *Joseph Andrews* is not a novel of action, it is a character-novel, in the true sense of the word.)

It is remarkable that in speaking of him we should be led to use the language of *dramatic* criticism. When he begins to write novels, Fielding is already an experienced dramatist. His plays—whether we like them or not—are skilfully constructed. And *Joseph Andrews* is constructed exactly like the plays of the French classical writers, with a regular, solid and sure plan. The four books are like four acts, of which the first contains the ' exposition ' and the knot of the problem, the second and third the ' peripeteia ' or incidents, and the fourth gives the *dénouement*. In the course of the first chapters each of the characters appears on the scenes in turn, Adams after Joseph, then Mrs Slipslop, then Lady Booby; these characters meet, the struggle which is about to break out between them is at first faintly discerned, and then declared in all its violence. " The scene opens itself by small degrees ", says our author (p. 57). He does it gradually and methodically. No other English novelist had as yet constructed and assembled his work so clearly [1].

The plot thought out, and the protagonists flung into the highway, there remains nothing for the author but to hold

[1] In the preface of *Incognita* ; *or Love and Duty Reconciled*, after the well-known passage where he draws the distinction between *Novel* and *Romance*, Congreve had, as it were, foreseen this discipline to which Fielding was to subject the English novel : " Since all traditions must indisputably give way to the drama, and since there is no possibility of giving that life to the repetition or writing of a story that it has in the action, I resolved in another beauty to imitate dramatic writing, namely in the design, contexture, and result of the plot. I have not observed it before in a novel. . . In a comedy this would be called unity of action ; here it may pretend to no more than the unity of contrivance." Congreve certainly did not follow this splendid programme in *Incognita*. But the theory of submitting the inorganic novel to the living laws of the drama, is a curious one. In *Joseph Andrews* and *Tom Jones* Fielding succeeded where Congreve, a pure dramatist, had failed.

them there and retard the *dénouement* by suitable incidents. Fielding, as a great artist and realist, employs only the simplest means. Rain and a storm force our folk to stop at an inn (II, 12, p. 179), their poverty keeps them there, thieves rob them, and a judge arrests them arbitrarily. There is nothing here but what was common and customary at the time ; it was the usual small crop of adventures of the English highroad.

The perfection of artistry is particularly striking when this economy of dramatic devices is compared with the complications, the entanglement of *motifs* in Richardson.

But, although the devices are so simple, nothing remains unexplained. No sooner does Dame Slipslop find Mr Adams and his companions at the inn than she hastens to tell us the why and the wherefore of this meeting, and at the same time an opportunity is afforded the author of painting this inexhaustible chatterbox (II, 13, p. 187). There comes a moment when " perhaps the reader may wonder how Mr Adams was able to produce a sufficient sum for so many days ". This again is explained (II, 2, p. 107). Elsewhere Adams and Fanny are arrested by mistake and taken before the judge ; a paragraph explains how pardonable was the mistake of those who arrested them (II, 10, p. 168). Nay, the second edition amends the first on this point, and brings its complement of explanations and likelihoods.

This is where his dramatic schooling has been most useful to Fielding. He subjects the novel to the discipline of the drama, to the rules for solid construction, which had been formed by a collective experience already old. The theatre of the Restoration was dying of the abuse of methods and formulae, of excessive ' craftsmanship '. But this craftsmanship, which was outworn in the theatre was new in the novel ; it gave it life.

We have called it a character-novel, in which the action, vigorous as it appears, does not, however, take the first place. Indeed, *Joseph Andrews* suffers from the fault which prevails

all too often in comedies of character. The ending is
necessarily the weak point in works of this kind. It is almost
always engineered from without ; for passions never stop
working nor come to an 'end'. *Tartuffe* terminates by the
intervention of the ' prince '. To prevent Harpagon from
marrying Marianne, a daughter has to be miraculously
discovered by her father [1]. Fielding resorts to a similar form
of *dénouement* in *Joseph Andrews*. Joseph is found to be the
son of a gentleman, Mr Wilson, while Fanny, far from being a
foundling, is the daughter of Gaffer and Gammer Andrews.
Bourgeois proprieties are saved (strange concession, at the
eleventh hour, to the prejudices of the time), and no one
henceforth opposes the marriage, which brings the book to
a happy ending. And yet feeble as it is, this *dénouement* is
by no means clumsily brought about. Fielding has been at
pains to lead on to the surprise gradually. First of all, Fanny
is found to be the daughter of the Andrews, so that for some
time everyone believes that she is Joseph's sister, which
allows the novelist to show us the different reactions of the
chief characters to the situation. We have already noticed
the grief of Joseph and Fanny ; Parson Adams also has his
word to say ; and hope blossoms once more in the heart of
Lady Booby. Is it necessary once again to point out how
classical is this form of construction ? One is often tempted
to believe that Fielding had read Boileau [2]. Finally Mr Wilson
arrives, and through a mark like a strawberry on Joseph's
chest, recognizes the young man as his long-since kidnapped
son. It should finally be noted that this arrival of Mr Wilson,

---

[1] In his translation of *L'Avare*, Fielding has amended this *dénouement* and has tried to make it more believable, which curiously enough,
shows us how full his mind was of these questions of verisimilitude,
cf. *supra*, p. 12-15.

[2]   " D'un secret tout à coup la vérité connue
        Change tout, donne à tout une face imprévue." *Boileau.*
In any case, even if Fielding did not know Boileau himself, he was at
least well acquainted with his eighteenth century successors, Le Bossu,
Bellegarde, etc.

which takes place in Chapter XV, had been announced as early as Chapter V.

If we fully understand this constructive method, we shall more easily realize why so much importance is given to certain characters, whose part in the action sometimes seems to lay too heavy a burden on their shoulders. It is clear for instance, that the chief mission of a Joseph Andrews and a Lady Booby is to carry the plot along ; and the great drawback of this system is that the people who thus form the centre of action are not always the centre of interest. To take a modern comparison (which, I confess, I am not making unintentionally) Joseph here plays a part somewhat analogous to that played in one of Anatole France's works by the excellent and simple Jacques Tournebroche. Joseph is a pretext for Parson Adams, just as Tournebroche is a pretext for Abbé Jérome Coignard, and the Joseph-Fanny intrigue plays the same important part in the economy of the earlier work, which the modern book assigns to the less modest loves of Tournebroche and the fair Jahel. As for Lady Booby, Book IV shows her desperate and quick to profit by all the obstacles which stand in the way of the young couple's happiness. She retreats step by step, and only yields when her resistance has shown us all the characters of the novel, revealed under all their aspects by conflicts which lay bare the soul. She is a ' utility-man ' in the most favourable sense of the word ; she bears upon the action, now retarding and now precipitating it.

Such in this book so often called a ' novel of adventure '. is the part actually played by adventure, by plot. Adventures are not often there for their own sake and the plot would be thin were it not filled out with characters. The essential thing is that there should be no hitch in it, so that we may give our whole attention to these characters, as it reveals them in high relief.

We have now seen how closely this art is allied to that of the theatre. In what way is it different ? The author tells us that it is to comedy what the *Iliad* and the *Odyssey* were to

Greek tragedy [1]. Fielding claims that he is writing " a comic epic poem in prose ". He has now the advantage over the drama, in that he is no longer hampered by the conditions of the stage, and can, therefore, give free rein to his imagination. In drama characterization must keep within certain limits and the lines be clearly drawn ; what is gained in vigour and distinctness, is lost perforce in richness [2]. The novelist, on the contrary, can work at length upon a less rigid design, he can linger over his painting, retouching is not forbidden him. He can explain apparent contradictions, can surround his protagonists with a whole atmosphere of secondary characters who appear upon the stage for an instant, just long enough to make one speech, to say a few words. But those few words pronounced by some ephemeral person, will have served to add to the picture an infinitesimal yet essential touch, which remains forever there. In short, the novelist is not condemned like the dramatist to unity and sobriety.

Yet some secret exigency of his free genius seems to have made Fielding constrain himself to this discipline. Never does this appear more clearly than when we study the character of Adams. Although it is without doubt one of the fullest and richest upon which a novelist has ever expended the wealth of his imagination, yet this admirable fulness is in no way confused ; nothing overlaps ; the figure is admirably wrought. Never did a more abundant genius restrict itself by a more rigorous method.

[1] Congreve had already made an analogous comparison in the preface to *Incognita* (quoted above) where he distinguishes between ' novel ' and ' romance '. " Romances give more of wonder, novels more delight. And with reverence be it spoken and the parallel kept at due distance, there is something of equality in the proportion they bear in reference to one another, with that between Comedy and Tragedy."

[2] This is particularly true of the Comedy of that time, which was limited to set types. In the *Museum* of August, 1747, a writer gave the following recipe for making a comedy : " Take a Coquette, a Beau, a Lover, a Valet, a miserly Father, and mix them well. . . Let the Coquette use her Lover like a dog for a long time, then marry him unaccountably to his great wonder and astonishment, then put in a Song and a Dance, and you have a complete Comedy."

JOSEPH ANDREWS

We make Adams's acquaintance progressively. He pene-
trates us gradually, each chapter adding a new characteristic,
retouching and correcting an old one, modifying a shade
And so this delightful soul reveals itself to us, this soul which
pours itself out so lavishly, and is forever springing into new
life. Now that I have to set my hand to it, I almost hesitate
to touch it.

Mr Adams is a curate. Influence has won him a parish
and he, and his wife, and his six children subsist on an annual
stipend of twenty-three pounds sterling ! But he never thinks
of deploring his poverty, for his mind is teeming with treasures
more precious than any material wealth. He knows much,
though his learning has not been acquired in schools or
universities, but by assiduous reading ; and that reading has
been almost entirely confined to ancient writers and the
authors of sacred works. He knows Homer from beginning
to end. The only modern tragedy of which he is not ignorant
is Mr Addison's *Cato*, which he admires greatly, and the only
comedy which he has ventured to see is Mr Richard Steele's
Conscious Lovers, in certain passages of which, he owns,
" there are some things almost solemn enough for a sermon."
By reading so many ancient authors, he has acquired their
habits and their philosophy of moderation. He is always
ready to reason about everything, enjoys talks and discussions, enters into conversations with any chance-met
stranger, knowing that every opportunity offers some sort of
profit ; or, if he is alone, he sits by the roadside and reads
Æschylus, an Æschylus in manuscript, which he has carefully
copied with his own hand. He has built for himself an ideal
world, the only world in which he cares to live. The other,
the world of reality, seems to him difficult. He often forgets
it and his moments of abstraction are delightfully amusing.
He leaves his village for London in order to sell ten volumes
of sermons, which he hopes will bring him money and fame.
When he is halfway through his journey, he suddenly finds
that he has left them behind. He is not, however, inordinately

63

annoyed ; the lapse will furnish him with the opportunity for a journey on foot, which he adores [1]. Another day he leaves an inn, forgetting in pure simplicity of heart to pay the bill ; several days pass before he remembers his horse, which he has left in the stable of a hostelry. Or again, hurrying to Fanny's aid, he accidentally flings the book which he was reading into the fire, alas, it is his precious Æschylus, and he can save only a miserable relic, the beautiful sheepskin binding.

It must not, however, be thought that this portrait is caricatured or laboured. Adams is not absent-minded in the sense that La Bruyère's Ménalque is. Ménalque's mind is empty, while that of Adams is, on the contrary, always busy and interested in everything. We should like him less if he were not so spontaneous. At the age of fifty he still has the fresh soul of a child, who looks out upon our old world with young eyes. For instance, he cannot imagine for one moment that a man and a woman can live together without being married (IV, 12, p. 385). Credulous and simple, he allows himself to be deceived with disarming ease [2], as though he were actually inviting people to deceive him. He is introduced to a bookseller, a possible purchaser of his sermons ; and " to induce the bookseller to be as expeditious as possible, as likewise to offer him a better price for his commodity, he assured him their meeting was extremely lucky to himself ; for that he had the most pressing occasion for money at that

---

[1] This is not the only characteristic which he has in common with Rousseau. In speaking of *Tom Jones* we shall analyse Fielding's naturalism (or love of nature). Let us keep in our minds the suggestion that Nature is something essentially good. This idea is very clearly developed in the story of Mr Wilson, (III, 4).

[2] This is obviously one of the ways in which he most resembles Don Quixote. Let us note some others : (a) his great height, which makes his feet touch the ground when he is on horseback ; (b) his great love of fights, in which he is often the victor. Last, and most important of all, the cause of their misfortunes is the same ; Adams pictures the world according to the books which he has read, just as Don Quixote does. Both make mistakes in such good faith and are so well-meaning that they awake in the reader the same sympathetic response.

time, his own being almost spent, and having a friend then in the same inn, who was just recovered from some wounds received from robbers, and was in a most indigent condition. ' So that nothing ', says he, ' could be so opportune for the supplying both our necessities as my making an immediate bargain with you '." (I, 17, p. 93). One can imagine the result of discussing business thus astutely with a crafty tradesman [1]. Another time, because he knows neither malice nor subterfuge, the good man unconsciously discloses secrets which have been confided to him, at the very moment when he is expressing a desire to keep them, (II, 3, p. 117).

Herein lies his greatness. There may be a kind of holy glory in being a dupe, and humanity's deep sympathy goes out to a Don Quixote (and later to a Pickwick) who cannot tread the tortuous paths of the clever. It is only the virtuous people in the book who love Parson Adams ; fools and rogues deride and persecute him. But he is always in the right. He believes, in all good faith, the promises made by a wag, (II, 16, p. 205). Any hypocrite whom he meets has no difficulty in throwing dust in his eyes, (III, 12, p. 317). He cannot see through the most flagrant rogue. During the whole of one evening a squire and his friends subject him to the most grotesque buffooneries or the most odious practical jokes ; they drive a pack of hounds between his legs, draw away his chair from under him, and " overturn a plate of soup into his breeches " ; but " the inoffensive disposition of his own heart made him slow in discovering " jests of this kind. Even when he does discover what is happening, the dear man always forgives. In their last joke, however, they go too far, and he is flung into a tub full of water. Then Mr Adams gets angry ; he drags his malicious host into the tub after him, and after a few high-sounding curses on the house, departs with Joseph [2].

[1] This may be reminiscent of the simplicity with which Gil Blas sells his mule, (Ch. 1).

[2] The original of this practical joker may well be John Duke of Montagu, of whom his mother-in-law, Sarah, Duchess of Marlborough,

THE NOVELS OF FIELDING

To tell the truth, if he is irritated it is not so much on account of the harm to himself, as because the lie has been given to his philosophy. Here, indeed, lies the secret of the artistic balance of this character, which is at once sympathetic and ridiculous. We may laugh without too much remorse when Parson Adams is jolted, ill-used and distressed by realities which he has disregarded. Far from confessing his inexperience, he actually claims to have more knowledge of life than anyone else. Adams is no exception to the rule that everyone has some particular affectation. But he is so ingenuously affected that we can but smile, without finding it in our heart to rebuke him. His host at the inn relates how he himself was fooled by the very maker of promises of whom Adams has just been a victim. " O fie ! " says Adams, " O, fie ! He is indeed a wicked man ; but God will, I hope, turn his heart to repentance. Nay, if he could but once see the meanness of this detestable vice ; would he but once reflect that he is one of the most scandalous and pernicious liars ; sure he must despise himself to so intolerable a degree, that it would be impossible for him to continue a moment in such a course. And to confess the truth, notwithstanding the baseness of this character, which he hath too well deserved, he hath in his countenance sufficient symptoms of that *bona idoles*, that sweetness of disposition, which furnishes out

writes : " All his talents lie in things only natural in boys of fifteen years old, and he is about two-and-fifty ; to get people into his garden and wet them with squirts and to invite people to his country houses, and put things into their beds to make them itch, and twenty such pretty fancies like these." (*Walpole's Letters*, ed. Cunningham.) Montesquieu was the victim of one of these pretty fancies. When he arrived it was decided that they should play at ambassadors, which meant, I imagine, that the duke was to receive his guest with great ceremony. The duke had conceived the idea of placing a tub of water in a hole on the spot where Montesquieu was to kneel to him. When the latter came forward to salute Marlborough, he stumbled and fell headfirst into the tub. " I thought it odd, to be sure ", said Montesquieu when he told the tale many years afterwards to Charlemont, " but a traveller, as you well know, must take the world as it goes." (Churton Collins, *Voltaire, Montesquieu, and Rousseau in England*). These practical jokes are precisely similar to those played upon Parson Adams.

a good Christian." "Ah, master, master !" says the host,
"if you had travelled as far as I have, and conversed with
the many nations where I have traded, you would not give any
credit to a man's countenance. Symptoms in his countenance,
quothà ! I would look there, perhaps, to see whether a man
had the small-pox, but for nothing else." He spoke with so
little regard to the parson's observation, that it a good deal
nettled him ; and, taking the pipe hastily from his mouth,
he thus answered : "Master of mine, perhaps I have travelled
a great deal farther than you without the assistance of a ship.
Do you imagine sailing by different cities or countries is
travelling ? No,

Caelum non animum mutant qui trans mare currunt.

I can go farther in an afternoon than you in a twelvemonth.
What, I suppose you have seen the Pillars of Hercules, and
perhaps the walls of Carthage. Nay, you may have heard
Scylla, and seen Charybdis ; you may have entered the
closet where Archymedes was found at the taking of Syracuse.
I suppose you have sailed among the Cyclades, and passed
the famous straits which take their name from the unfortunate
Helle, whose fate is sweetly described by Apollonius Rhodius ;
you have passed the very spot, I conceive, where Daedalus
fell into that sea, his waxen wings being melted by the sun ;
you have travelled the Euxine Sea, I make no doubt ; nay,
you may have been on the banks of the Caspian, and called
at Colchis, to see if there is ever another Golden Fleece."
"Not I, truly, master", answered the host "I never touched
at any of those places." "But I have been at all these ",
replied Adams. "Then, I suppose ", cries the host, "you have
been at the East Indies ; for there are no such, I will be sworn,
either in the West or the Levant." "Pray, where's the
Levant ?" quoth Adams, "that should be in the East Indies,
by right." "Oho ! you are a pretty traveller ", cries the
host, "and not know the Levant ! My service to you, master ;

you must not talk of these things to me ; you must not tip us the traveller ; it won't go here." " Since thou art too dull to understand me still ", quoth Adams, " I will inform thee ; the travelling I mean is in books, the only way of travelling by which any knowledge is to be acquired. From them I learn what I asserted just now, that nature generally imprints such a portraiture of the mind in the countenance, that a skilful physiognomist will rarely be deceived." (II, 17, p. 213).

His books, however, have not prepared him to find mankind so wicked. Its perversity astonishes and scandalizes him. " Good Lord ! " says Adams, " what wickedness is there in the Christian World ! I profess almost equal to what I have read of the heathens." Yet he never profits by any of the lessons of experience. This is the conclusion which he draws from an adventure in which he has been fooled : " You say right, Joseph, knowledge of men is only to be learnt from books, Plato and Seneca for that ; and those are authors, I am afraid, child, you never read." (II, 16, 210). No, Joseph certainly has not read them but his brief experience as a footman has taught him more than all his master's books.

This indeed is Adams' chief vanity. He is more learned than those among whom he moves and so he thinks himself wiser. This results in a sort of ingenuous pedantry, the manifestations of which are most delicious when they are least expected. On one occasion, although he is in a difficult position, he cannot prevent himself from raising a point of grammar, (II, 11, p. 173). He breaks the thread of an interesting story to correct the pronunciation of a proper name, (IV, 10, p. 373). And he does not lose the opportunity of giving us a long lecture on Homer and his chief perfections, (III, 2, p. 231).

These are very small eccentricities and are easily forgiven. They amuse us all the more since neither theories nor books have withered Adams' soul. We have seen how he persists

JOSEPH ANDREWS

in nourishing an incurably optimistic philosophy in the face
of all the shocks and contradictions of life. But it must not
be imagined that the outside world is always to blame. It is
Adams himself, whose actions contradict his theories in the
most delightful way. One day his friend, Mr Wilson, gives
him a long dissertation on vanity, and the important part which
it plays in human life. " Adams now began to fumble in his
pockets, and soon cried out, ' O la ! I have it not about me.'
Upon this, the gentleman asking him what he was searching
for, he said he searched after a sermon, which he thought his
masterpiece against vanity."

" ' Fie upon it, ie upon it ! ' cried he,' why do I ever
leave that sermon out of my pocket ? I wish it was within
five miles ; I would willingly fetch it to read it to you '."
Mr Wilson answered that there was no need, for he was cured
of the passion. " ' And for that very reason ', quoth Adams,
' I would read it for I am confident you would admire it :
indeed, I have never been a greater enemy to any passion
than that silly one of vanity.' Mr Wilson smiled [1]."
(III, 3, p. 252).

These contradictions make Adams very human. He is
arrested by some villagers, who think him guilty of an offence,
and is proved innocent ; the judge apologizes and there is a
general reconciliation over a few pots of beer. Suddenly
sounds of quarrelling are heard ; the villagers have begun to
fight. The judge goes out to pacify them and returns saying
that " the occasion of the quarrel was no other than a dispute
to whom, if Adams had been convicted, the greater share of
the reward for apprehending him had belonged. All the
company laughed at this, except Adams, who taking his
pipe from his mouth fetched a deep groan, and said, ' He was
concerned to see so litigious a temper in men '." He then

[1] Adams, having denounced vanity, shows that he himself is vain.
This is a touch dear to Molière : M. Jourdain's master of philosophy
inveighs against anger, and then flies into a rage, Vadius jeers at verse-
makers and proceeds to take a book of verses out of his pocket, etc.

69

tells a story and concludes with " some philosophical observations on the folly of growing warm in disputes in which neither party is interested ".

Several minutes pass and the judge (who has cut a very poor figure throughout the whole business), begins to " sing forth his own praises and to value himself exceedingly on his nice discernment. . . He was quickly interrupted by Mr Adams, between whom and his worship a dispute now arose, whether he ought not in strictness of law, to have committed him, the said Adams ; in which the latter maintained he ought to have been committed, and the justice as vehemently held he ought not. This had most probably produced a quarrel (for both were very violent and positive in their opinions), had not Fanny, etc." (II, 12, p. 179).

On another occasion, Joseph who is beginning to weary of waiting, asks the parson to hasten his marriage, whereupon Adams preaches a long sermon in two heads, which ends thus : " ' You are too much inclined to passion, child, and have set your affections so absolutely on this young woman, that, if God required her at your hands, I fear you would reluctantly part with her. Now, believe me, no Christian ought to set his heart on any person or thing in this world, but that, whenever it shall be required or taken from him in any manner by Divine Providence, he may be able, peaceably, quietly, and contentedly to resign it.' At which words one came hastily in, and acquainted Mr Adams that his youngest son was drowned. He stood silent a moment, and soon began to stamp about the room and deplore his loss with the bitterest agony. Joseph, who was overwhelmed with concern, likewise, recovered himself sufficiently to endeavour to comfort the parson ; in which attempt he used many arguments that he had at several times remembered out of his own discourses, both in private and public (for Mr Adams was a great enemy to the passions, and preached nothing more than the conquest of them by reason and grace), but he was not at leisure now to hearken to his advice. ' Child, child ', said he, ' do not go about impossibilities. Had it been any other of my children, I could have borne it with patience ; but my little prattler, the darling and comfort of my old age '." and Mr Adams continues thus to pour out his sorrow with a tender and familiar abundance [1], when suddenly news is brought that the child has indeed fallen into the river, but has been rescued. " When these tumults were over, the parson, taking Joseph aside, proceeded thus : ' No, Joseph, do not give too much way to thy passions, if thou dost expect happiness.' The patience of Joseph nor perhaps of Job could bear no longer ; he interrupted the parson saying it was easier to give advice than to take it ; nor did he perceive he could so entirely conquer himself, when he apprehended he had lost his son, or when he found him recovered ; ' Boy ', replied Adams, raising his voice, ' it doth not become green heads to advise grey hairs. Thou art ignorant of the tenderness of fatherly affection ; when thou art a father thou wilt be capable then of knowing what a father can feel. . . .' ' Well, Sir ', cries Joseph ' and if I love a mistress as well as you your child ? ' Whereupon Mr Adams again rebukes him : ' Every man ought to love his wife, no doubt ; we are commanded so to do ; but we ought to love her with moderation and discretion '." This time it is Mrs Adams who settles the question and proves that her husband is contradicting himself. . . " ' You do not preach as you practise ; for you have been a loving and cherishing husband to me ; that's the truth on't ; and why you should endeavour to put such wicked nonsense into this young man's head, I cannot devise. Don't hearken to him, Mr Joseph '." (IV., 8, p. 368.)

If Mr Adams frequently contradicts himself, it is chiefly because he does not know himself. We find our own minds reflected in his, with our constant illusions about ourselves, our wavering resolutions and our attempts to achieve another

[1] In February, that is to say, when *Joseph Andrews* was appearing, the registers of St Martin's in the Fields mention the burial of little Charlotte Fielding. She had been ill all the winter (cf. preface to *Jonathan Wild*), and Fielding had often been anxious about her.

ego. The stoicism which he has chosen as his ideal is something of which he is quite incapable. It would have needed a stern and arid nature, and his teems with goodness. It is one of those natures which know not evil, because they have never seen it in themselves, and which find no merit in doing good because they do it without effort. He is not a saint, as we rather too theoretically conceive saints to be, straining their wills to follow the rugged paths of perfection. His habits are, on the contrary, full of freedom and gaiety [1]. If he is happy he stamps and skips like a child (p. 183), walks with a swinging stride (188, 344), or snaps his fingers in a favourite gesture. He likes romantic tales, his ears are " the most hungry part about him ", his curiosity " insatiable." And, if the story is edifying to boot, he " licks his lips ", " I could willingly hear it over again ", he says (262). He laughs in the amusing places, groans when occasion demands (240). As a story-teller he gives, and as a listener demands, the most minute details : " Madame, if it be not impertinent, I should be glad to know how this gentleman was dressed." (126). Mr Wilson tells him the story of his life, full of regrets for the loss of a kidnapped son. Adams reflects for a few minutes in silence, then suddenly cries " ' No, that won't do.' The gentleman inquired into his meaning. . . He answered, ' He has been considering that it was possible the late famous King Theodore might have been that very son whom he had lost '; but added, ' that his age could not answer that imagination. However,' says he, ' God disposes all things for the best ; and very probably he may be some great man, or duke, and may one day or other revisit you in that capacity '. " (III, 4, p. 264).

[1]This ease of manner is found in many contemporary portraits of virtuous men. " In all cases alike these personifications were prompted by a desire to make virtue appear simple and to impart to morality a commonsense complexion. . . Hence the object aimed at was not so much edification as simplification, or more truly, the former by means of the latter. There is nothing mysterious or incomprehensible in the life of virtue—such in nearly all these pattern instances is the presupposition either expressed or implied." Whittuck, *The ' Good Man ' of the eighteenth Century.* London, Allen, 1901 pp. 6-7

Fortunately, he enjoys a physical health as vigorous as his moral health. For this reason his love of romance takes the shape not of vague romanticism but of a pronounced taste for adventure [1]. " Though I am not afraid of ghosts ", says he, " I do not absolutely disbelieve them [2]." And when certain moving lights prove to be shepherds' lanterns and not souls in pain, Adams muttered to himself, ' He was convinced of the truth of apparitions for all that '." (III, 2, 230). This worthy parson, a good drinker, a great eater and a great smoker, has something adventurous in his nature, which allies him with Don Quixote [3]. He adores rescuing unfortunates in distress, he is a knight-errant of the by-ways. His fist lights in turn upon innkeepers, upon seducers, upon the moustached face of Dame Slipslop, whom he takes for a demon. Drubbings multiply about him, whether he be the attacker or the attacked ; by day and by night battles follow hot upon one another, pots are emptied over divers heads, an innkeeper's wife getting short of arguments throws a basinful of hog's blood in his face ; blows rain down, thick and fast ;

[1] cf. Meredith, for good health as a remedy against romanticism. Adams is a great enemy of what he calls " nonsense and enthusiasm ". This is his objection to Methodism, which had just appeared, which he praises elsewhere for its return to primitive Christianity. This resistance premature to romanticism, this criticism of ' enthusiasm ' to which ' commonsense ' was opposed, was a characteristic common to the time ; cf. article entitled *Enthusiasm*, in *Eighteenth Century Literature*, *an Oxford Miscellany*.

[2] The romantic and modern attitude of melancholy, the ' happiness of being sad ' is expressed by the curiously inverted opinion of Mme de Stael on the subject of ghosts : " I do not believe in them ; but I am afraid of them ", (*je n'y crois pas, mais j'en ai peur*).

[3] There is a certain physical resemblance between them which must not be exaggerated, for Adams, so fond of good living, is not to be compared with the Knight of the Sad Countenance. Adams may be ' original ', but he is not mad like Don Quixote. Yet *Joseph Adams* is written ' in imitation of the manner of Cervantes '. The humorous titles of the chapters recall those of Don Quixote and [without any direct borrowing there is a general air of similarity between the two books. One feels that Fielding is steeped in Cervantes. But his reading has been admirably ' transposed '. If Adams is deceived through innocence, like Don Quixote, there is nothing Spanish about the deceptions. *Joseph Andrews* is not even as international as *Gil Blas*, which is hardly international at all. It is thoroughly English.

the men use fisticuffs or sticks, the women scratch ; in the struggle Mrs Slipslop's hair is torn out by the handful. The valiant clergyman is always in the vanguard of these burlesque fights and beats people with the very hand which blesses them. Fragments of his ten-year-old cassock are left to the dogs, but his soul remains entire, true to itself in the midst of dangers. In spite of ourselves, we cannot forbear laughing when he visits his odious colleague, Trulliber, and the pigs, rushing against him, precipitate him into the mire, or when, in the course of an Homeric battle, he receives a muddy rag full in the face. Although we love him, we laugh, because we know that these ridiculous adventures do not belittle him, any more than our sympathy for Don Quixote is diminished by the thrashings which he receives [1]. We have learnt Fielding's lesson, that a poor, badly-dressed man, humble and scorned, can play the part of a hero, if he carries beneath his rags a beautiful soul and a courage superior to his fortune.

He is a comic hero, indeed a hero pure and simple, if occasion demands. So high does Parson Abraham Adams rise in the fourth book of *Joseph Andrews*. His heroism is noiseless, good-natured, prevented by the very simplicity of his ways from becoming pompous. When Lady Booby wishes to intimidate or bribe him so as to stop him from marrying Joseph and Fanny, he opposes her with simple nobility : " Madam, I would obey your ladyship in everything that is lawful ; but surely the parties being poor is no reason against their marrying. . . Madam, I know not what your ladyship means by the terms *master* and *service*—I am in the service of a Master who will never discard me for doing my duty. . ." (IV, 2, 333). And what is even more deserving, he dares oppose his wife in order to obey his conscience.

---

[1] Meredith, *Essay on Comedy* : " You may estimate your capacity for comic perception by being able to detect the ridicule of them you love without loving them less. . . . If you detect the ridicule and your kindliness is chilled by it, you are slipping into the grasp of Satire." Alone perhaps, among the Victorians, Meredith sometimes gives the impression of the pure comedy of Fielding, in all its robustness and deep sanity.

JOSEPH ANDREWS

His religion is broad. At the risk of being taxed with heresy he refuses to admit that a good Turk must necessarily be damned (96). He is a clean, vigorous Christian[1], with a Christianity which pays less heed to pure dogma than to active sympathy for the weak and disinherited of this world.

It must not be supposed, however, that this nobility of nature, which grows increasingly more marked, outweighs all other characteristics in such a way as to destroy the balance of this richly delineated figure. Fielding's artistic genius and his sense of reality have succeeded admirably in making this note harmonize with the whole. The burlesque adventures of the night succeed the heroic adventures of the day. The portrait moves and changes, as full of subtle shades as Life itself[2].

Such is Adams. As a finishing touch to his portrait I cannot forbear to quote the happy phrase in which M. Anatole France has characterized his Abbé Jérôme Coignard, when he speaks of " that sweet sublimity, that amazing richness of a soul always overflowing and pouring itself forth[3]." There would

[1] There is no suggestion of the rationalist about Adams : " Adams in fact goes as far in the way of belief as it was possible in the eighteenth century for a man to be represented as going by any but a purely devotional writer, such, *e.g.*, as William Law. Yet, the importance which he attaches to the practical side of Christianity, no doubt to a large extent determines his view of its other sides." (Whittuck, *op. cit*). For his religious opinions see particularly I, 17. We should also note that if Adams is simple in manner, he has, nevertheless, very high ideals ; cf. his frequently expressed opinions oṅ submission to Providence, the luxury of the Church, service of God, impurity of the theatre, pity for the poor, and his scorn for hypocrites and rogues. The essential point to remember is that this portrait of a virtuous man has a Christian basis.

[2] In a letter to Mrs Donnellan (February 22nd, 1752) Richardson writes " Parson Young sat for Parson Adams, a man he knew and only made a little more absurd than he is known to be." This William Young was parson at East Stour from 1731-40. Fielding evidently met him there. Young followed him to London and they planned to translate Aristophanes and Lucian together. Many of Adams' characteristics are borrowed from Young, impenitent Bohemian and needy Hellenist. Mr Paul de Castro has thrown some new light on this character, in *Notes and Queries*, 12 S.I., 224-5 (March 18th, 1916).

[3] Cette douce sublimité, cette étonnante richesse d'une âme toujours éparchée et ruisselante." *La Rôtisserie de la Reine Pédauque*, p. 385.

be no lack of analogies between the two heroes, were it not that behind the figure of the French abbé, with all his refined culture, one is too often conscious of the malice of his ironical biographer. I will leave to those who enjoy piquant comparisons the task of drawing a parallel which should prove enlightening.

A whole world of secondary characters moves round Adams. Fielding may have acquired at the theatre his faculty for putting into the mouths of his characters, the words which they *must* say and which reveal their state of mind better than a long analysis. Hence his rich gallery of individual types, all clearly characterized. A traveller in a coach, a post boy, an inn-keeper, appear but for one instant, yet they remain firmly engraved upon the mind.

We already know Lady Booby. Her companion, Mrs Slipslop, is one of the most delightful creations of the book. She has the foible, which Sancho Panza had in a lesser degree, of liking to use difficult words, which she distorts. " Having made a small slip in her youth, she has continued a good maid ever since." Having attained an age, which places her beyond the reach of accidents, she decides to break a fast which has been all too long. Her attempts to assail Joseph's virtue are a delicious parody of those of her mistress. As soon as she knows Lady Booby's secret, her customary attitude of hypocritical humility in the presence of her superiors, changes to insolence. And we see her, now hard on her inferiors, now crafty and cunning when her own interest is involved ; or prudent and careful when she is not blinded by passion [1].

The dialogue shows the same gifts of characterization which belong rather to the dramatist than to the novelist. Most of the sayings of the characters are not humorous in

---

[1] cf. especially I, 7. In Chapter V, Joseph is shown in the clutches of Lady Booby, in chapter VI, in those of Dame Slipslop. Chapter VII confronts the two women, both in the same state of mind, and displays the different reactions produced by differences of temperament and education ; cf. the ' parallel ' scenes in Molière's *Dépit amoureux*.

themselves. There is very little wit [1] in this novel of Fielding's, but there are, on the other hand, many of those reflections which enable us suddenly to plumb the depths of some conscience or to tear away a mask [2].

I dare not make a special choice from among this great collection of country types. It is all the England of the Western counties which passes before us, as Fielding saw it during his sojourn at East Stour. In such a way, Molière too observed French provincial life at Pezenas or Montpellier. Fielding was a Londoner and the contrasts, the violent clashes between these highly-coloured rural figures, struck him more forcibly than they would have done a countryman. Boorish squires, village tyrants, like the man who amuses himself by killing a little house-dog, on the ground that it destroys his game ; great sportsmen, hearty feeders, heavy drinkers, with no interests beyond their horses and dogs ; illiterate surgeons and ignorant physicians, in the true lineage of Molière's doctors [3] ; male and female inn-keepers, of every sort and kind, from the excellent Timotheus who keeps the Lion Inn, " well-known to the traveller round the Western circuit ", and is " well-versed in history and politics, hath

[1] The most characteristic and almost unique example of this is the very licentious speech of a lawyer who is in the coach when Joseph is met, naked, on the road. Even the wit itself is of a legal nature, as Fielding himself observes : " The lawyer likewise made several very pretty jests, without departing from his profession." (I, 12, 65).

[2] This is Molière's precept, " Pour ce qui est des enfants par l'oreille . . . ., l'auteur n'a pas mis cela pour être de soi un bon mot, mais seulement pour une chose qui charactérise l'homme." *Critique de l'Ecole des Femmes*, sc. 6.

[3] Among many reminiscences of Molière, we may single out the following as directly borrowed from him : A doctor says, " Veniente occurrite morbo : that is my method. I suppose brother, you understand Latin ? " " A little ", says the gentleman. " Ay and Greek now, I'll warrant you. Ton dapomibominos poluflosboio thalasses ", and further on " The contusion on his head has perforated the internal membrane of the occiput, and divellicated that radial small, minute invisible nerve, which coheres to the pericranium ; and this was attended with a fever at first symptomatic, then pneumatic, etc." (I, 14.) We must remember that Fielding had translated *Le Médecin malgré Lui*. It is obvious that he was equally well acquainted with *Le Malade Imaginaire*.

a smattering in law and divinity, cracks a good jest and plays wonderfully well on the French horn ", to the Tow-Wowse couple, who are humble with the rich and harsh with the poor [1].

We leave their inn and take the coach, after waiting for the ladies who are late. When the horses have started the travellers begin to talk. Miss Graveairs simpers, Mrs Slipslop replies with impertinence, another lady begins a long story, there is some talk of brigands, and a lawyer, who is courageous before the danger occurs, recovers his bravery when once it is past. Silhouettes appear and disappear ; servant girls with easy morals, carters, innkeepers and post boys. A thief is arrested, and the whole town is in an uproar, everyone has his word to say ; they scream and jostle and quarrel, the thief is searched and nothing is discovered, he is then believed innocent and cheered ; a gold coin, which he had stolen, is found upon him and immediately he is guilty and insulted ; meanwhile the innkeeper rubs his hands at the thought of so many prospective customers. The whole episode ends with the escape of the thief, whom the village constable, Tom Suckbribe, allows to slip through the window (I, 12-16).

All these people move before us and we know them as though we had lived with them for a long while. We visit Mrs Adams, a good mother and excellent housewife, who apologizes for the untidiness of her house when she sees such fine folk. She is a prudent woman, who is aware of the difficulties of poverty, and, therefore, opposes her husband's heroic resolutions. The parson for once does not yield to her and quotes numerous texts from the scriptures to prove that a wife should obey her husband. But how much must it cost him to do so, and how often must the gentle creature, when duty is not at stake, allow his wife to lead him by the nose !

---

[1] Fielding's names are all expressive, Slipslop, Miss Graveairs, Peter Pounce the miser, Lawyer Scout. Tow-Wow, in a pamphlet of 1725 on the highwayman Blueskin, has the same meaning as ' comment-a-nom ' in Rabelais. Fielding was not the man to shrink from coarseness.

What accommodating habits she has induced in him, too! One intimate detail which is here reported, will show this better than all the commentaries in the world. " Adams groped out the bed, and turning the clothes down softly, a custom Mrs Adams had long accustomed him to, crept in and deposited his carcase on the bed-post, a place which the good woman had always assigned him ¹."

There is scarcely any description of Gaffer and Gammer Andrews, but could any analysis equal the few sentences which describe their actions when they find their long-lost daughter ? " Gammer Andrews kissed her, and said she was heartily glad to see her ; but for her part she could never love anyone better than Joseph. Gaffer Andrews testified no remarkable emotion : he blessed and kissed her, but complained bitterly that he wanted his pipe, not having had a whiff, that morning." (IV, 16).

A squire, for fun, sets his hounds on Adams and Joseph. The two men defend themselves, and do great slaughter with their cudgels. When the battle is over the huntsman arrives and is soon " busy cutting the ears of his dogs, and endeavouring to recover them to life ; in which he succeeded so well, that only two of no great note remained slaughtered on the field of action. Upon this the huntsman declared, ' Twas well it was no worse ; for his part he could not blame the gentleman (Adams), and wondered his master would encourage the dogs to hunt Christians ; that it was the surest way to spoil them and make them follow vermin instead of sticking to a hare." (III, 5). Thus can Fielding's rich imagination pass from truculent comedy to sober irony. Rare indeed are the writers who can, without any pedantry of technique, make their working men speak each according to his trade and with so sure a touch. Once more he reminds us of Molière, the Molière of the *Bourgeois Gentilhomme.*

---

¹ This is a delightful touch, and at the same time is a useful addition to the verisimilitude of the narrative ; for Adams, who has mistaken the bed, has to sleep beside Fanny without waking her.

It is, however, impossible to pass in review all the secondary characters of the book, for in analysing them thus, all the point and savour of their words and actions would disappear. Here are no portraits of subtle souls. The only one which the author has attempted, that of Lady Booby, fails, precisely because it is too theoretical. The people with whom this book deals live their lives before our eyes. The reader has the pleasure of penetrating their affectations and seeing how absurd they are. It is only by reading the book that one can really appreciate the meticulous art with which the characters are grouped, react upon one another, set one another off by their contrasts and analogies, until finally Adams is made to stand out as the central figure.

It needs careful reading, too, for all this strict and self-imposed arrangement marvellously escapes stiffness; the play of the characters remains supple; and the whole movement is carried along with a swing which neither flags nor ceases.

It was the theatre which moulded Fielding's genius: we are always brought back to this. It was at the theatre and by writing polemics and newspaper articles, that he acquired the habit of a vigorous style. Since the flow of his prose is simple, the least touch leaves its mark. A word is enough to put the attentive reader on his guard [1] Take, for example, all the finesse and the ironical innuendoes of the following conversation, the first between Joseph and Lady Booby. The young man has just told her that he is indifferent to all women : " ' Oh, then ', said the lady, ' you are a general lover. Indeed, you handsome fellows, like handsome women, are very long and difficult in fixing ; but yet you shall never persuade me that your heart is so insusceptible of affection ; I rather impute what you say to your secrecy, a very commendable quality, and what I am far from being angry with

---

[1] For example, the word ' accidentally ' in this sentence : " The lady being in bed, called Joseph to her, bade him sit down, and having accidentally laid her hand on his, etc." (I, 5).

you for. Nothing can be more unworthy in you men, than to betray any intimacies with the ladies.' 'Ladies! Madam', said Joseph, ' I am sure I never had the impudence to think of any that deserve that name.' 'Don't pretend to too much modesty ', said she, ' for that sometimes may be impertinent '.'' Now he gives us a full and realistic description [1], now is content with a single detail : " The uplifted hanger dropped from his hand and he fell prostrated on the floor with a lumpish noise, and his halfpence rattled in his pocket."

Comic effects are rarely absent, and the comedy smells sometimes of the lamp. Scarcely anything is borrowed directly, but it is. obvious that the author is extremely well-read ; one can often guess whom he has been reading. This passage is written after the manner of Lucian, that battle is reminiscent of the author of *Hubibras* or of Cervantes [2], something else recalls Scarron [3]. Side by side with these models, Fielding also mentions Le Sage and Marivaux. But he often goes further back still, to Homer, whose *Odyssey* was the first great romance of adventure on the highway, the great highway of the sea [4].

[1] cf. especially, the description of Mrs Tow-wowse, (I, 14). " Her person was short, thin and crooked. Her forehead projected in the middle, and thence descended in a declivity to the top of her nose, which was sharp and red, etc." I insist less on this realism which is the current coin of the picaresque writers.

[2] cf. II, 5, 138. It is scarcely possible to make comparisons save in the case of certain very general characters, or, on the other hand, of infinitesimal details, for example the fact that there is a puppet showman in *Don Quixote* and in *Joseph Andrews*, or again that Sancho Panza often uses long words in the wrong sense, like Mrs Slipslop ; or, possibly certain literary dissertations. For comparisons of this kind, many of which are for that matter erroneous, cf. the books of Bosdorf and Dibelius.

[3] cf. IV, II. The adventure of Beau Didapper going to see Mrs Slipslop by mistake, has its analogy in *Guzman d'Alfarache* (VI, I). It is obvious that many of these adventures are not new. What *is* new, is the way in which they are used.

[4] Here is the homeric battle : " No sooner did Joseph perceive the distress of his friend, when first the quick-scenting dogs attacked him, than he grasped his cudgel in his right hand ; a cudgel which his father had of his grandfather, to whom a mighty strong man of Kent had given it for a present in that day when he broke three heads on the

But the surpassing merit of Fielding's style does not lie in these reminiscences. It is to be found rather in its directness, its strength, which is at times almost massive. It is not the subtle and delicate prose of a Marivaux, with its weighing of imponderable nothings [1]. Fielding's realism is always broad, expressing itself in passionate dialogues [2], rough words, simple and familiar gestures—a judge, before listening to the witnesses, takes time to light his pipe—or in scenes of profound and irresistible comedy like that in which Adams, who has been arrested, is condemned upon the sight of his manuscript copy of Æschylus, which an illiterate judge takes for a book written in cipher [3]. Here, for instance, is the speech in which Lady Booby defends herself before Dame Slipslop from the charge of sensuality :

" ' I believe my conduct may defy malice itself to assert so cursed a slander. If I had ever discovered any lightness, any wantonness in my behaviour ; if I had followed the example of some whom thou hast, I believe, seen in allowing myself indecent liberties, even with my husband ; but the dear man who is gone ', (here she began to sob) ' was he alive again ' (then she produced tears) ' could not upbraid me with any one scene of tenderness or passion. No, Slipslop, all the time I cohabited with him he never obtained even a kiss from me without my expressing reluctance in the granting it. I am sure he himself never suspected how much I loved him. Since his death, thou knowest, though it is almost six weeks (it

stage. It was a cudgel of mighty strength and wonderful art, made by one of Mr Deard's best workmen, whom no other artificer can equal and who hath made all those sticks which the beaus have lately walked with about the park in a morning ; but this was far his masterpiece. On its head was engraved a nose and chin which might have been mistaken for a pair of nut-crackers, etc." The rest of the battle is painted with the same brush, (III, 6); see also I, 6, where Dame Slipslop is compared to a tigress.

[1] It was Voltaire who said of him : " Il pèse des riens avec des balances de toile d'araignée."

[2] For example (I. 9), the dialogue between Lady Booby and Slipslop, or (II, 5), between Slipslop and Miss Graveairs.

[3] The whole of this scene was added in the second edition.

wants but a day) ago, I have not admitted one visitor '."
(IV, 6). How exactly she has calculated the length of her
mourning. How cold and hard is the irony which put such a
speech into her mouth ! These effects of style owe their
peculiar quality to their sureness and restraint, and such simplicity is all the more striking when one recalls the affectedly
sentimental ' fine style ' of certain pages in Richardson.

All this is highly characteristic of Fielding. This working
up of a simple matter ; this conscious and organic development of a slight plot ; this dramatic power of characterization ;
this careful composition of the various personages of the
story, grouped at different levels, round a central character,
whom they bring out in high relief ; and, finally, this power of
clear and classic expression, the frankness, the bold brutality
of this laughter ; all these qualities are by Fielding united
for the first time. Boileau, wishing to pay Racine the highest
possible compliment, speaks of his ' *savants ouvrages* '. [In the
same sense of the word *Joseph Andrews* might be described as
a ' learned work '. It is the ' masterpiece ' of a journeyman,
who, after a long and adventurous apprenticeship, is about
to pass out a master-craftsman.

It is by this manner of his, more even than by his ideas,
that Fielding places himself in direct opposition to Richardson,
The letters, which preceded *Pamela*, insisted on the romantic
interest and the truth of the story and on the moral benefit
to be derived from it. Fielding's ambition is different ; in
the preface to *Joseph Andrews* he merely explains his artistic
aim. His design, he tells us, has not been to write a burlesque,
a caricature which raises laughter by distorting reality [1] ; and
this at once distinguishes him from the picaresque writers.]
The utmost concession he will make is that burlesque shall
be admitted as an exception : " in the diction, I think

---

[1] This is the French classical theory, the theory of Boileau on the
burlesque, which Fielding first met in Molière, and notably in the work
of Abbé Bellegarde ;   cf. the English translation of Bellegarde,
Reflections upon Ridicule, or what it is that makes a man ridiculous ;
and the means to avoid it . . . in 2 volumes (5th edition),London, 1739.

burlesque itself may sometimes be admitted, of which many instances will occur in this work. . . not necessary to be pointed out to the classical reader, for whose entertainment those parodies or burlesque imitations are chiefly calculated." As for characters and sentiments, these shall never be burlesqued but shall merely reproduce life, which " everywhere furnishes an accurate observer with the ridiculous."

His work, then, has only to remain realistic in order to be comic, effortless, but not so without deliberate choice ; for Fielding distinctly claims to control reality, and to select from it. It is this which makes his work artistically something new. Defoe, Richardson, and even the author of *Gulliver*, essay to create the illusion of truth ; they pretend to have discovered a travel diary, some memoirs, a bundle of letters ; their object is to make a romance pass for reality, by means of external proofs. Fielding seeks no such effects. He tells the story himself and conducts it as he pleases. He brings a new artistic formula, his own, into English literature.

Does this mean that he confines himself to his literary aim and has no moral purpose ? Were this so, he would not be an Englishman—above all, not an Englishman of his time. There is in Fielding an impenitent essayist, who reappears on the slightest pretext, and develops moral commonplaces with the occasionally wearisome complacency of a Johnson or a Goldsmith. But his ambition flies higher than this. Laughter is a weapon. He who uses it, must do so wittingly, and must distinguish between the enemies whom he strikes with it. Some are merely ridiculous, others are odious. But how many nuances there are between the one and the other ! Fielding laughs first at affected persons, and here, one may say, he is making fun of the whole of humanity, if it be true that we are all guilty of affectation. He ruthlessly exposes the secret egoism which lies behind our apparently most disinterested actions, and which prompts us to choose one side rather than another. An admirable scene in the novel shows this to the life.

84

JOSEPH ANDREWS

Thieves have robbed Joseph of all his clothes and have left him for dead, by the roadside. The coach drives past. " The postilion told the coachman, he was certain there was a dead man lying in the ditch, for he heard his groan. ' Go on, sirrah ', says the coachman, ' we are confounded late, and have no time to look after dead men '." A lady intervenes, the coachman stops, the postilion alights and returns, saying " that there was a man sitting upright as naked as ever he was born. ' O Jesus ! ' cried the lady, ' a naked man, dear coachman, drive on and leave him.' Upon this the gentlemen got out of the coach ; and Joseph begged them to have mercy upon him : for that he had been robbed and almost beaten to death. ' Robbed ! ' cries an old gentleman, ' let us make all the haste imaginable or we shall be robbed, too.' A young man who belonged to the law answered, ' He wished they had passed by without taking any notice ; but that now they might be proved to have been last in his company : if he should die, they might be called to some account for his murder. He therefore, thought it advisable to save the poor creature's life, for their own sakes, if possible '." And so the conflict of egoisms continues throughout the length of a pitiless chapter (I, 12), which I should like to quote in full.

We are all egoists, in different degrees, but some of us are merely vain egoists, and the most inoffensive form of vanity is affectation ; above all, we pride ourselves upon qualities which we do not possess. The virtuous Adams himself is vain at times. At the other extreme are the hypocritical egoists, such as Trulliber, the coarse, cruel clergyman, and Peter Pounce, the malicious miser [1]. Already the supreme importance of kindness begins to appear in Fielding's moral code, and characters who are deficient therein are painted

[1] Tradition has it that Trulliber is the portrait of a certain Parson Oliver, who was Fielding's schoolmaster and of whom he preserved a very unpleasant memory. Peter Pounce undoubtedly represents Peter Walter, a rich usurer who lived at Stalbridge Park, a few miles from East Stour ; cf. *Quarterly Review*, 1855, p. 116. Fielding has mentioned him elsewhere under the name of Peter Gualterus, and Pope cites him as a notorious miser, (*Epistle III*, v. 123 *et seq*).

in the darkest colours. It is evident that this novel is the work of a man to whom life has not been tender. It is a plea on behalf of the poor who are crushed by the world, of the simple and innocent, of a Joseph Andrews and a Parson Adams. Fielding shows us the world as the humble see it, from below, and seen from this angle this brilliant world of eighteenth century England, is not beautiful. The wicked often triumph in it, to the dismay of Adams who believes in a virtuous humanity just as Don Quixote believed in a chivalrous one. And if sometimes in this wicked world kindness is to be found, it is only among the poor and wretched. A postilion destined for the gallows and a chambermaid at an inn, who is no better than she should be, are the only people who show the unfortunate Joseph any compassion. The reason is that the poor, possessing nothing to which their egoism can cleave, draw from within themselves great treasures of charity. Mr Adams, repulsed by Trulliber his rich and terrible colleague, finds a poor pedlar, who empties the contents of his wretched purse into that of the parson. Such is the lesson which life teaches to our social prejudices.

Are we perhaps to see in this a reflection of the great industrial and commercial crisis, which swept through the Western counties about the year 1739, and was one of the possible causes of the Puritan awakening of 1740 [1]. It may be that in Fielding's pity there is, as it were, an echo of this great distress. But there is also, more simply, the tone of a man personally acquainted with poverty. He knows how the humble are received by innkeepers and how they are treated by justices of the peace. And, for a moment, he is moved.

In this very sensibility, in this capacity for being moved, he may, in spite of himself, be compared with Richardson. They were, it is true, deadly enemies, and our examination has shown that they were at the very antipodes of art. Fielding is a writer who sets out to amuse ; with him there

[1] cf. Elie Halévy, *La naissance de méthodisme en Angleterre, Revue de Paris*, August, 1906.

is not a dimple which does not smile, nor a character which is not, in some degree, comic. Richardson is a moralist whose object is to instruct ; with him every wrinkle is grave and every character serious. It is as though, in these two novelists, were personified the two Englands which were in collision with one another about 1740. Richardson is the new England, religious, serious, sensitive, and priggish, respectful of the established order, at once passionate and prudent, narrow and enthusiastic, secretly a little anxious, and, above all, careful of what ' people will say '. The new mentality of bourgeois Puritanism, which was to reach its zenith in the Victorian age, was then in embryo. Richardson is one of the first writers to express it [1], in any case the first novelist, to represent it at all clearly. Against this new tendency Fielding raises the protest of the old England, which some forty years earlier, had triumphed in the theatre with Congreve and Wycherley. Driven from the theatre, it takes refuge in the novel and infuses new life into it [2]. Fielding revolts ; he roars with laughter in Richardson's grave face ; he scouts the idea of a man who glories in his chastity. The people whom he paints seek to enjoy themselves, even the women, particularly

[1] The Victorians often preferred Richardson. Tennyson, writing of Clarissa Harlowe, said that he liked these " great still books ", adding " I wish there were a great novel in hundreds of volumes that I might go on and on. . . ." Fitzgerald wrote : " That Richardson (with all his twaddle) is better than Fielding, I am certain. There is nothing at all comparable to Lovelace in all Fielding, whose characters are common and vulgar types of Squires, ostlers, ladies' maids, etc. . ." (*Letters of Edw. Fitzgerald*, II., p. 131).

[2] During the course of the first year *Pamela* went through six editions, but we do not know the number of copies. On February 15th, 1742, *Joseph Andrews* was published in an edition containing 1,500 copies. The second edition, May 31st, 1742, contained 2,000, and after February, 1743, a third of 3,000 was necessary, the total being 6,500 copies. In 1771 *Pamela* had reached its tenth, and in 1769, *Joseph Andrews* its ninth edition (tenth if we include the edition of Fielding's complete works published in 1762). Apparently the success of Richardson's work, which was superior during the first year, diminished palpably on the appearance of Fielding's book, which was to end by attaining an equally wide circulation. The numbers of the first editions were copied by Mr Paul de Castro from the printers' registers (cf. *Notes and Queries*, November, 1917).

the women. The sole punishment which the vice of incontinence brings, is an occasional visit to a doctor for the man, and for the woman a bastard. He constantly amuses himself with somewhat indecent scenes, which he takes as a joke ; and if a pretty girl's kerchief slips from her throat, he does not fail to keep the reader's eye for some time upon the charming spot. Robust and insolent health, the John-Bullism of men who are not afraid of their three bottles ; in everything the material side of things writ large ; this was the old Merry England of Fielding.

The two books were contradictory. Yet the public liked them both, and their success was almost equal. What is more, they often had the same readers. Lady Mary Wortley Montagu, for example, puts Fielding quite plainly above Richardson as an artist. In 1755 she praised him in these high terms : " Since I was born, no original has appeared excepting Congreve and Fielding." And yet she cannot tear herself away from Richardson. " This Richardson is a strange fellow. I heartily despise him and eagerly read him, nay, sob over his works in a most scandalous manner." Precious confession, which recalls Mme de Sèvigné acknowledging with lowered eyes that she loves La Calprenède.

The public hesitated, torn between the two tendencies, when it did not follow both at once : trained by the dramatists in an appreciation of comedy, it was, nevertheless, ready to weep over the adventures of a man of feeling [1]. Does not Fielding himself show signs of weakness in this parody of Richardson ? He is not so far from going over to the enemy. A Mr Wilson whom Adams meets, gives us a long account of his life, and it is an edifying tale [2]. After a stormy youth he has fled from the society of men to the bosom of nature and

[1] In two articles published in the *Revue Germanique* (*Autour de Fielding*, R.G., July and December 1920) I have given several typical examples of this divided admiration.

[2] There are many autobiographical reminiscences in Mr Wilson's story, particularly in the passages which deal with his literary début in London.

cultivates the fruits of the earth. The story is as touching and as insipid as certain passages in Rousseau's *Nouvelle Héloise*. And here already we catch a glimpse of the old generation rallying to the new, in a sentimental conception of morality and nature.

This consummation is already clearly hinted at here, but it is only a hint. We shall see much more easily in *Jonathan Wild* how the new Fielding emerges from the old.

But although it is true to say that his moral standard will gain in definition and precision in the works which follow, we may be certain that he has found the form of his art in his first novel ; the expression may be fuller in the later works, the construction more skilfully engineered, but the framework remains the same. *Joseph Andrews* has already all the essential characteristics of the novel which we call Fielding's, the ' prosai-comi-epos ', the comic epic in prose.

Richardson had not, properly speaking, created any new form. He had contented himself with pouring into the epistolary novel, as it already existed (for example, in the *Letters of a Portuguese Nun*) a passion and a morality unknown to it. But Fielding altered the very texture of the novel. One is tempted to hail him, as an admirer hailed Molière : " *Courage, Fielding, voici le vrai roman.*" The spirit which animates him is indeed the spirit which animated Molière. He has Molière's methods, he speaks of his characters and of his art in the same terms. How is it that no one has noticed this ? It is the pure discipline of the great French classics, which he imposes upon himself [1]. His is the genius which

---

[1] According to the testimony of Goldsmith who saw them at Covent Garden (*Remarks on Our Theatres*, from *The Bee*, October 6th, 1759) Fielding's translations of *L'Avare* and *Le Médecin malgré lui*, *The Miser*, and *The Mock Doctor* were still being acted in 1759. The very great influence of Molière on the English drama, particularly on that of Fielding, cannot be discussed here. Here are two parallel passages. Molière had said : " Ces sortes de satires tombent directement sur les moeurs, et ne frappent les personnes que par reflexion. N'allons point nous appliquer à nous-mêmes les traits d'une censure générale ; et profitons de la leçon, si nous pouvons, sans faire semblant qu'on parle

THE NOVELS OF FIELDING

wills and dominates, which when it has learnt its aim, marches straight towards it. No character in his later works will surpass Parson Adams in life and in artistic and human truth. He is the first live and authentic son of Fielding.

à nous . . . Ce sont miroirs publics, où il ne faut jamais témoigner qu'on se voie. . ." (*Critique de l'Ecole des Femmes*, sc. VI). Fielding using the same image writes that he desires " to hold the glass to thousands in their closets, that they may contemplate their deformity, and endeavour to reduce it, and thus by suffering private mortification may avoid public shame. . ."(*Joseph Andrews*, III, I.). Molière " disait que son dessein est de peindre les moeurs sans vouloir toucher aux personnes." (*Impromptu de Versailles*, sc. IV). Fielding writes : " I declare here, once for all that I describe not men but manners." (*Joseph Andrews*, III, I).

The whole dialogue between the poet and the actor(*Joseph Andrews*, III, 10), so interesting from the point of view of Fielding's literary ideas, is inspired by the Trissotin-Vadius dialogue in the *Femmes Savantes*.

Fielding also quotes Balzac and Voltaire, Scarron, Marivaux and, of course, Cervantes.

CHAPTER III

JONATHAN WILD THE GREAT (AND THE MISCELLANIES)

Chance plays a great part in literary history. It was pure coincidence that *Pamela* was published just at the moment when Fielding, prevented from writing freely for the theatre, was seeking a new outlet for his inspiration ; and by another singularly happy chance, he was then, thanks to all his earlier experiments in literature, at the height of his talent. The *Miscellanies*, which we are about to study, show the direction which he might have continued to follow, had he not been turned aside by Richardson's heroine. For *Joseph Andrews* revealed him to himself. He had written from inspiration and straightway had produced a masterpiece, which instantly satisfied him and which he " valued above all his writings [1]."

It may seem surprising that he did not profit by the success of *Joseph Andrews* to undertake another novel in the same style. Seven years elapsed before the publication of *Tom Jones*. The probable explanation of this is that Fielding had really no choice in the matter. Before publishing *Joseph Andrews* he had solicited subscriptions for three volumes of

---

[1] Joseph Warton writing to his brother, in October, 1746, says : " I spent two evenings with Fielding and his sister, who wrote *David Simple*, and you may guess I was very well entertained. . . I find he values, as he justly may, *Joseph Andrews* above all his writings." (Wooll's *Biographical Memoirs of Warton*, p. 215).

Miscellanies, the plan of which he had previously published. The success of *Joseph Andrews* would not absolve him from carrying out his previous engagements, however small his inclination to do so. He worked energetically at the *Miscellanies* during the winter ; and in April, 1743, they were ready [1]. The pages were padded with old compositions, fragments, rough sketches, some of which were printed without his having had the inclination or the time to revise or finish them. He rapidly emptied his drawers of anything which he could find in them.

Besides being a profitable expedient, the *Miscellanies* were a liquidation of his literary past. Fielding's art had ripened slowly, the *Miscellanies* give us a strange medley of his successive attempts. Like Pope he had written moral epistles in verse and translations of the ancient poets ; like Defoe he had taken up and was to keep practising political journalism ; he had also written essays after the manner of Steele and Addison. But the principal outlet for his energies had been the drama. He had thus tried, one after another, all the literary forms cultivated in his time, all those which his experience showed him might make a writer famous. Even the two important works contained in the *Miscellanies* fall in this category. The *Journey from this World to the Next*

---

[1] Although the exact date of the first application for subscribers has not yet been discovered, it must, if the time necessary for the printing of the books be taken into account, have been very much earlier than the publication and perhaps even than the composition of *Joseph Andrews*. Indeed, the publication of the *Miscellanies* must have been promised for the winter of 1741-2, or the spring of 1742, if we are to believe the excuse added by Fielding to his announcement of June 5th, 1742 : " The publication of these volumes has been hitherto retarded by the Author's indisposition last winter, and a train of melancholy accidents scarce to be parallel'd ; but he takes the opportunity to assure his subscribers [they were thus already in existence] that he will most certainly deliver them within the time mentioned in his last receipts [thus there were other receipts which announced an earlier date] *viz.*, by the 25th of December next." This announcement appeared in the *Daily Post*, and a translation of the prospectus was published in the *Nouvelles Littéraires* (p. 209) of the *Bibliothèque Britannique, ou histoire des ouvrages des savants de la Grande Bretagne*, for the months of April, May, and June, 1743 at the Hague.

treats a theme as old as Lucian, and *Jonathan Wild* is essentially a picaresque novel, the offspring of an ancient tradition. It is strange that a writer of genius should hesitate for so long before finding the form of art which must allow him the fullest self-expression.

The *Journey from this World to the Next* describes a visit to Hades, and the avatars of a soul, that of the Emperor Julian, whom Minos has condemned to pass through a series of existences on earth. The idea is far from being new and it is probable that Fielding borrowed it from Lucian, with whose works he was very familiar. It is true that he makes a no more literal use of the *True History, Menippos* or *The Cock* here than he makes of *Don Quixote* in *Joseph Andrews*. Here he is most indebted to Lucian, but he does not neglect the example of Rabelais' description of topsy-turvydom in the nether world, of Scarron in the *Virgile travesti*, of Le Sage in the *Diable Boiteux*, nor possibly that of the many other picaresque writers who develop this theme [1]. It is curious to note that the same idea came about the same time to Montesquieu, whose *Histoire Véritable* also shows the vicissitudes of a soul migrating from body to body of either sex. But the similarity of the two works lies only in the basic idea [2].

The general design of all these romances is almost identical ; they bring before our eyes a procession of characters more or less representative of various social classes. They belong to the class of the *roman à tiroirs*, the expanding novel which can be prolonged to infinity ; its very nature precludes unity.

Fielding must often have abandoned and resumed his

[1] cf. particularly Antonio Enriquez Gomez who in his *Siglo Pitagorico* (1644) " replaced the passage of a servant from master to master by the transmigrations of a soul from body to body ", (Chandler, *The Literature of Roguery*, p. 13). Chandler's book gives numerous details regarding all these works of the picaresque school. In English literature Donne's poem *The Progress of the Soul* should also be noted. It describes the adventure of a soul passing from form to form until it reaches its final incarnation in the body of a woman.

[2] This *Histoire Véritable* was published from a new manuscript, in 1902 at Bordeaux, by L. des Bordes de Fortages.

work on the *Journey*. Side by side with passages which frankly are dull and diffuse, he gives us better inspired pages, amusing characters, carefully, if superficially observed, with a feeling for the telling trait, which he had learnt in the service of the drama. This is how a Fop tells the story of his life :

" My next scene of action was Rome. I was born into a noble family and heir to a considerable fortune on which my parents,thinking I should not want any talents,resolved very kindly and wisely to throw none away on me. The only instructors of my youth were, therefore, one Saltator, who taught me several motions for my legs ; and one Fiers whose business was to show me the cleanest way (as he called it) of cutting off a man's head. When I was well accomplished in these sciences, I thought nothing more wanting, but what was to be furnished by the several mechanics in Rome, who dealt in dressing and adorning the Pope. Being, therefore, well equipped with all which their art could produce, I became at the age of twenty, a complete and finished beau. And now during forty-five years I drest, I sang and danced, and danced and sang. I bowed and ogled, and ogled and bowed till in the sixty-fifth year of my age, I got cold by overheating myself with dancing and died." It is all a little breathless, and the humour is rather jejune, as often happens with works composed after ancient models. The fact is that this tale, which I must persist in believing to be a youthful work [1], is mainly interesting for the promise which it shows. Many characteristics of the later Fielding are already there, and will only become more definite in the future. Hatred of the military, for whom there is no place in the Elysian Fields,

[1] The proofs given by Mr Cross in his recent biography of Fielding only tend to show that several passages were certainly written, or modified, in 1741 or 1742. He concludes that " the *Journey*, though probably begun before *Joseph Andrews*, was mainly written during the weeks immediately succeeding ". (Cross, I, p. 396). For the reasons of internal evidence which I am giving here, I believe the *Journey* was a much earlier work, taken up again later and revised. An author does not ' undertake ' to write three volumes of *Miscellanies*. The very suggestion of *Miscellanies* presupposes the collection of works already in existence, or at least planned, and doubtless partially drafted.

94

a broad-minded and anti-Puritan morality which slams the gate in the face of a parson of strictly virtuous repute (" for no man enters that gate without charity "), and refuses eternal happiness to prudes ; such ideas would bring no reproof to the lips of Parson Adams. Elysium, says Minos, was never made for those " who are too wise to be happy "— a phrase which has already the true Fielding ring. And, to whom will Minos open wide the door ? " I confessed I had indulg'd myself very freely with wine and women in my youth, but had never done an injury to any man living, nor avoided an opportunity of doing good ; that I pretended to very little virtue more than general philanthropy and private friendship. I was proceeding when *Minos* bid me enter the gate and not indulge myself with trumpeting forth my virtues." (Ch. VIII). This might almost be the ' good ' rake, Tom Jones.

One has the impression that the *Journey* was abundantly, I might almost say desperately, touched up until the last moment. Some of the passages were certainly written at the same time as the best parts of *Jonathan Wild*. See how the tailor is spoken of, in terms which seem worthy of Swift. " The prince, indeed, gives the title but it is the taylor who makes the man. To his labours are owing the respect of crowds, and the awe which great men inspire into their beholders. . . I was just set up in my trade, when I made three suits of fine clothes for King Stephen's coronation I bustled on the day of the ceremony through the crowd, and it was with incredible delight I heard several say, *as my clothes walked by* [1], ' Bless me, was ever anything so fine as the Earl of Devonshire '." Almost, one might say, a foretaste of *Sartor Resartus*.

There are other pages which are probably contemporaneous with *Joseph Andrews*. It was certainly Parson Adams who overheard that dialogue of the immortals, in which Homer,

[1] The italics are ours.

Virgil, Dryden, and Addison, each had his say [1]. A delightful touch will suffice to show its subtlety. Addison's ignorance on a certain point has just been proved by Virgil : " Upon this I thought the critic looked a little out of countenance, and turned aside to a very merry spirit, one Dick Steele, who embraced him and told him he had been the greatest man upon earth ; and he readily resigned up all the merit of his own works to him. Upon which Addison gave him a gracious smile, and clapping him on the back with much solemnity, cried out, ' Well said, Dick." (Ch. VIII).

A few delightful touches are not, however, sufficient to save the book which the reader, will too often find dull. So did the author, for he never finished it. But does not this very fact allow us to observe how great was the progress made by Fielding ? There is all the difference in the world between the loose construction of this *roman à tiroirs* and the more compact, judicious and self-imposed plan which we have admired in *Joseph Andrews*. And how wide is the gulf between this superficial observation, the. current coin of the makers of literary ' portraits ', and that rich picture of English life and English oddities.

The third volume of the *Miscellanies* is entirely occupied by the *Life of the late Jonathan Wild the Great*. It is the only first-class work which they contain. The *genre* to which it belongs, the biography of thieves and vagabonds, was an old one in England, as the well-known books of Nash and Greene testify. But during the course of the seventeenth century the indigenous stock of romances of roguery was enormously enriched by the advent of the Spanish novelists and of their successor and popularizer, Le Sage. From 1600

---

[1] It will be remembered that during his visit to Laputa, Gulliver made a journey to Glubdubrib, the Governor of which was a necromancer who called up before him the spirits of Homer and Aristotle followed by all their commentators. This form of irony places the *Journal* among the works of the first half of the century, from which *Joseph Andrews* had not yet broken completely loose.

For a page which recalls the one about the tailor, cf. *A Tale of a Tub*, section II.

to 1740, twelve editions of *Guzman d'Alfarache* appeared [1]. Rogues became popular. Their picturesque life and ingenious tricks charmed the public, and their biographies were soon enriched by incidents borrowed from the picaresque novels. A special literature thus kept their glory alive ; Abbé Le Blanc who travelled in England about 1738, was quite surprised to find that thieves were there regarded as heroes. Every notorious gallows' bird was the subject of a broadsheet or ballad ; his memoirs (more or less apocryphal) and his last confidences to the Newgate Ordinary were published. There was a whole literary *genre*, and a very abundant one, which pandered to the same sort of curiosity as the columns of police court news in our daily papers.

We know how easily parody came to Fielding. It is not impossible that his first intention was to parody the grandiloquence and pretentiousness of these biographies of rogues, and indeed some of the works of which we have been speaking may even have given him the idea ; for some of them, as we shall see, were not devoid of irony.

Jonathan Wild, who was executed in May, 1721, is an important figure in this police court literature. The numerous biographies in the British Museum are not always consistent, and legend is often mingled with history. The most significant was published in Northampton in 1725, under the following title : *The Life of Jonathan Wilde, Thief-Taker General of Great Britain and Ireland, from his Birth to his Death, containing his Rise and Progress in Roguery ; his first acquaintance with Thieves, by what arts he made himself their Head, or Governor ; his Discipline over them ; his policy and great cunning in governing them ; and several Classes of Thieves under his Command. In which all his Intrigues, Plots, and Artifices, are accounted for, and laid open. Intermix'd with variety of*

[1] cf. Chandler, *The Literature of Roguery*, and C. E. Morgan, *The rise and development of the novel of manners*, pp. 44-6. In England there was a taste for these works rather than a consistent literary production of them, which was usually confined to the translation of French and Spanish books.

*diverting Stories ; taken chiefly from his own private Journals,
and daily transactions of his Life, as found amongst his papers
since his first being apprehended.* The preface states, with a
somewhat ironical enthusiasm : " . . . We need make no
apology for collecting these Materials, and offering them to
the Publick. For here they will meet with a system of
Politicks unknown to Machiavel ; they will see deeper
Stratagems and Plots form'd by a Fellow without Learning
or Education, than are to be met with in the Conduct of the
greatest Statesmen, who have been at the Heads of Govern-
ments. And, indeed, when Things are rightly compared, it
will be found that he had a more difficult game to play ; for
he was to blind the Eyes of the World, to find out Tricks to
evade the Penalties of the Law ; and on the other Side, to
govern a Body of People who were enemies to all government." It is true that the paradox of the brigand-genius and
the comparison between the criminal and the statesman are
rather clumsily handled, but they are present, all the same,
and that is the main point. Elsewhere the author assumes
an attitude of mocking admiration of his hero. " He show'd
early signs of a forward Genius, and, whilst a Boy, would
commit a thousand little Rogueries . . . in which he discover'd a ready Wit, and a Cunning much above his Years."
(p. 6). " It was not long after this, that he found the making
of Bucklers too mechanick an Employment for him ; his
Soul was too great to be confin'd to such servile Work . . ."
Finally, after a very clever forgery, he is put in prison and
" here he laid the Foundation of all his future greatness "
(p. 12). He becomes the chief of a gang and then, very
cleverly, plans to act as intermediary between the robbers
and the robbed, to whom he returns, for a monetary consideration, the goods which have been stolen from them. At the
same time he publicly declares himself an informer, and hands
over his rebellious ' subjects ' to the police.

It is strange to observe how this worthless pamphlet,
written almost immediately after Wild's execution, fore-

shadows the ironical attitude of Fielding. The thing was, however, of fairly frequent occurrence. " Faith, Sirs ", cries the Guzman of Le Sage, " ye are still but apprentices in your trade. I will show you that a superior genius has far better lights than yours. If you so desire it, I will take charge of this enterprise ", (V. I). The ' enterprise ' is a carefully organized swindle.

It was a part of the tradition that tales of thieves should be told with a smile. Their life ended in a ballad, and thus the public avenged itself for having feared them. Because Jonathan Wild had been considered one of the most formidable of thieves, he was one of the most widely mocked. His biographers are pleased to jest ; they tell how he asked, upon the eve of his execution, how the great men of Rome and Athens behaved on similar occasions ; they relate his matrimonial misfortunes at length. Many dialogues and ballads were composed in his honour [1]. Swift dedicated some verses to him [2] and Defoe [3] wrote his biography. He won such a lasting fame that thirteen years after his death Pope could still refer to him as a well-known character [4].

Such was the historical personage whom Fielding makes his hero. No finer hypocrite could be found than this informer, honourably known as ' thief-catcher ', and secretly at the head of a gang of thieves. Being a hypocrite, he is, therefore, odious and not merely ridiculous (we must remember the theories set forth in *Joseph Andrews*) ; so he will not be let

---

[1] *News from the dead, a dialogue between Blueskin, Sheppard and Jonathan Wild* (no date). The following two lines are from a ballad entitled *England's Ingratitude* (Dublin, 1725) :

" Ye Britons, curst with an unthankful mind,
Forever to exalted merit blind ! "

[2] *Newgate Garland.*

[3] *The life of Jonathan Wild*, by H. D., late clerk to Justice R. . ., London, 1725.

[4] " Down, down, proud satire, though a realm be spoiled,
Arraign no mightier thief than wretched Wild."
Epilogue to the Satires, dialogue II, I, 38-9. Pope, Courthope edit. : III, 474.

off lightly. From the very beginning Fielding adopts towards him a determined attitude of severe irony. He is about to relate the history of a ' great man ' ; and the very terms in which men are wont to speak of an Alexander or a Caesar, will serve him for his rascal.

Once more we are faced with a parody. It is really remarkable what a fascination parody, or, more generally, satire has for realistic writers, either at the beginning or the end of their careers. It would seem that they take a certain time before they perceive that reality will suffice them, or else that a moment comes when reality suffices them no longer. Thus Marivaux begins by burlesquing the *Iliad* and *Télémaque*, and Flaubert ends with *Bouvard et Pécuchet*. In the same way Fielding's first two novels are parodies.

Jonathan Wild is a ' great man ', a complete ' great man '. He is even more perfect than Alexander ; for whereas Alexander is reported to have acted sometimes with comparative goodness, the wickedness, nay, the greatness of Wild is unblemished. His life from his birth to his death on the scaffold, is a perfectly harmonious work of art, unmarred by a single good action. Such is the philosophical basis of the book ; a simple, clear and accessible idea, a development familiar to rhetoric.

The idea of the criminal conqueror is a commonplace, which is found here and there throughout antiquity. It occurs again in Boileau (Satire VIII) and the French classics ; Maundeville (*Fable of the Bees*, vol. I, p. 26) and Pope (*Essay on Man*, IV, 222) call Alexander ' Macedonia's madman '. The classical commonplace, however, acquired a new vogue in England about 1720. To what was this vogue due ? Alarm had already been aroused by the danger to public security involved in the ambitions of a Louis ' the Great '. But upon English minds the deepest impression seems to have been made by Charles XII[1]. Voltaire, it will be remembered, was

---

[1] Charles XII died in 1718.

in London when he first thought of writing his *History*. If he is to be believed, " during the first years of the century the public knew no other hero in the North than Charles XII ", that soldier " who left behind him nothing but ruin [1]." Else-where he informs us that his work " has for a long time been a subject of debate in the English newspapers ", " party-writers have used it as a pretext ", and finally that the English public was much interested in it, " as it has been translated twice and printed more often in London than in Paris [2]." Thus revived, the idea that ' great ' conquerors are criminals pursued its way. It corresponded so closely to the general aspirations of the time and to the development of liberal ideas, that it could not fail to be accepted with enthusiasm. The mere conqueror became more and more unpopular. The really great man must henceforth be a good man [3]. A lady, later on, wrote to Richardson to thank him for showing in Grandison that " greatness and goodness are synonymous terms "[4]. The question was in the air ; indeed it was at the core of all the speculations of a philosophic era which was to conceive an ' enlightened despotism '. Fielding alluded to

[1] Voltaire *Histoire de l'Empire de Russie sous Pierre le Grand*, init.

[2] *Notes sur les Remarques de la Motraye*. The translation of Voltaire's *Charles XII* reached its seventh edition in 1740 and the résumé published in 1734 was reprinted in 1739 and 1750.

[3] Pope wrote :   " Heroes are much the same, the point's agreed,
From Macedonia's madman to the Swede
The whole strange purpose of their life to find
Or make an enemy of all mankind."
(*Essay on Man*, IV, 217-23).
Voltaire, to bring himself into line, wrote a ' discourse ' as preface to the English edition of *Charles XII*, in which he, too, speaks of ' true greatness '. " The memory of bad princes is preserved like that of fires, plagues, inundations. Conquerors are all of a species between good kings and tyrants but partake rather of the last . . . and such is the unaccountable folly of mankind, that we admire those who have done any glorious mischief, and are better pleased to be talking of the destroyer of a State than of its founder."

[4] Lovelace writes : " I have not the art of any of our Christian princes who every day go from infraction to infraction, from robbery to robbery ; commit devastation upon devastation and destroy—for their *glory* . . . and are dubbed Le Grand ; praised and even deified by orators and poets for their butcheries and depredations." (*Clarissa*, V, letter 136).

it on more than one occasion ; and so fashionable was this great idea, that after flowering too luxuriantly it was to grow old and wither ; in 1763 the *Correspondance littéraire*, reviewing the French translation of *Jonathan Wild*, criticized these comparisons of a thief with Alexander or Caesar as ' old-fashioned ' and ' tedious '. After all, in 1763, Charles XII had been a long time dead !

But when Fielding took it up the topic was still a living thing. Charles XII was still very much in the public mind, and in 1740 our author himself translated, in the capacity of what he calls a ' hackney-writer ', a certain insipid *History of Charles XII* [1] by Adlerfeld. If this be true he must in a few months (from March to October) have put into English some thousand pages of military history, an impassive schedule of massacres. If Fielding really thus, in company with the conscientious Adlerfeld, followed Charles XII through slaughter after slaughter there is nothing surprising in the savage irony with which he sometimes draws a parallel between the warrior and the butcher, nor in the personal note of his mockery when he praises Wild for his ' greatness of soul ' and his ' perfect insensibility '. For if we are to believe honest Adlerfeld this is how Charles XII hears of the death of a beloved sister : " He shed a few tears, the only tears that had fallen during the whole of his life. Yet when the prince had yielded, for a short space, to the first feelings of grief which nature inspired, he recovered that greatness of soul for which he had always been conspicuous " etc. (Vol. III, p. 275). It is perhaps to these naive lines and to the impression which they made upon their translator that we owe some of the fine flights of ironical eloquence, which abound in *Jonathan Wild*.

[1] cf. E. Green, *Henry Fielding* (1909), and J. E. Wells *Journal of English and Germanic Philology*, published quarterly by the University of Illinois, October, 1912. The majority of the notes added to this translation of Adlerfeld correct and control his assertions and are based upon Voltaire's *History*. Fielding cited Voltaire's *History of Charles XII* in *The Prolegomena* which he printed with *The Covent Garden Tragedy* in 1732. See also an article by Mr J. E. Wells (*Publications of the Modern Language Association of America*, 1913) on the general political trend of *Jonathan Wild*.

JONATHAN WILD

Genius is often a personal arrangement of pre-existing data. Fielding found himself faced with two literary traditions, on the one hand, the joking tone of rogues' biographies, on the other, the commonplace of the criminal conqueror. He was the first to combine these two hitherto isolated elements into a new and consummate creation. The low joke, in the service of a general idea, is transmuted into philosophical irony, while the commonplace ceases at once to be banal.

Moreover, Fielding gives it a personal twist. The comparison of the conqueror to the thief was a convention of the school, but he reverses it. He gives us the inversion of the travesty *à la Scarron,* of which everyone was tired. No longer is Aeneas a rogue, it is the rogue who is Aeneas [1]. The irony thus gains in subtlety. Mr Jonathan Wild is treated all through as a fine gentleman. The joke is aimed straight at him, but it rebounds from the poor devil, and strikes the fine gentleman, his neighbour. The stone is not cast at the great man, but it is he who is bespattered with the mud which splashes from it.

But none of this is yet enough to account for the virulence of the outburst. What was the point of attacking Jonathan Wild ? He was dead. Or Charles XII ? He was dead, too. One does not become as indignant as this, against two corpses. Behind them Fielding envisaged a living figure, and that living figure was without any doubt the Minister, Walpole.

[1] I do not forget *The Beggar's Opera,* the success of which was immense (1728). Several of its characteristics may have influenced Fielding but its laughter is very gay and far removed from the deep and severe irony of *Jonathan Wild.* Yet occasionally Fielding's work contains reminiscences of speeches such as the following, made by Peachum when he arrests Macheath : " But really, my dear, it grieves one's heart to take off a great man. When I consider his personal bravery, his fine stratagem, how much we have already got by him and how much more we may get, methinks I cannot find in my heart to have a hand in his death " (I, 11). When Macheath is betrayed by the women, Peachum says : " Your case, Mr Macheath, is not particular. The greatest heroes have been ruined by women " (I, 24). It appears that Gay, too, was referring to Walpole, cf. Lewis Melville, *Life and Letters of John Gay.*

It must be well-understood that I am not attempting here the impossible task of discovering the 'sources' of *Jonathan Wild*. But though such positive evidence be lacking it is, however, permissible to try to appraise the sentimental value, the moral undercurrents of a work which is, in the main, somewhat obscure. The question is this : instead of the picaresque novel, gay and copious, which might have been expected of him, a novelist's version of Gay's *Beggar's Opera*, Fielding writes a bitter book, full of corrosive irony, a novel so harsh that it has disturbed or frightened many of his readers. How are we to explain this remarkable exception to all the rest of his known work ?

He had a thousand reasons for hating Walpole. Their relations had begun with courtesy. In 1730, Fielding addressed an epistle in verse to the Minister, and in 1731 dedicated to him his comedy, *The Modern Husband*. Did Walpole fail to respond to these advances ? In 1734, Fielding inserted an election-scene in his comedy, *Don Quixote in England*, and proclaimed, in his dedication to Chesterfield, that his design was to expose the calamities brought on a country by general corruption. He had by this time passed over to the Opposition, and his attacks were becoming more and more violent. *Pasquin* played in 1736, contained a ruthless satire on election scandals. The play was a great success and Fielding, sure of finding favour in the eyes of the public, returned to the attack a few months later with an even more severe criticism in *The Historical Register for 1736*. In this a certain Quidam is made to appease some over-noisy patriots by giving them a bag of money. The preface contained some singularly violent sentences. "Corruption hath the same influence on all Societies, all Bodies . . . whoever attempteth to introduce corruption into any Community, doth much the same thing and ought to be treated in much the same Manner with him who poisoneth a Fountain . . . which he is sure Everyone will drink of. . . I shall be asked, who is this Quidam, that turns the Patriots into Ridicule and bribes them out of their

Honesty ? Who but the Devil could act such a part ?. . Indeed it is so plain who is meant by this Quidam that he who maketh any wrong Application thereof might as well mistake the Name of Thomas for John, or old Nick for old Bob.''

Fielding intended to continue the attack. For once, Fortune smiled on him ; he was the manager of a company, and his works, played in his own theatre, were enjoying a great success. He announced certain improvements to the public and even set to work to recruit new actors : " If Nature hath given me any Talents at ridiculing Vice and Imposture, I shall not be indolent, nor afraid of exerting them, while the Liberty of the Press and Stage subsists.''

But he soon had to change his tune. Walpole, annoyed by these violent attacks, suppressed the liberty of the stage by the Licensing Act of June, 1737. Fielding, against whom the law had been especially directed, was gagged in a brutal and indeed, it would seem, in rather an ugly manner [1]. What was more natural than that he should continue elsewhere the struggle which was forbidden in the theatre ? The public which had recognized Mr Quidam would have no difficulty in identifying Jonathan Wild, the member of a social class composed of " conquerors, thieves, and Prime Ministers ". And this no doubt is the reason for the extreme irony, the caustic satire of certain passages in *Jonathan Wild*. A chapter such as that headed ' of Hats ', the title of which is reminiscent of Molière " surpasses, short as it is ", says Coleridge, " *Lilliput* [2] or the *Tale of a Tub*."

" As these persons [the thieves in Wild's gang] wore different *Principles*, *i.e.*, *Hats*, frequent dissensions grew among them. There were particularly two parties, *viz.*, those who wore hats *fiercely* cocked, and those who preferred the *Nab* or trencher hat, with the brim flapping over their eyes. The former were called *Cavaliers* and *Tory-Rory-Ranter Boys*,

[1] cf. p. 41, No. 1.
[2] It will be remembered that Swift speaks of the two great political parties of Lilliput, one of which stood for high heels and the other for low (*Gulliver's Travels*, IV).

etc., the latter went by the several names of *Wags, Round-heads, Shakebags, Old-nolls,* and several others. Between these, continual jars arose, insomuch that they grew in time to think there was something essential in their differences, and that their interests were incompatible with each other, whereas, in truth, the difference lay only in the fashion of their hats." Wild calls them together one day and addresses them in these terms : " Gentlemen, I am ashamed to see men embarked in so great and glorious an undertaking, as that of robbing the public, so foolishly and weakly dissenting among themselves. Do you think the first inventors of hats, or at least of the distinctions between them, really conceived that one form of Hats should inspire a man with divinity, another with law, another with learning, or another with bravery ? No, they meant no more by these outward signs than to impose on the vulgar, and instead of putting great men to the trouble of acquiring or maintaining the substance, to make it sufficient that they condescend to wear the type or shadow of it. You do wisely, therefore, when in a crowd, to amuse the mob by quarrels on such accounts, that while they are listening to your jargon you may with the greater ease and safety pick their pockets : but surely to be in earnest, and privately to keep up such ridiculous contention among yourselves, must argue the highest folly and absurdity [1] ", (II, 6).

On another occasion a ' captain ' mutinies, saying that he is tired of seeing the chief (' providentially ' at the head of the gang) always take the major part of the booty. Wild replies : " You are talking of a legal society, where the chief magistrate is always chosen for the public good, which, as we see in all the legal societies of the world, he constantly consults, daily contributing, by his superior skill, to their prosperity and

---

[1] cf. " I remember in the reign of the late Queen Anne, when disputes ran high between Whig and Tory, some persons suffered party to mix in their minutest action. A Tory would not cock his hat in the same manner that a Whig did, etc." (Joe Miller's *Jests* (No. 589). Joe Miller speaks as though the custom no longer existed. His book was well-known to all, particularly to Fielding, who quotes it in *Jonathan Wild.*

not sacrificing their good to his own wealth, or pleasure, or humour : but in an illegal society or gang, as this of yours, it is otherwise ; for who would be at the head of a gang unless for his own interest ? . . . Surely there is none in the whole gang who hath less reason to complain than you : you have tasted of my favours : witness that piece of ribbon you wear in your hat, with which I dubbed you captain. Therefore, I pray, Captain, deliver the watch." There are many passages such as these in *Jonathan Wild*. And we should do but scant justice to so philosophical an irony were we to see in it merely a vulgar libel. The irony may have been roused by the ephemeral actions of a Prime Minister, but it soon went further and higher. Even so, Pascal, scribbling down thoughts on the foundations of justice, was reminded of the Fronde which he had witnessed and the dangers to which it exposed public order ; but very soon the Fronde was to him only a fragment of eternal history. Fielding begins by caricaturing Walpole in the figure of Wild, a notorious thief ; but his personal anger is quickly transformed into a universal anger, the anger of humanity. One day he thinks of the great massacrer of men, Charles XII [1], whom he despises ; then his thoughts turn to Charles I and he speaks of Wild in terms analogous to those which Clarendon applied to his king [2], making the thief leave, after his death, certain Maxims on greatness, which Fielding himself compares with those which the author of *Eikon Basilike* claims to have found after the execution of Charles I.

But this is not all. After the elections of 1741, the fall of Walpole began to appear imminent. And now his great

[1] The passages in Chapter III which deal with the education of Wild are very definitely reminiscent of those in Voltaire which describe the education of Charles XII.

[2] This similarity has been noted by Mr Gerould, editor of a very good selection of Fielding's *Essays*, who draws attention to the fact that Chapters I, 1, and IV, 16, bear a curious resemblance to the character and death of Charles I, in Clarendon's *History of the Rebellion*. From these passages and others, he concludes that Fielding " had Clarendon in mind and half mockingly copied his style ".

adversary, the journalist of the *Champion*, the pamphleteer of so many virulent attacks, published a poem entitled *The Opposition : a Vision*, in which he expresses infinitely more moderate opinions. Here he predicts that the principles of patriotism in the name of which the Prime Minister has been opposed will soon be forgotten, that there will be place-hunting, and ingratitude towards the good fighters who have won the victory. At last in February 1742, Walpole falls. Would Fielding, who had written his *Jonathan Wild* with this ' great man '[1] in mind, now vent his rage upon the dead ? No, for suddenly the satire takes a new direction. When Jonathan Wild arrives at Newgate he finds a certain Roger Johnson, who is king of the thieves. Wild makes an inflammatory speech, demanding ' the liberties of Newgate ', overthrows Johnson and takes his place. The prisoners soon find to their disgust that the new master is worse than the old [2]. Wild even wants to dress himself in the spoils of his predecessor but the fine velvet cap is too heavy for his head and the embroidered waistcoat is so big for him that it hangs in folds. Walpole has now become Roger Johnson and Wild represents Wilmington. The same mask now conceals another face. Walpole's successor was proverbially a nonentity. With what interest must Fielding have watched the scenes which accompanied the fall of a ministry which had lasted so long ! Can we wonder at the political scepticism which we encounter in *Jonathan Wild* [3] ?

[1] The titles of ' great man ' and 'Prime Minister ' were traditionally applied to Walpole by the pamphleteers of the age. " Speaking in the House in 1741 he said of his opponents : Having invested me with a kind of mock-dignity and styled me a Prime Minister, they impute to me an unpardonable abuse of that chimerical authority which only they created and confirmed." (Doran, *London in the Jacobites times*, II, p. 89).

[2] If it were indispensable to find a ' source ' for this passage, one might compare it with the rivalry between Guzman d'Alfarache and Soto, his companion in the galleys, over whom Guzman finally triumphs. (*Guzman d'Alfarache*, VI, 9).

[3] Even if we were limited to presumptions alone we might well suspect that this portrait was added on purpose to deflect the caricature from Walpole to Wilmington. But Fielding writes in *the second edition*

JONATHAN WILD

It is a difficult and complex book, for those who would decipher and follow all the author's intentions. If it were worth while to look for them and if we could know the whole secret history of the period, a hundred other allusions might be discovered. We have only pointed out the most obvious, those which could not be neglected without mistaking the real character of the book. A famous thief, Charles I, Charles XII, Walpole, Wilmington, and others still, these are not contradictory interpretations ; they are all gathered into Fielding's Jonathan Wild. We can, we ought even to read the book without thinking of them, but we needs must study them if we would understand why it is that this book is not the mere cold development of an abstract topic ; its whole life and strength is mysteriously drawn from a thousand actual realities. By fathoming these realities we fathom the deep secret of its life.

The miracle is that from all these scattered elements, there should emerge the harmonious unity of a book ; a unity so vigorous and so perfect that some have thought that the book was written ' at a sitting '[1]. Again let us try to surprise the secret of this artistic synthesis. " My design ", says the author, " is not to enter the lists with that excellent historian, who from authentic papers and records, etc., hath already given so satisfactory an account of the life and actions of this great man." Fielding will take Wild as a type and will depict, he tells us, ' roguery and not a rogue '. This claim immediately places him on a different plane from Defoe. As we observed in the case of *Joseph Andrews*, he is writing a novel

of *Joseph Andrews*, after the fall of Walpole : . . . " She suspected he had used her as some very honest men had used their country ; and had rescued her out of the hands of one rifler in order to rifle her himself" (II, 10 init.). On the other hand the preface of the 1754 edition of *Jonathan Wild* refers those who seek for personal applications to the chapter on the sedition—which may perhaps prove that this chapter was written on purpose to discourage them. " To such persons . . . I would particularly recommend the perusal of the fourth book."

[1] cf. G. T. Bispham, *Fielding's Jonathan Wild* in *Eighteenth Century Literature, an Oxford Miscellany*, (Oxford. At the Clarendon Press, 1909).

and not pseudo-memoirs, a pseudo-correspondence or a pseudo-biography. Nor does he make use of any of these pretences which are designed to give an air of reality to such works ; his aim is rather to reject reality when it proves a hindrance, to add to it at need, to be more true than nature. " My narrative is rather of such actions which he might have performed, or would or should have performed, than what he really did ; and may in reality as well suit other such Great Men as the person himself whose name it bears." Nor does the author hesitate, as Coleridge profoundly observes, to put into the mouth of his hero speeches which the real Jonathan Wild would never have uttered, for these speeches and reflections conform to the author's secret purpose of making his story unreal [1] in order to give a transcendental reality to the truths which he wishes to convey. Everything which idealizes Wild, everything which lifts him out of the crapulous mediocrity of the real man, serves but to give more weight and universality to his example. This is a clear use, and possibly the first conscious one in literary history, of the synthetic method employed by the great realistic novelists of the nineteenth century.

Fielding must thus choose from the true history of Wild only those few characteristics which will enable him to bring out clearly his conception of the ' great man '. For example, he keeps the attempt at suicide whereby Wild aspires to imitate the heroes of antiquity [2]. He keeps the public stoning at the execution [3]. Such a circumstance is well-suited to this hero, so misunderstood by the crowd. Other features are

---

[1] " Whether the transposition of Fielding's scorching wit (as Book III, ch. 14) to the mouth of the hero be objectionable on the ground of *incredulus odi*, or is to be admired as answering the author's purpose by unrealizing the story, in order to give deeper reality to the truths intended, I must leave doubtful, yet myself inclining to the latter judgment." (February 27th, 1832, Coleridge's *Miscellanies, aesthetic and literary*, London, Bell, 1885, p. 339).

[2] cf. *The history of the lives and actions of Jonathan Wild, thief-taker, Joseph Blake, alias Blueskin, and John Sheppard*, London, 1725.

[3] " They pelted him with stones and dirt all the way." (*Captain Alexander Smith's relation*, etc., p. 18).

modified. Wild had been married several times and had shown himself at once brutal and lascivious towards women. Fielding keeps only the lasciviousness and his hero is deceived by the women whom he loves. Such is often the fate of great men ! Again, according to history, Wild was accused of stealing a box of lace and of helping to steal another and was condemned on the evidence of a certain Margaret Morphew, who asserted that she had gone one morning about midday to Wild's house to give his wife a pair of shoes and had heard him speaking of the theft. None of this appears in Fielding's work ; such an end would have been too undignified for so great a hero. Life does not grant each man the fate which his character deserves, but the novel can correct this and in this respect is ' more philosophic than history '.

Fielding thus chooses and *composes* the life of his hero. Jonathan Wild has inherited every quality which constitutes heroism. Of noble birth, since his genealogy goes back as far as one of Hengist's companions, many of his ancestors have been remarkable for their expert thieving ; and his mother's fingers possessed a certain ' glutinous quality ' which was most useful. Formed by these examples, giving in his school-days indications of a precocious genius, young Wild one day meets at the house of his uncle, the bailiff, a certain Count La Ruse whom a ruthless tailor is keeping in prison for debt. Wild plays cards with him and cheats. The count, instead of being annoyed as a meaner spirit might have been, congratulates himself on having found someone more ingenious than himself. The two men begin a conversation, a noble conversation in alternate speeches, a conversation worthy of tragic heroes. " You cannot, I apprehend, Mr Wild, be such a stranger to your own capacity as to be surprised when I tell you I have often viewed, with a mixture of astonishment and concern, your shining qualities confined to a sphere where they can never reach the eyes of those who would introduce them properly into the world and raise you to an eminence where you may blaze out to the admiration of all men . . . for those abilities which would entitle you to honour and profit in a superior station, may render you only obnoxious to danger and disgrace in a lower " (I, 5). There follows a most philosophical debate. The count exhorts Wild to work in a sphere worthy of the ' greatest genius of the age ', for the same qualities that make a good ' prig ' or thief often make a Prime Minister. But, objects Wild, is it more profitable to be a Prime Minister than a thief ? Certainly, answers the count, there is less risk of being punished, and " there is a crowd oftener in one year at Tyburn than on Tower-Hill in a century [1]." But in an extremely sarcastic speech Wild weighs the two professions in the balance and ends by proving that the thief is the happier of the two. His last argument—very characteristic of Fielding—is that the thief's conscience can never prick him for the theft of a few shillings, while that of the Prime Minister may reproach him for having " betrayed a public trust and ruined the fortunes of thousands, perhaps of a great nation ". But the count has fallen asleep during this noble discourse, and Wild picks his pocket before leaving him.

This splendid education continues. Even travel, tradition-ally necessary to the formation of a gentleman, is not omitted. And His Gracious Majesty finds an opportunity of sending Mr Wild to see his American plantations.

So Wild's character is formed. He is none of your dull pickpockets who steal without finesse. He only likes a masterly and well-planned fraud. We find him trying his method first in a small deal. One evening the count, adept in giving fortune a helping hand, has reaped a fine harvest ' at the hazard-table ' ; Wild arranges for a certain Bagshot to rob him as he leaves the gaming-house. When the time comes to divide the booty Wild proves irrefutably that the whole sum belongs to him. " Pray, who proposed or counselled the taking ? Can you say that you have done more than executed

[1] Thieves were executed at Tyburn and prisoners of State at Tower Hill.

my scheme ? . . . Your hire I shall not refuse you, which is all that the labourer is entitled to or ever enjoys. . . It is true that the farmer allows fodder to his oxen and pasture to his sheep ; but it is for his own service, not theirs. In the same manner the ploughman, the shepherd, the weaver, the builder, the soldier, work not for themselves but others ; they are contented with a poor pittance (the labourers' hire), and permit us, the *Great*, to enjoy the fruits of their labours. Aristotle, as my master told us, hath plainly proved in the first book of his Politics that the low, mean, useful part of mankind are born slaves to the wills of their superiors, and indeed are as much their property as the cattle. It is well said of us, the higher order of mortals, that we are born only to devour the fruits of the earth ; and it may be as well said of the lower class that they are born only to produce them for us. Is not the battle won by the sweat and danger of the common soldier ? Are not the honour and fruits of the victory the general's who laid the scheme ? Is not the house built by the labour of the carpenter and the bricklayer ? Is it not built for the profit only of the architect and for the use of the inhabitant, who could not easily have placed one brick upon another ? Is not the cloth or the silk wrought into its form and variegated with all the beauty of colours by those who are forced to content themselves with the coarsest and vilest part of their work, while the profit and enjoyment of their work falls to the share of others ? Cast your eye abroad and see who is it lives in the most magnificent buildings, feasts his palate with the most luxurious dainties, his eyes with the most beautiful sculptures and delicate paintings, and clothes himself in the finest and richest apparel ; and tell me if all these do not fall to his lot who had not any the least share in producing all these conveniences, nor the least ability so to do ? Why, then, should the state of a ' prig ' differ from all others ? Or why should you who are the labourer only, the executor of my scheme, expect a share in my profit ? '' (I, 8). At last, after a scene of alternate intimidation, doubtless inspired by the interview between Maître Jacques and Valère, Bagshot[1] yields to threats and gives up his booty. What a comic string of deceptions ! La Ruse, who has thieved at the gaming table, is despoiled by Bagshot, Bagshot in turn by Wild, Wild . . . one might continue, and Fielding actually does so, but Wild is not robbed vulgarly. He hurries to place the money at the feet of Miss Laetitia Sharp to whom he pays ' urgent addresses '. Indeed he becomes so urgent and brutal that ' to confess the truth ', Laetitia was " more indebted to her own strength for the preservation of her virtue than to the awful respect or backwardness of her lover ". But there is yet another surprise in store for us. The rejected lover has scarcely left the room before Miss Laetitia liberates another wooer from his hiding-place, and grants him everything that she has just refused our ' great man '. The series of robbers robbed ends with Wild himself.

By the end of the first book Wild's system is complete. He has observed that men are divided into two classes : those who work themselves, and those who make others work. Wild, of course, wishes to take up his position in the second class. This comprises two sub-divisions according to whether one makes others work for the common weal or for one's own interest. The first section includes merchants and the second " conquerors, absolute princes, Prime Ministers and prigs (thieves) ". So Wild must recruit a gang which will work for his benefit.

Such is the first book. The figure of Wild is harshly drawn, with a cruel and naked irony ; the execution is that of an engraver rather than of a painter. For it is necessary to avoid any possibility of a misunderstanding on the part of the reader. In a certain passage of *Tartuffe*, Molière has thought it advisable to add a note that a hypocrite is speaking, ' *c'est un hypocrite qui parle* '. The heavy lines in which

---

[1] In *The Beggar's Opera* there is a Bagshot, also a Sukey Straddle, possibly the kinswoman of Fielding's Molly Straddle.

Fielding draws his hero fulfil the same function as Molière's note.

Wild alone fills the first book. And the figure which Fielding has made of him is so deeply impressed upon us from the beginning that a few reminders in the rest of the novel suffice to keep him vividly before us. The second and following books are enriched by new characters and different adventures, a few honest men even appear upon the scene, the novel flows in a wider and more complex stream, but, from time to time, there reappear pages and chapters written in the same vein as the first book. Just as a geologist finds a stratum appearing in a sudden outcrop and then reappearing once again further away, so does this vein of sharp irony reappear from place to place with great distinctness in the midst of the more abundant flow of the other pages. With a little care it is easy enough to isolate these chapters. There is only one in the second book, the chapter entitled ' of Hats ' which we have already mentioned. Chapters III, VI, VII, VIII, IX, XIII-IV, of the third book, which deal with Wild's marriage ; and in the last book, Chapters II, III (the mutiny in Newgate) and XIII-V (Wild's last hours) are successive outcrops of this vein. In addition to their peculiar quality of cynical and implacable irony they have another characteristic in common. They are concerned with Wild's personal destiny. None of the events which they narrate are ever referred to in the other chapters, while on the other hand they are never concerned with episodes related in the other chapters, (*i.e.*, mainly the Heartfree swindle) with the exception perhaps of some connecting link at the beginning or end of a chapter. If one were to take out of the whole work the first book and the few chapters which I have enumerated in the others only a few links would be needed to make of them a complete and self sufficient novel, a simple biography, mordant and restrained, of Jonathan Wild.

I am convinced that we should then possess the primitive vein, the original form in which Fielding conceived his novel, and probably the form in which he first drafted it. In the absence of other proofs the internal evidence is decisive. For the pages of revolt against society, of caustic Swift-like irony, came naturally to the first Fielding, to the journalist hampered by want, the genius wounded by life. To the first Fielding, also to the dramatist of scandalous gossip, to the author of *The Modern Husband,* belong the pages which describe Wild's conjugal misfortunes. Certain conversations written in dialogue form (in particular III, 8) could, with the names of the interlocutors detached, be put straight into a comedy.

The most violent political allusions are to be found in this original nucleus of the novel, or rather in what remains of it in the final version. But in the meantime Fielding's talent was maturing, he was developing into the author of *Joseph Andrews.* And the pages which remain to be described are undoubtedly the work of the hand which produced *Joseph Andrews.*

It was the new Fielding who feared to weary his readers by such continuous villainy, such unrelieved and inexorable irony. The moment has come when he discovers his true genius. Onto the picaresque biography which he had begun, he now grafts a novel according to his own fashion. And this is why, parallel to the fate of Wild, we are told the story of his victim, Heartfree. A few remarks will enable us to appreciate the consummate art with which this story is connected with the other and woven intimately into the very texture of the work.

Observe, first of all, that as soon as Heartfree and his wife are presented to us at the beginning of the second book, above all, as soon as they are clearly portrayed as the future victims of Jonathan Wild, we are given the impression that everything which preceded was mere preparation and that we are now about to witness the central incident of the novel. The whole development of Wild has become nothing more than the first act of a four-act drama. The second ' binds ' the plot, and sets Wild at grips with his victim Heartfree. Wild, with the complicity of Count La Ruse, robs Heartfree and then has him imprisoned, abducts his wife and carries her away on a ship. Privateers seize them and abandon Wild to the mercy of the sea ; but ' Providence ' watches over the hero and brings him safely back to England. The third book, despite several shadows in the picture, shows the progress of Wild's greatness. He is on the point of victory and Heartfree on the eve of being condemned to death ; Wild is still posing as Heartfree's intimate friend. With the fourth book comes the catastrophe. Wild is arrested. Mrs Heartfree who has been lost for a long time, returns and confounds him by her evidence [1]. His wife and his old friends desert him ; and Jonathan Wild wins the glorious death which should be that of all ' great men ', present and future ; he is hanged by the neck till he is dead.

Directly the unfortunate Heartfree is introduced into the novel, it no longer seems possible to do without him. He acts as a foil to the figure of Wild, gives it its true value, and buttresses it. Heartfree is a jeweller. He is one of those men (like Parson Adams) " whom experience only, and not their own natures, must inform that there are such things as deceit and hypocrisy in the world ". He suffers from " several great weaknesses of mind, being good-natured, friendly, and generous to a great excess : he had, indeed, too little regard to common justice, for he had forgiven some debts to his acquaintances only because they could not pay him. . . He was withal so silly a fellow that he never took the least

[1] The episode of Mrs Heartfree, carried far from her husband by a disloyal friend, and forced to make an extraordinary journey, is very much like the story told by Abbé Prévost in *Cleveland*. Fanny, the virtuous wife of Cleveland, is abducted by his false friend Grelin, who persuades her that her husband is deceiving her. On board the vessel which is taking them away he makes love to her and she resists, just as Mrs Heartfree resists Wild. At the ports she breaks the hearts of many lovers, and finally rejoins her husband more frightened than hurt, exactly like Mrs Heartfree. These stories of extraordinary journeys were very common ; cf. Le Sage's *Beauchene* and *L'Histoire générale des Voyages*, begun about 1736 in England. Fielding parodies them all, without aiming at any one of them in particular.

advantage of the ignorance of his customers, and contented himself with very moderate gains on his goods ".

The irony is a little heavy, but nevertheless we have here already Fielding's characteristic method, which is to be resumed with a finer sense of humour in *Tom Jones*. This method consists essentially in painting two contrasting figures, an honest man persecuted, and a rascal prospering. The malice of fate and the naughtiness of the world will have it that the good seems always wrong and the wicked right. The final catastrophe, however, sets everything straight and the hypocritical rascal is unmasked in the end. Yet the catastrophe is only there to satisfy man's conception of justice ; from the very beginning of the story, in the midst of his greatest misfortunes, the honest man has never ceased to be happier than the successful rascal, for his conscience brings him joys which are greater than any material prosperity.

So it will be with Tom Jones and Blifil, as it is already with Wild and Heartfree, though the contrast is less flexible. Here we are undoubtedly nearer to the scheme of *Tom Jones* than we were in *Joseph Andrews*. And this consideration may complete our conviction that a large part of the work, the part dealing with Heartfree, was written after the parody of *Pamela*. Reviewing the circumstances, we see that *Jonathan Wild* was certainly begun, but as certainly unfinished, when *Joseph Andrews* appeared. Fielding was not the man to keep a finished work without publishing it. Most of the other contributions to the *Miscellanies* are obviously youthful work. The *Journey*, which brings the second volume to an end, was probably kept until the last minute and given to the printers unfinished. The subscribers were waiting ; as early as June 5th, 1742, the author reassured them, and the *Miscellanies* were only finally ready in April, 1743. In his preface Fielding apologizes for his delay in satisfying his readers. He has passed the winter, he says, working " with a favourite child dying in one bed" and his wife " in a condition very little better on another ", not to mention other ' circumstances ' which were doubtless bailiffs' writs. Now on which of the items, published in the *Miscellanies*, could he have been working so feverishly ? We have seen why a work like the *Journey* could no longer interest the author of *Joseph Andrews*. He was never to return to it, and was in future to be completely uninterested in its fate. No, the book on which Fielding was working so desperately during the winter of 1742-3 was his old *Jonathan Wild*, his short picaresque novel, which he recast by adding the story of Heartfree, so obviously written in his new manner.

Thus internal evidence, which alone can be consulted here, may help us to solve the vexed riddle of the composition of *Jonathan Wild*. Such evidence is decisive, and through neglecting to investigate it Fielding's biographers left the question as obscure as they had found it [1].

Unlikely though it may seem, we ought, perhaps, to go back to the very morrow of Wild's death in order to find the earliest inspiration from which the book was to emerge. Mr A. F. Robins [2] has discovered in *Mist's Weekly Journal* of

[1] Edmund Gosse attributes the composition to 1740 ; Dobson—a part at least—to 1740. Bispham (*An Oxford Miscellany*) to 1737. The latest of Fielding's biographers, Mr Cross, seems to place it at 1742, though he notes at the same time that the Wild-Walpole parallel had been frequent. Examples of it are already to be found in *The Beggar's Opera*,1728, and in the political articles of the *Champion*, which Fielding was editing. These circumstances seem to confirm our opinion.

[2] cf. *Notes and Queries*, October 1st, 1910: the following are passages from the article quoted : " I suppose it will be granted that a person may be a rogue, and yet be a great man, which may excuse me from employing more gentle terms when I only speak of him as a man of parts. . . Mr Wild (like other great men), had a turn of thought peculiar to himself . . . the authors he studied most were Machiavel, *the English Rogue*, the lives of the highwaymen, Cooke upon Lyttleton, Echard's *History of England*, a collection of session papers, and Cornelius Tacitus.

" He found out that there were more wise men to be met with in these times than any former age could boast of, for heretofore it appeared to him as if men were apt to give in to some foolish prejudices which hinder a man's thriving and growing great in the world, such as honour and conscience, which now, says he, your busy and pushing people look upon to be chimeras and, therefore, you see that —— and —— and many more, who are rising people, don't make the least pretence to either."

June 12th, 1725 (Wild has been executed on May 24th), a somewhat perplexing article. The author's attitude towards Wild is precisely that which was to be adopted by Fielding. The quality of the irony is tolerably similar and certain expressions are almost textually the same as those used by Fielding. Now at that time Fielding was eighteen years of age. We can scarcely imagine that he wrote this article on leaving Eton. Did he imbibe the first idea of his novel from it ? It is impossible to say.

In any case, though the starting point must remain a mystery, it is possible to state with something like certitude, that a considerable part of *Jonathan Wild* was written about 1737, the date of the Licensing Act. Whole sentences of the book in its present form clearly refer to this measure and defend the liberty of the Press, now threatened with the same fate as the liberty of the theatre.

But the fall of Walpole effaces many of the grievances which Fielding might have laid at his door. Little by little, time calms the writer's rancour and he softens certain effects and obliterates allusions which are too direct ; yet in spite of this he still leaves too many, and is careful to expunge them from the corrected version of his book, published in 1754. The 1754 edition uses the much more general term ' Statesman ' in every place where the 1743 version speaks of ' Prime Minister ' (and almost always couples the words with the epithet ' thief ').

Thus the work was composed gradually in the intervals of a life full of movement, of incessant dramatic and journalistic production. For many years, side by side with pages which he knew were ephemeral, he polished this more powerful work, expressive of the bitter but vigorous philosophy of a man avenging himself on fate with the sword of irony. Little by little, his novel grew richer. Starting from the theoretical standpoint common to young men who know their Juvenal, it rose to the richer satire of one who has lived. Fielding interrupted this work to publish others. At last, one day in the heat of a new inspiration, he began to write *Joseph Andrews*, and *Joseph Andrews* succeeded ; he was fain to profit at once by this kind reception. And now, having found himself, he hastened to add to his work or else to finish, in the few months of the summer of 1742 and that feverish winter of 1742-3, the whole history of Heartfree, fuller and less polished than the rest [1], more palpitating too with life and personal experience. For I cannot forbear to think that when he describes the clumsy despair of Heartfree, robbed by Wild, Fielding is remembering sights seen a dozen years earlier, when a swindling banker absconded with the Fieldings' fortune [2], and I feel sure that his enthusiastic sympathy for Heartfree, the jeweller, is a reflection of his fondness for the jeweller Lillo, on whose death he wrote : " He had the spirit of an old Roman joined to the innocence of a primitive Christian [3]." Again he throws pell-mell into his novel, in certain animated if rather extravagant chapters, those scribblers of adventure-stories, as insipid as they were far-fetched, who had multiplied to such an extent after the success of Robinson Crusoe [4]. Never was book so worked and re-worked. Even in 1754, when Fielding was ill and at the point

---

[1] It is in these chapters that the second edition of 1754 makes most corrections of form.

[2] cf. p. 6, n. 2.

[3] George Lillo, jeweller, had already put upon the stage with great success *The London Merchant*, a bourgeois drama, which marks an epoch in the history of the theatre. On the contrary, his *Christian Hero* had no success (1735). In 1736 Fielding presented *Fatal Curiosity* at his theatre in Haymarket. From that moment Lillo became one of his great friends and it was one of Fielding's habits to put his friends into his books. Was Lillo, as a jeweller, the victim of a big swindle ? At any rate his character corresponds to that of Heartfree.

[4] cf. The way in which Johnson in his translation of the *Travels of Lobo in Abyssinia* (1734) speaks of travellers' exaggerations. Fielding deals with the subject in *The Champion*, March 29th, 1739-40. These foreign travels were long popular ; cf. Quarll's *Voyages*, Aphra Behn's novels, *Oroonoko, The Black Slave*, etc., or Daniel Defoe's *Singleton*. Lucian's *True History* had long ago contained the account of a journey in the course of which the hero and his ship were swallowed by an enormous monster, the entrails of which contained towns, lakes, islands, etc. Mrs Heartfree has a similar adventure.

of death, he sent the printer a new edition, extensively corrected and with two chapters omitted.

The student of Fielding might find it profitable to compare the work in its two forms, the one belonging to the beginning and the other to the end of his literary career [1]. Here we are dealing only with the first version ; it already shows a marvellous perfection of form, which is explained by its long incubation.

By a parody of the severely impassive style of the historian, Fielding is able here to obtain certain ironical effects which do not recur in his other novels ; namely, the continuous and restrained mockery produced by the impact of short sentences, an occasional touch of Voltaire.

" His only hopes were now in the assistances which our hero had promised him. These unhappily failed him : so that the evidence being plain against him, and he making no defence, the jury convicted him, the court condemned him, and Mr Ketch executed him." (II, 5).

" There was in the gang a man named Blueskin, one of those merchants who trade in dead oxen, sheep, etc., in short, what the vulgar call a butcher. This gentleman had two qualities of a great man, *viz.*, undaunted courage and an absolute contempt of those ridiculous distinctions of meum and tuum. . . The common form of exchanging property by trade seemed to him too tedious : he therefore resolved to quit the mercantile profession." (III, 14).

" For a rogue, he wisely said, like gunpowder, must be used with caution." (*ibid.*)

" The cart now moved slowly on, being preceded by a troop of horse-guards bearing javelins in their hands, through streets lined with crowds all admiring the great behaviour of our hero, who rode on, sometimes sighing, sometimes swearing, sometimes singing, or whistling as his humour varied."

" When he came to the tree of glory, he was welcomed by

---

[1] We have tried to do this in another volume, *Le Texte des Romans de Fielding*, Hachette et Cie, Paris, 1923.

a universal shout of the people, who were there assembled in prodigious numbers to behold a sight much more rare in populous cities than one would reasonably imagine it should be, *viz.*, the proper catastrophe of a great man." (IV, 14), and so the story continues. The tone is seldom raised as high as indignation ; the irony remains cold and incisive, applied to a subject firmly detested but treated artistically, to a character which Fielding wishes to be complete because unfaltering. It is the height of the pure satirist's art, the Fielding who is the peer of Congreve as a dramatist, of Swift and Voltaire as a stylist.

But this irony which is the dominant note in *Jonathan Wild* is even so but a part of his comic genius. Although the subject may not allow of the noisy and epic gaiety of *Joseph Andrews*, yet the gaiety of battles and drubbings, good-humour, at least, makes a frequent appearance. Again Fielding, like Molière, and possibly for the same reasons of haste, never hesitates at need to repeat himself. The string of robbers robbed, which we have already mentioned, is to be found in the second as well as in the first book ; Mr Wild, having arranged for Heartfree to be plundered, is in turn robbed by the Count, who is himself finally dispossessed by the legitimate owner and a chance acquaintance, who in turn, etc. Indeed, this second series of thefts is infinitely better arranged and infinitely richer in droll surprises and ridiculous disappointments than the first [1]. The same sort of progress may be traced in Molière's well-known scenes of lovers' quarrels which are reproduced from one play to another.

Whatever may be their cause these repetitions add to the artistic harmony of the novel ; they are linked into a progression. In the first book, Wild has the effrontery to visit the Count in prison, after having caused him to be robbed. The same scene is repeated when he goes to see his victim Heartfree. But compare the one scene with the other, and

---

[1] If our hypothesis be true and the first book written some time before the second, this progress is all the more easily explained.

you will observe how a thousand subtle nuances make the second proceeding seem far more extraordinary, more scandalous, and 'greater', than the first.

The novel does not flow with a smooth and equal tide towards its close. It rises and billows like a wave ; Wild becomes greater and greater : he will have the further to fall. Similarly Heartfree grows in importance, as he must if he is really, as we have seen, the counterpoise of Wild. Indeed, Heartfree is, at first, only described in relation to the principal hero ; then Fielding becomes interested in the honest jeweller ; Heartfree is described for his own sake and we hear about his family and his apprentice. Little by little the author grows so attached to them that he sometimes forgets his original design. At the beginning, whenever he addresses the reader, he apologizes for introducing a character as stupid and as deficient in 'greatness' as this worthy man. But as the *dénouement* draws near, he almost allows his irony to relax. If any fortunate incident favours Heartfree he hastens to assure the reader that " there is no passage in this whole story that can afford him equal delight ", and he praises the good judge who releases Wild's victim. Thus the mask is sometimes slightly withdrawn, which is a further proof that the work was not written ' at a sitting '.

Even Mrs Heartfree who was, at first, nothing more than a ' mean-spirited ' woman, gradually acquires a more marked personality, (particularly in the course of the second book). She is given individual features, and has her peculiarities, which sometimes make us smile. I cannot resist the pleasure of quoting the beginning of a chapter, were it but to show that Fielding is not always a man of big effects, but that his style is often full of wit and delicacy. Mrs Heartfree who has just been interrupted continues the story of her adventures : " If I mistake not, I was interrupted just as I was beginning to repeat some of the compliments made me by the hermit." " Just as you had finished them, I believe, Madam ", said the justice. " Very well, Sir ", said she ;

" I am sure I have no pleasure in the repetition." (IV, 11). Other amusing touches such as Heartfree's continual fears throughout this story for his conjugal honour [1] and his wife's dangerous—and comical—voyages would perhaps almost tend to change the atmosphere of the novel towards the end. But, as we have seen, chapters of pure and incisive irony recur at regular intervals to restore the dominant note, and the very contrast only serves to throw them into stronger relief.

In *Jonathan Wild* the ' real ' Fielding is not as yet entirely revealed. But the evolution is beginning and, little by little, it alters the earlier man. We have pointed out the parts of this work which seem to us to belong to his youth. On the other hand there are several characteristics which distinctly foreshadow the author of *Tom Jones* and *Amelia* [2]. To begin with, there is the general construction of the novel, the two complementary figures, the good and the bad man. The difference is that in *Tom Jones* the proportion will be reversed. Of the two characters introduced in *Jonathan Wild* it is the bad man who attracts all the artistic and moral interest. The book remains a satire. On the contrary, of the two personages depicted in *Tom Jones*, the weak and theoretical figure will be that of the wicked Blifil, and the living character, which absorbs all the moral and psychological

---

[1] There is a similar point in Le Sage's *Bachelier de Salamanque* (part VI, chap. 9) : Blandine, wife of Toston, the Bachelier's servant, is found by him after she has been carried off on a ship by Captain Cope. The husband allows himself to be reassured by his wife but nevertheless makes certain reservations : " If your account is true—it is hardly likely." " I agree with you ", replies his wife, " I had a narrow escape." " I'll warrant you ", answers her husband. " During your story I broke out into a cold sweat which lasts till this moment. Besides the danger to which the English captain exposed you, you were in a no less perilous situation with those two rascally sailors. . . You are lucky to have lost nothing but your money. And now, my dear wife, let us say no more about it." The situations are somewhat similar, and even more so is the bantering tone. This is natural here, but rather less so in *Jonathan Wild* ; Mrs Heartfree is treated with a lightness which is rather astonishing, but which is explicable if Fielding was thinking of Le Sage's *Blandine* when he wrote this part of his story.

[2] Amelia will resemble Mrs Heartfree almost as much as Sophia Western.

interest, will be the honest man. But what an honest man!
He is already foreshadowed, by contrast, in Wild's funeral
oration : " The character which he most valued himself upon,
and which he principally honoured in others, was that of
hypocrisy. . . He said there was little greatness to be
expected in a man who acknowledged his vices but always
much to be hoped from him who professed great virtues :
wherefore, though he would always shun the person whom he
discovered guilty of a good action, yet he was never deterred
by a good character which was more commonly the effect of
profession than of action : for which reason he himself was
always very liberal of honest professions and had as much
virtue and goodness in his mouth as a saint . . . ."

This hatred of hypocrisy and this assertion that he who
professes to be virtuous is therefore suspect, how clearly they
show that the hand which wrote *Jonathan Wild* was indeed
the hand of Richardson's rival and *Pamela's* parodist !

In *Jonathan Wild* Fielding, the novelist, bids farewell to
pure satire. He has attacked Walpole bitterly, has seen him
replaced by another and is now heartily sick of these struggles,
the sole object of which is to put one ' great man ' in the
place of another. As for the small and the weak, they are
always oppressed ; it is from them that reform must come.
" Nothing sure can be more justly ridiculous than the conduct
of those who should lay the lamb in the wolf's way and then
should lament his being devoured. What a wolf is in a sheep-
fold a great man is in society. Now, when one wolf is in
possession of a sheep-fold, how little would it avail the simple
flock to expel him and place another in his stead. . . Perhaps
some would say " Is it then our duty tamely to submit to
the rapine of the *prig*, who now plunders us, for fear of an
exchange ? Surely no : but I answer, it is better to shake
the plunder off than to exchange the plunderer. And by
what means can we effect this but by a total change in our
manners ? " (IV, 3). So says the ' grave man ', drawing his
lesson from the revolt at Newgate which has replaced Johnson

by Wild. Henceforward Fielding hopes far more from moral reform than from any political change. The moralist emerges more and more clearly from the pure satirist.

When discussing a work as profound and as rich in various lessons as *Jonathan Wild*, one must of necessity select. I have tried to isolate its peculiar characteristics and have not been able to insist as I could have wished on perfections already noted elsewhere, such, for instance, as the admirable skill with which the secondary characters who form the background, a chaplain, a courtesan, a bailiff, a thief, a sailor, are made to stand out by one or two vivid details.

We cannot, however, complete this chapter without pausing before one other consideration. Many of Fielding's readers, among them Walter Scott, and even Coleridge, have not been able to avoid a certain feeling of discomfort in reading *Jonathan Wild*. It is true that this book, by reason of its very depth, is cruel. It belongs to the type which Bernard Shaw calls ' unpleasant '. Is the cause to be sought in its advanced democratic aspirations, which had struck Byron [1] ? I think not, for all Fielding's readers, whatever their opinions, experience this uncomfortable feeling in a greater or less degree. Neither is it due to the crudity of certain expressions ; the realistic novelists have taken the edge off our susceptibilities in that matter. No, I am inclined to think that the undeniably uncomfortable sensation which may still come over the modern reader of *Jonathan Wild* arises from the character of the book, which is at bottom purely anarchical. It probes deep down into our souls and there, like Swift, stirs up certain beliefs which we neither dare nor desire to disturb.

[1] " I have lately been reading Fielding over again. They talk of Radicalism, Jacobinism, etc. in England (I am told), but they should turn over the pages of *Jonathan Wild the Great*. The inequality of conditions and the littleness of the great were never set forth in stronger terms, and his contempt for Conquerors, and the like, is such, that had he lived *now*, he would have been denounced in the *Courier* as the grand Mouthpiece and factionary of the revolutionists. And yet I never recollect to have heard this turn of Fielding's mind noticed, though it is obvious in every page." (1821) (*Works*, Murray, 1904, *Letters and Journals*, Vol. V, p. 465).

It is an intellectual pastime, a lawyer's game, wherein the concepts of honour, virtue and social distinctions are roughly handled. Judged as dangerous by those who believe in 'necessary prejudices', it may also shock those who accept them without believing in them, or who deem it imprudent to destroy them. Like Pascal's, his doubt sometimes leads us into depths which terrify the ordinary swimmer.

CHAPTER IV

TOM JONES

Posterity will always think of Fielding as " the author of *Tom Jones* ". He expressed himself for all eternity in this immense work, of which Stendhal said that it is to other novels what the *Iliad* is to epic poetry. For my own part, when I seek to analyse the impression left upon my mind by *Tom Jones*, I feel no impulse to compare it with any other book, but rather there rises before my eyes a vision of one of the great ships of old ploughing with spread sails and laden hold over a sunlit sea. The winds blow fair, and from her deck, as she speeds upon her way, the deep voices of sailors fling to the air some lusty old chantey, simple and victorious.

Tom Jones resumes the great road of *Joseph Andrews*, and this time Fielding's genius carries him as far along it as he can go. Indeed, after his first two novels we no longer expect a literary revelation, for he has found himself as a great creator of character in the first, and in the second as a master of style. But we have already observed that these two books, particularly *Jonathan Wild*, leave an uncomfortable moral impression upon the reader's mind. *Joseph Andrews* attacked Richardson and the doctrine of profitable chastity, but it was almost entirely lacking in any positive lesson ; the worthy Adams could hardly be cited as a model. *Jonathan Wild* attacked the Pharisees, and some others, but its decent folk showed themselves such pitiable dupes that no one could possibly think of imitating them. Laughter in itself is negative; what ideal lay behind the author's mockery?

Tom Jones is the answer to this question. After this parody, after this destructive irony, it is a work of reconstruction, in which at last we have the moral ideal of Fielding.

I

Although the book is less polemical, it is by no means devoid of hostile intent. To begin with, the attack on Richardsonian tendencies is resumed. True, it is a more courteous battle, in which the insulting laughter of *Joseph Andrews* is no more heard. Fielding is greater now and has no need of weapons which are the resource of the weak. He merely asserts himself; but it is interesting to observe that he still asserts himself against Richardson. Richardson again! Yet I do not know a single biographer who has thought to point out, save by a few anecdotes, how close is the interaction between these two literary careers [1]. *Joseph Andrews* follows *Pamela.* Then there is a long silence (1742-8). Within an interval of a few months *Tom Jones* follows *Clarissa Harlowe* [2]. Two years pass and this time Fielding is ready first; *Amelia* precedes *Grandison.* These six great works go in pairs, and in order that nothing may be lacking in the picture, after two male portraits by Fielding had followed upon Richardson's two female portraits, Fielding was to end his career as a novelist with the picture of a woman, to which Richardson was to reply by that of a man [3]. There is more here than mere coincidence. In these works two types of genius, two

---

[1] The intermediary between these two novelists was Fielding's sister, Sarah. I have made a study of their relationship in two articles in the *Revue Germanique*; cf. *supra* p. 27, n. 1.

[2] *Jonathan Wild*, was written earlier, and therefore has no part in this evolution.

[3] Richardson was furious at the success of *Tom Jones* and thought of confronting it with the portrait of a really good man. All his admirers wanted him to do this, but he needed pressing. He wrote to

artistic conceptions, two techniques, two moral ideals and two conflicting temperaments, deliberately confront one another. But nowhere is the opposition as clear as in this : that while Fielding remains essentially " the author of *Tom Jones* ", Richardson faces him, essentially " the author of *Clarissa Harlowe* ".

Richardson began to write his novel in 1744. He continued to work from 1744 to 1748 amid discussions and controversies, upon which his correspondence throws considerable light. A wide circle of admirers, (one might almost call them collaborators), both men and women commented on the smallest incidents. There is, moreover, no doubt that Fielding's sister Sarah kept him in touch with the progress of the work ; he knew the plot and he gave his opinion (of which Richardson was by no means ignorant) on the ending [1]. Austin

Lady Bradshaigh : " But for what should I set about the work I had once in view ! To draw a good man, a man who needs no repentance, as the world would think ! How tame a character. Has not the world shown me that it is much better pleased to receive and applaud the character that shows us what we are (little of novelty as one would think there is in that) than what we ought to be ? . . . I will only say, that when the world is ready to receive writings of a different cast, I hope writers will never be wanting to amuse, as well as instruct. Nor perhaps may the time be very far off." The concluding sentence of his letter is curious. It seems to indicate that at this date (December, 1759) Richardson knew that Fielding was preparing to write *Amelia*, many scenes of which pass in prison, ". . . Newgate or the Tower ; in the former of which (removed from inns and ale-houses) will some of his next scenes be laid : and perhaps not unusefully ; I hope not. But to have done for the present with this fashionable author." (Richardson's *Correspondence*, Vol. IV, p. 285, seqq.).

[1] On November 7th, 1748, Richardson wrote to Aaron Hill sending him volumes 6 and 7 of *Clarissa*. (*Tom Jones* had not yet been published but some copies of the first volumes were ready and had been shown to various friends. People discussed them a great deal). It is easy to see that Richardson was thinking of Fielding, the writer of ' novels '.

" These will show you, Sir, that I intend more than a novel or romance by this piece ; and that it is of the tragic kind, In short, that I thought my principal characters could not be rewarded by any happiness short of the heavenly. But how have I suffered by this from the cavils of some, from the prayers of others, from the entreaties of many more, to make what is called a happy ending. Mr Lyttleton, the late Mr Thomson, Mr Gibbes, and Mr Fielding have been among these." The picture of Fielding asking Richardson . . . to write *Tom Jones* is curious. Let us be thankful that as Richardson had refused, Fielding preferred to write it himself.

Dobson [1] has proved that *Tom Jones* was not begun before the autumn of 1746. The dates do not preclude the suggestion that Fielding knew of the existence of *Clarissa Harlowe* and of his rival's plans, at the moment when he himself began to work. Is it rash to go further and to suppose that he was moved to write a new novel by the thought of this ' *Nescio quid majus* ', which was at that moment coming to birth in the workroom of his rival, and the progress of which he could follow step by step ?

Too much faith must not be placed in a presumption, however well-founded it may be [2]. Even if Fielding had not composed *Tom Jones* with *Clarissa Harlowe* in his mind, it would be impossible to discuss the one without first speaking of the other, and if we wish to-day to taste the full flavour of *Tom Jones* and to know all its riches, we must, like its contemporaries, have fresh in our minds *Clarissa*, a study of the same set of people from another point of view, a conflict rising out of a similar situation, but among persons whose sensibilities are different.

The plot of Richardson's novel is well known. Clarissa Harlowe, wishing to avoid an odious marriage which her pitiless father, brother, sister, and uncles are trying to force upon her, elopes with Lovelace. But Lovelace is a debauchee who treats her infamously. In the end she dies of grief and despair, unwilling to seek a reconciliation with him, and unable to win one with her family.

Here, on the other hand, is the plot of Fielding's novel : Sophia Western, also wishing to avoid an odious marriage, which her brutal father and half-crazy aunt want to force upon her, runs away from home. The dissolute young man, Tom Jones, whom she loves, rejoins her after numerous escapades. Since he proves to be better than his reputation,

---

[1] cf. A. Dobson, *Life of Fielding*, p. 117. Mr Cross gives further arguments confirming this date.

[2] It is more than a presumption. Further numerous examples quoted later on, prove that Richardson was never far from Fielding's thoughts.

Sophia is reconciled to him, and when her father learns that the young man's bastardy is honourable, he allows his daughter to marry him.

Such are the contrasting *dénouements* which Richardson's tragic, and Fielding's comic, spirit drew from a situation which was materially the same.

The inevitable logic of the sentimental [1] drama rules all the details of Richardson's book. In order that Clarissa's misfortunes may win our sympathy and that her persecutors may have no excuse, she must, first of all, be the model of all feminine virtues, for young girls will receive a much more efficacious warning against seducers, if even a paragon, a Clarissa, is unable to defend herself. Then again, the treatment of Clarissa by the Harlowes must be of such a prodigious and unheard-of cruelty as to make her forget her high principles and think of an elopement ; yet she will not consent to her abduction but will be tricked into it. In contrast to her, again, Lovelace must be an unnatural and diabolical rogue [2], to be capable of treating a Clarissa with such odious brutality, and so on. It would be possible to justify, on these lines, by a process of logical deduction, most of what seem the most unlikely touches in the novel. Is this the result of that assiduous discussion which has already been mentioned ? Does it signify a desire to reply to Fielding's denunciation of the epistolary novel [3] ? At all events Richardson is here making a

[1] Lady Bradshaigh, writing to Richardson, asks in a postscript the meaning of the word " *sentimental*, so much in vogue amongst the polite both in town and country ".

[2] cf. Part III, letter 34, where Lovelace plans to abduct Miss Howe and her mother by taking them on board ship, to seduce them, and throw Hickman overboard. From time to time, examples of Lovelace's appalling potentialities are given, cf. the letter to Joseph Leman where he enumerates in the most cold-blooded way, all his mistresses who have died in childbirth—or again the end of letter 35.

[3] In the preface which Fielding wrote to *Familiar Letters between the principal characters in David Simple and some others*, published in 1747 by his sister Sarah, he condemns the epistolary novel in the following terms : " Sure no one will contend that the epistolary style is in general the most proper to a novelist, or that it hath been used by the best writers of this kind " and lower down " to conclude this point I know not of any essential difference between this and any other way

visible effort at composition ; it is shown in many footnotes, in many references from one letter to another. The artistic construction is far more carefully handled than that of *Pamela ;* it would be more difficult to ' skip ' when reading *Clarissa.*

But however interesting the story may be, Richardson declares that it was not his purpose to write a ' mere novel or romance '. The essence of his work lies in its moral lesson [1]. And this was a pretention which Fielding could no more admit than he had admitted it in the case of *Pamela.* I look forward with confidence, to the day when an authentic document will be discovered, proving that *Tom Jones* was really written to oppose *Clarissa.*

I know of few works which are richer in pathos than *Clarissa Harlowe.* In saying so, I pass over all the melodrama of the novel, its pseudo-tragedy, and its vain attempts to reach the sublime. Richardson lacks one thing to be a classic, that ' grand manner ' of which Matthew Arnold speaks. His characters, a Lovelace, a Clarissa, are greater than he, and they overwhelm him ; they are weighed down, indeed, by a whole heritage of religious struggles ; the conflict of their two prides [2] evokes and reawakens the deep harmonic

cf writing novels, save only that, by making use of letters, the writer is freed from the regular beginnings and conclusions of stories, with scme other formalities, in which the reader of taste finds no less ease and advantage than the author himself."

[1] It should be noted that Richardson's name figures in the list of subscribers to *Familiar Letters.* Richardson was obviously thinking of Fielding's reproaches when he wrote a certain ' Postscript ' to *Clarissa.* To those who wished to see him give up the epistolary style, he replied, that it had already brought him considerable success. He was not writing a ' mere novel or romance '. He warned his readers that " the story (interesting as it is generally allowed to be) was to be principally looked upon as the vehicle of the instruction ". Scorn for the ' epistolary style ' is answered by scorn for the ' mere novel '. The intention is obvious.

[2] The following are two passages among many : Lovelace writes " Let me first to gratify *my* pride, down *hers* . . . " (III, i, 70) and for Clarissa's pride : " I cast myself at her feet. Begone, Mr Lovelace, said she. . . My soul is above thee, man ! with both her hands pushing me from her !—urge me not to tell thee how sincerely I think my soul above thee—Thou hast in mine, a proud, a too proud heart to contend with ! Leave me, leave me forever ! Thou hast a proud heart to contend with." (III, Letter 27).

vibrations of that great conflict which for so long divided the English soul, and ranged against each other, like two brother enemies, pride of Puritan and pride of Cavalier. Into what subtleties, what refinements of sadism, are they not drawn ! Lovelace goes so far as to violate the woman whom he loves, to see if she loves him enough to forgive him for having humiliated her. He evolves the most complicated situations, makes plans, piles lie upon lie for the pleasure of being different from the common herd, of showing that he has neither their sensations nor their sentiments, and of flying from reality. Such maniacs need bromide or a douche. But what a point of feverish and artificial excitement must have been reached by a society which could accept such pictures as true to life !

Clarissa shows the same unhealthy love of the romantic. Her sadism is complementary to that of Lovelace. She indulges in an ecstasy of suffering, which she has no desire to alleviate. One wonders that she never seems to want to profit by Lovelace's good intentions in order to obtain her marriage, but this is no mere unskilfulness on Clarissa's part [1]. The explanation is worse : from the beginning, from the moment when she opposes her family, one can trace in her actions that Puritan pride which thinks that it has been singled out by God to suffer special ordeals. She stands apart and looks at herself and this is why she is so ready to write ; she enjoys what she is describing. Nor shall we be surprised by Clarissa's prolonged and detailed preparation for death, her ordering the coffin to be carried up to her room and decorating it with symbols and mottoes. She revels in it all with a strange and morbid pleasure.

Here, in my opinion, is the secret of the deep pathos of

---

[1] Miss Howe, her friend, has a healthier mind. She often advises her to accept Lovelace and to be less punctilious. Richardson's women-readers found Clarissa too particular. He wrote in a note (Letter 32 of the second part) : " Many of the sex, (we mention it with regret) have been readier to censure her for over-niceness . . . than him for artifices and exultations not less cruel and ungrateful than ungenerous and unmanly."

this book, which is also, as Coleridge has observed, 'unhealthy'. It is charged, perhaps unconsciously, with all the complex and restless sensibility which filled the minds and hearts of its contemporaries. Henceforth these refinements of passion were to disappear from literature. Puritans and Cavaliers alike were aristocrats, and it was in wider and more airy spheres that conflicts of sentiment were henceforward to be fought out. Clarissa Harlowe is the last expression of an age, its swan song; and in its music we may at the same time catch, as yet faint and half lost among the old themes, the first notes and chords which prelude the great sentimental symphony of romanticism.

But what of the moral of *Clarissa*, that moral which Richardson declared to be the 'essence' of his book? It was in truth not very clear and his contemporaries did not conceal their perplexity from the author. The lesson miscarried. Lovelace won all hearts, and Clarissa was deemed now prudish and affected, now rash and a coquette [1]. And it was the good who were punished in this 'moral' novel! Richardson, indignant and astonished, was reduced to explaining that the virtuous Clarissa would find her reward in Heaven.

The truth is that Richardson, for all his moral theories, has an entirely a-moral conception of love [2]. He really ought to hold Corneille's view; a Clarissa, endowed with every

---

[1] "Why, I attempted to draw a good woman, and the poor phantom has set half her own sex against her. The men more generally admire her, indeed, because bad men, as I have quoted above from Lovelace, admire good women. But with some of the sex, she is a prude; with others a coquette; with more a saucy creature, whose life, manners and maxims, are affronts to them. Mr Fielding's Sophia is a much more eligible character." (Richardson's *Correspondence*, Vol. VI, p. 83, to Lady Bradshaigh). Like all his contemporaries, Richardson speaks of Clarissa as parallel with Sophia.

[2] cf. *Clarissa Harlowe*, Letter XL, where Clarissa gives a lengthy explanation of the state of her heart to her friend, Miss Howe. As a corollary to this, Miss Howe does not love Hickman, although he is endowed with all the virtues. Richardson published *Grandison* as an answer to those who had reproached him with immorality. After this Lady Bradshaigh, in an access of enthusiasm wrote: 'Sir, you ought to have been made a Bishop.' (MSS., Forster Collection, March 22nd, 1754).

perfection, should only fall in love with a man whom she could recognize as a hero. Yet in spite of herself she is in love with the unworthy Lovelace, just as Pamela was in love with the brutal Squire B. What a humiliation for virtue ! Here, the psychological truth spoils the moral lesson, and this is indeed the great weakness of *Clarissa*. It is less a novel, says Richardson, than " a vehicle of instruction ", and it is precisely as a " vehicle of instruction " that it fails [1].

Fielding did not fail to see all this clearly, to point it out to his rival—or to cause others to do so—and to write about it on occasion. Richardson's delight in insulting him both in conversation and correspondence, is well known. Yet, if his biographers are to be believed, Fielding was either ignorant of these insults, or knew of them and did not take the trouble to reply. Such forbearance accords ill with what we know of him, and if we were in possession of his correspondence, I feel sure that we should find there some very frank expressions of opinion on the subject of Richardson. In the absence of such letters, how is it that no one has thought of commenting on the preliminary chapters of *Tom Jones*, where Fielding speaks of his art, and where there are undeniable attacks on, and sundry allusions to, his great literary rival ? His condemnation of the epistolary novel, has already been mentioned. Elsewhere he speaks in terms which it is impossible to misunderstand, of characters which are ' all of a piece ', completely vicious or entirely virtuous, angelically perfect or diabolically depraved. " Nor do I indeed conceive ",

---

[1] Lady Mary Wortley Montagu's opinion is very characteristic. She thought *Clarissa* very moving but not particularly moral : " I was such an old fool as to weep over Clarissa Harlowe like any milkmaid of sixteen, over the ballad of the Lady's Fall. . . but on the whole it is most miserable stuff. . . Even that model of affection, Clarissa, is so faulty in her behaviour as to deserve little compassion. Any girl who runs away with a young fellow, without intending to marry him, should be carried to Bridewell or Bedlam the next day. Yet the circumstances are so laid as to inspire tenderness, notwithstanding the low style and absurd incidents : and I look upon this and *Pamela* to be two books that will do more general mischief than the works of Lord Rochester." (To the Countess of Bute, March 1st, 1752).

says he, " the good purposes served by inserting characters of such angelic perfection or such diabolical depravity, in any work of invention." Is this not a deliberate blow at Richardson[1]? Later a complete chapter is given up to showing that love must not be confounded with an appetite for " delicate white, human flesh "[2], after the manner of the prurient Lovelace. Elsewhere he laughs at authors who are without " birth or fortune or, what is equivalent to both, the honourable profession of a gamester," and yet paint the manners of the aristocracy, without having had any opportunity of observing them. He adds that he, " whose province is comedy ", has no such pitfalls to avoid[3]. Again, in a severe paragraph, he points out that modern society is not even capable of the vices of which it is accused, that people are vain rather than lewd, and frivolous rather than vicious[4].

[1] " We must admonish thee, my worthy friend . . . not to condemn a character as a bad one, because it is not perfectly a good one. If thou dost delight in these models of perfection, there are books enow written to gratify thy taste," and he adds, " nor do I conceive the good purposes, etc." (*Tom Jones* X, i).

[2] *Tom Jones*, VI, i.

[3] cf. XIV, i, and also a passage (XI, i)which shows that Fielding knew of letters (analogous to those which Richardson was to write later to Hill or Lady Bradshaigh, in which his adversary refuses, in advance, to read him and brands him as ' low '. Had *Tom Jones* been shown to Richardson in manuscript, by those who had already read it, and had he refused to look at or read it ?" I think I may boldly object to the censures of any one passed upon works he has not himself read. Such censurers as these, whether they speak from their own guess or suspicion, or from the report and opinion of others, may properly be said to slander the reputation of the book they condemn.

Such may likewise be suspected of deserving this character who, without assigning any particular faults, condemn the whole in general defamatory terms : such as vile, dull, d——d stuff, etc. ; and particularly by the use of the monosyllable ' Low ': a word which becomes the mouth of no critic who is not ' Right Honourable ' . . . " if we judge according to the sentiments of some critics, and of some Christians, no author will be saved in this world and no man in the next."

[4] cf. XIV, i, (last paragraph) : " There is not indeed a greater error than that which universally prevails among the vulgar who, borrowing their opinion from some ignorant satirist, have affixed the character of lewdness to these times. . . . . In my humble opinion the true characteristic of the present Beau Monde is rather folly than

TOM JONES

It is probable that while he was writing *Tom Jones*, Fielding had only an indirect knowledge of *Clarissa*. He knew the subject and the main lines of the narrative, he condemned its tendencies and had nothing but antipathy for Richardson's point of view ; and it seems probable that he decided to write a novel on an analogous theme with the object of drawing from it a different moral lesson, and one which he thought healthier. Then, when the first two books of *Clarissa* were published, he was moved to the heart, as no one could help being moved, by the pathetic grandeur and psychological realism of these portraits, and expressed his sincere admiration in two articles in the *Jacobite's Journal*[1].

It is in their moral interpretation that the two writers are so decidedly opposed. The society which they paint is essentially the same, a society of egoisms upheld by conventions. The brutality of Clarissa's parents differs very little from that of Sophia's father or aunt. In both novelists is to be found more or less disguised, the same protest against unlimited parental tyranny, and the same vindication (which foreshadows romanticism) of the rights of personality. At first there is scarcely any difference between Tom Jones and Lovelace[2]. The real difference lies in the author's point of

vice, and the only epithet it deserves is that of frivolous." It is curious to note that he is in agreement with Brown, author of the famous *Estimate of Manners and Principles of the times* (1757), who writes (pp. 27 and 29) : "Now the slightest observation, if attended with impartiality, may convince us that the character and the manners of this age and nation is by no means that of abandoned wickedness and profligacy . . . but that of a vain, luxurious, and selfish effeminacy."

[1] *The Jacobite's Journal*, January 2nd, 1748, and March 2nd, 1748.

[2] The descriptions are curiously alike. Miss Howe imagines young Lovelace to be "a curl-pated villain full of fire, fancy and mischief ; an orchard robber, a wall-climber, a horse-rider without saddle or bridle, neck or nothing : a sturdy rogue in short, who would kick and cuff and do no right and take no wrong of anybody ; would get his head broke, then a plaster for it, or let it heal of itself ; while he went on to do more mischief, and if not to get, to deserve broken bones, etc." (Letters XLVI).

[2] cf. *Tom Jones* (III, 2) : "He had been already convicted of three robberies, *viz.*, of robbing an orchard, of stealing a duck out of a farmer's yard, and of picking Master Blifil's pocket of a ball."

view and in his appreciation of moral values. Richardson has the tragic outlook, the fatality of his characters dominates him ; in spite of himself he admires them, or at the least he submits to them. Fielding, on the contrary, always keeps his detachment. He never loses that critical faculty, which is essential to the comic spirit, he always sees his characters intellectually and is never in their power.

He desires to see life steadily and see it whole ; and he succeeds. In contrast to Lovelace, a creature diabolically depraved, a symbol of vice as seen by a Christian visionary, he draws his Tom Jones, a real person, a human mixture of vices and virtues. His protagonists are deliberately opposed to those of Richardson, just as the happy ending of his novel raises a sort of protest against the intensely gloomy close of *Clarissa* [1].

To deliver us from the spell of the wicked nobleman, he gives us his foundling. Tom Jones, brought up by Mr Allworthy, who found him one day on his bed, is a hardy country-bred youth, a lover of open air life and wide spaces, a natural vagabond. He is full of vigorous and lusty life. One day, rushing to the rescue of Sophia, he breaks his arm, but gives no sign of his suffering. His animal spirits are strong and simple ; he knows no better way to celebrate his guardian's recovery than to get drunk ; he would be running after women, were it not that he is in love, and even so his love is not always strong enough to triumph over his temperament and to make him refuse a good opportunity. He is of a ' sanguine ' nature, in the old sense of the term, living solely and with all his strength in the present. It is a characteristic of the savage, and Tom Jones is indeed very close to nature. In this he is the true child of his age, both French and English ; reading his adventures, strongly flavoured as they are at times,

---

[1] Fielding's advice to Richardson about a happy ending, must be remembered. In refusing, Richardson protested against the rather too universal opinion that ' a reformed rake makes the best husband ' ; cf. *Clarissa Harlowe*, Letter CXX. The *dénouement* of *Tom Jones* conforms exactly to this idea.

one is irresistibly reminded of Rousseau, of the brutal and
sometimes almost crapulous frankness of the *Confessions*,
and of the morality which pardons everything to the sinner,
if only he be sincere in his sin. By this simplicity alone Tom
Jones is infinitely far removed from Lovelace, who is always
calculating, always trying to humbug people. True, they are
both egoists, but the egoism of Tom Jones is that of a child.
His vice is always ingenuous. There is in him more than a
mere *joie de vivre ;* it is a very intoxication, with all the lack
of restraint which the word implies. Wide and full, his life
unrolls itself all about him ; he is fain to squeeze the brimming
measure of enjoyment from everything ; from Nature as he
sees it in Somerset, with its wide meadows shadowed by
beautiful trees, and its streams gushing everywhere ; from
men, for they interest his curiosity, and he will talk readily
and at length with anyone, an innkeeper, a puppet-showman,
a barber, a pedlar, a surgeon. He is curious too about women,
from no vicious motive but from a desire to learn about life,
to spend himself, to make the most of the fullness of his
strength. He is susceptible to a thousand impressions ; he
will break into an ungovernable rage, but his rage will not
be proof against a strong inclination to laugh ; he will laugh
uproariously and be just as ready to weep copiously if occasion
arises. He is a brave heart but how his conscience gets in
his way ! How much he would like to obey it, if only
obedience were not so difficult ! His heart is paved with good
intentions, and yet, for all his good will, we see him
by turns lying, poaching, drinking, quarrelling, fighting,
knocking a man down, sleeping now in prison, now beneath
the stars or anywhere else, on the slightest invitation ; and
since he is wretchedly poor in London, he will even go so far
as to take money from a certain Lady Bellaston, a beauty of
somewhat mature years, who, as Fielding gives us to
understand, has in addition unsweet breath.

" For all the rest, the best fellow in the world [1]." But what

---

[1] *Au demeurant le meilleur fils du monde."* (Clément Marot).

is the rest and what is it worth ? It is that this fine country
lad with his rather plebeian vigour, this child of nature, is
good. His faults are never more than errors, after which he
sooner or later finds the right path. If he errs it is because
he is not guided by ready-made principles, because he has to
learn life by living it. Yet, however far he strays, he is always
sound at heart. He has a natural horror of lying, yet he will
lie and hold to his lie under the whip, because by doing so he
can save a poor gamekeeper, whom his denunciation would
deprive of a living. Most of his actions are a similar mixture
of good and evil, but each one of them is a complete revala-
tion of his character in all the extraordinary complexity of
its impulses. His nature shows scarcely any evolution. His
first appearance is already a clear intimation of what he will
be like in the end. With far less wealth of intellect, far greater
wealth of feeling and an infinitely more highly developed sense
of reality, he nevertheless belongs to the race of Abraham
Adams, of those men whose personal reactions are so strong
that they resist all education. Men such as these have an
instinct anterior and superior to all experience, which, when
the moment comes, blazes its way straight ahead, overturning
the barriers of prudence and public opinion.

How strangely disordered is this mind, which conscience
alone can reduce to a sort of unity ! Tom Jones is not incapable
of renunciation. One day he discovers that he is in love with
Sophia, the daughter of his neighbour Western, and that she
returns his love. But he is already the lover of a poor girl,
Molly Seagrim, the daughter of the aforesaid gamekeeper,
who is expecting a child and is relying upon him. So much
the worse for him. He will give up the fair Sophia and do his
duty. But then he accidentally discovers his tutor, the grave
philosopher Square, squatting in Molly's room. Now that
the situation is altered he can set aside his scruples and freely,
though not without lapses, love his Sophia, until the day
when Western brutally refuses to bestow on him his daughter's
hand, and his adopted father at the instigation of Blifil,

drives him ignominiously from the house. Then Tom Jones is ready once more to yield to fate and loyally, like a man of honour, to remove himself from the young girl's life.

It is indeed a strangely disordered mind. At the very moment when he has not a shilling in his pocket, he keeps and refuses to touch a hundred pound note, which he has found in the road and which he knows to belong to his Sophia. But in order to avoid one indelicacy he is quite ready to commit another, by accepting from his mature mistress, Lady Bellaston, the money which he refuses to borrow from the girl. He then immediately squanders in lavish charity the sum which he has thus received.

What principle guides his actions? The essential rule for Tom Jones is to do no harm to anyone [1]. Nothing else matters. A young man of fashion is about to abandon a girl whom he has betrayed, so that he may make a rich marriage ; Jones sets his feet once again on the right path. " Tom, Tom ", answered Nightingale, " remember last night—— " " Lookee, Mr Nightingale ", said Jones, " I am no canting hypocrite, nor do I pretend to the gift of chastity. . . I have been guilty with women, I own it ; but am not conscious that I have ever injured any ; nor would I, to procure pleasure to myself, be knowingly the cause of misery to any human being " (XIV, 4). Here is the great principle : do harm to no one. Tom Jones, the sinner, is so actively and universally *kind* by the end of the novel that he finally assumes the air of a philanthropist *a la Diderot* [2].

[1] cf. *Journey from this World to the Next* and the passage quoted above. cf. also a certain speech of old Laroon in *The Jesuit caught* (1732). '" Besides, Sir, I have no sins to reflect on but those of ane honest fellow. If I have loved a whore at five-and-twenty, and a bottle at forty, why I have done as much good as I could in my generation ; and that, I hope, will make amends." (*The Jesuit caught*, last scene). In those " sins of an honest fellow " have we not already a forecast of the morality of *Tom Jones* ?

[2] cf. particularly Diderot : " *Est-il bon, est-il méchant* ? " Here again is a passage from Diderot which exactly expresses Fielding's moral philosophy : " Do you not think that a man can be so fortunately begotten that he finds great pleasure in doing good ?—I do.—That he can have received an excellent education which strengthens his

This is a vindication. If Tom Jones errs (we seem to be told) it is usually through sheer imprudence. He is no one's enemy but his own. Optimist as he is, he is ready to believe that all other men are as good as he (which is another characteristic of Adams). His imprudences are innumerable ; the most important which includes all the others, is that he trusts simply to the dictates of his conscience, without the slightest regard for appearances. This makes it all too easy for his enemies to put him in a bad light. He confides to one that his pocket is full of money, to another that he is in love with an heiress, to another that he has found favour in the eyes of a pretty woman, in fact he gives himself away to such an extent that any rogue can take advantage of him.

It is, of course, true that all these characteristics are to be found elsewhere ; this defenceless simplicity comes straight from *Gil Blas ;* nor could anyone be the friend of Lady Bellaston without having some characteristics in common with Marivaux's *Paysan parvenu* [1]. And, after all, Fielding was not the first to paint a fine lad, clear-eyed, with strong appetites, setting forth to live. But out of a thousand scattered traits he has made a synthesis that is all his own.

Once more, this is a vindication in reply to the indictment of the man who drew Lovelace : Tom Jones is a plea for indulgence on behalf of certain ' bad lots ', who may, perhaps, be branded as ' rakes ' by the world, but who do not deserve to be condemned without appeal. Side by side with those who are vicious through wickedness, pride, or diseased nerves (like Lovelace), there are (Fielding seems to tell us) men,

---

natural inclination to kindness ?—Assuredly.—And that, when we are older, experience will have taught us that, take it for all in all, there is greater wordly happiness to be won by being a good man, than by being a rogue ? " (*Entretien d'un philosophe avec la Maréchale de* . . .)

[1] Jacob receives a purse from a lady of mature years whom he loves : " Here my boy ", she added, " is something with which to pay your coach fares. When that is done, I will give you some more ", and his comment is : "I was delighted to be offered the money, but I blushed to take it. The one seemed to me flattering, the other mean." (Part IV).

sound in body and heart, who cannot always resist temptation, if it come to them with bright eyes and red lips. But such a man at least does not exult in his faults ; at least he is concerned that no one but himself shall suffer for them. At all events, he must not be condemned without a hearing, or an attempt to understand him.

What gives this tale its individual note and its depth is, often enough, the feeling borne in upon the reader, that it has all happened ; or at least that it must, could, or should have happened so. This Tom Jones, whose reputation is so bad and whom all ' right-minded ' people put to such shame that they even succeed in making his benefactor turn him out of the house, reminds us irresistibly of another sinner who never attempted to pose as a hero. Henry Fielding had some terrible enemies and a few benefactors, chief among whom was Ralph Allen, the prototype of Allworthy, Tom Jones's adopted father. The things which Fielding's enemies were never tired of saying, the calumnies which to this day cast a slur upon his reputation, the idle gossip which still mars his glory, are not unlike the spiteful remarks which people made about Tom Jones. Was the book a precaution ? Was Fielding making an ingenious plea *pro domo*, when he depicted Allworthy listening to false reports and driving Tom away ? Allen was a pious man, a philanthropist with a wide circle of friends, among whom were Richardson and others who pretended to look upon Fielding as a contemptible creature, vulgar and dissolute. The story of Tom Jones was an oblique answer to these libels. Let the hypothesis stand for what it is worth, it would at any rate explain the strange human depths of this character ; Tom Jones is the work of a novelist who can see the soul beneath its envelopes of flesh, who knows that mankind cannot be divided into two distinct groups, the very good and the very bad, who knows, too, that the best of men can find at times unsightly things in the hidden corners of his heart, and who refuses to let those dark corners remain hidden. His picture is a beautiful and a frank one.

Sophia Western, too, shows the same gay and calm courage in the face of life as the young women of Shakespeare or Molière. Upon those who had just read, or were in the midst of reading *Clarissa*, the contrast forced itself ; it is impossible to believe that it was unintentional. Contemporary readers did not fail to see it ; and, in his correspondence, Richardson refers to it a hundred times, without attempting to hide his bitterness. For the comparison is to the advantage of Sophia. The great reproach against her rival has already been pointed out ; if Lovelace parades his vice, Clarissa parades her virtue, and one excess is as bad as the other. Strange perversion of saintliness, turned to pride ! Clarissa is not in search of happiness, nor even, it is much to be feared, of goodness ; her one aim is victory, a complete victory involving the humiliation of her enemy and a surrender of arms, with drums beating, flags flying [1]. Ten times she has the advantage over Lovelace and ten times, for the most trifling reasons, she loses the opportunity of ending the whole matter and marrying. Lovelace has offered her his hand too cavalierly, the proprieties would be shocked at too early an acceptance, she must observe ' due decorum ' ! Johnson's judgment upon Clarissa was profoundly true ; " There is always something which she prefers to the truth." She never once consents to look her situation in the face and made a decision [2]. It is evident that at the bottom of her heart

[1] Lovelace has just offered her marriage on his knees : " in words the most tender and explicit, he tenders himself to my acceptance. . . But what could I say to this ! Extorted from him, as it seemed to me, rather as the effect of his compassion than his love ? What *could* I say ? I paused, I looked silly, I am sure I looked *very* silly, etc." (II, 60). She is always so much interested in how she looks. Lovelace is quite aware of this pride. " And I verily think I should be inclined to spare her all further trial . . . were it not for the contention that her vigilance has set on foot, *which* shall overcome the other " (II, 61).

[2] Her friend, Miss Howe, never ceases to give her this advice : " But if you cannot despise and hate him, if you care not to break with him, you must part with some punctilios . . . either he must mean well or ill ; if ill the sooner you know it the better. If well, whose modesty is it he distresses, but that of his own wife ? " (II, 65). To which Richardson adds, in a note, the reflection that Clarissa cannot act

TOM JONES

Clarissa is proud of all the vicious ingenuity which Lovelace
expends in order to conquer her, just as Pamela is inwardly
flattered at being bullied by B—— ; from beginning to end
of the book she is in the falsest and most difficult of positions,
and if she does not escape from it, it is because she is afraid,
afraid of what the world will say, of that great London, of
which she is ignorant, of life itself ; she temporizes and evades
difficulties ; when she is in a painful position she weeps
but she does not extricate herself ; when it becomes too
painful she at last decides to die of grief. She sulks
puritanically at life.

Sophia Western knows nothing of such subtleties. It is
true that when her father opposes her, she declares that she
is determined to die, but this is merely a *façon de parler*
and we know very well that she will do nothing of the kind.
Surrender is not a common habit with Fielding's people ;
they are made to act rather than to feel, or, at any rate, their
feelings do not impede their actions.

Sophia Western, who is motherless and therefore, perhaps,
old for her age, looks life in the face and knows how to make
a decision. Clarissa, when driven into a corner by the thought
of a marriage which she detested, was afraid to flee alone,
and at last, almost crazy and quite incapable of making up
her mind, allowed herself to be abducted by a man whom she
felt to be a blackguard. In a like situation Sophia weighs
the pros and cons, and finally decides to set out alone for
London, there to join her kinswoman, Lady Bellaston. What
a fine English girl she is, so energetic and so sane, and how
good it is to see her prepare for her flight ! She forgets
nothing, neither money, nor a change of linen, nor a brace of
pistols in case of some evil encounter ; she sets out at midnight
without a tremor, strong and firm in the saddle, above all,

this way : " It was not possible for a person of her true delicacy of mind
to act otherwise than she did to a person so cruelly and so insolently
artful." cf. another letter from the ' girl of spirit ', Miss Howe :
" Run away from him, my dear . . . or marry him if you cannot "
(II, 23).

147

THE NOVELS OF FIELDING

self-reliant [1]. She is, indeed, the spiritual daughter of the young hero, who at the age of fourteen ran away from Eton, and went to Salisbury.

But for all her firmness, she has no lack of delicacy. She adores music, has a good taste in it, and likes to play Handel [2]. She is charitable, with a fine, unprejudiced Christian charity ; this pure young girl has no sense of false shame when she goes to the help of an unhappy unmarried mother, even when this mother is Molly Seagrim, of whose child Tom is the reputed father. Morally she does not seek to gratify her pride by a victory over others or over herself ; as soon as she observes that she is looking upon Jones with favour she is quick to mistrust herself, and tries to see less of him ; claiming no superhuman virtues she will avoid temptations. She lives continually in the company of a father who is a coarse and brutal drunkard and who would even like to prevent her from cherishing the memory of her mother ; not indeed a situation likely to encourage romance in a girl's heart. But she loves her father as he is, without wasting her time in wishing him otherwise. Clarissa, on the contrary, perpetually avoids reality, to dream of what might happen, if only [3] . . .

Sophia has, in fact, the spirit of the realist who, without wasting time in fruitless computations of what life might have given, hastens to gather all that it gives, and joyfully to make the most of it. She loves Jones, which, certainly needs courage and even a certain amount of foolhardiness,

[1] For Clarissa's weakness and uncertainty, cf. Letter XV. It is impossible not to believe in Fielding's critical intent, in the face of such obvious contrasts as are apparent in the following details. Clarissa is left without any change of clothing and is thereby considerably embarrassed (II, 70). Sophia, on the contrary, takes everything that she needs. Clarissa is afraid of going alone to London. " People would wonder how I lived. Who knows, but I might pass for a kept mistress, etc. . ." (II, 5), and she is always repeating that she is afraid she may be taken for a kept mistress. When Sophia is taken for Jenny Cameron, the Pretender's mistress, her companion is very much shocked but she herself laughs heartily.
[2] Whenever he could, Fielding paid homage to Handel whom he loved and admired. Tom Jones is also a lover of music.
[3] cf., for a very striking example, *Clarissa Harlowe*, II, letter 68.

for every day some new act of Jones's seems to warn her against him ; yet she persists in loving him, openly, without subterfuge or pretence, ' in the country way ' Fielding tells us. Her love is forbearing ; it is in danger only once and then the unforgivable thing is not that Tom is incontinent, but that he has openly talked about her in an inn. Herein lies the delicacy of a really noble soul. She knows that the casual encounters of the highway may be pardonable, so long as the pure memory of the beloved remains enshrined in the inner tabernacle of the heart ; but if the veil be drawn aside and the image of the loved one associated for one instant with some doubtful escapade, it means that the man is not truly upright, nor worthy of love. Sophia's refusal would be final, did not Jones show her clearly that he has been wrongly accused, and that the blame lies with a gossiping servant.

Psychological discoveries such as this betray the master. The view held by so many, that Fielding is inferior as a psychologist to Richardson, is an extremely superficial one. I admit that he is less explicit than Richardson, a veritable *pointilliste* in sensibility. But it would be an error to suppose that subtle minds are always and of necessity rich or, *a fortiori*, profound. The secret lack of balance in Richardson's characters is due to the fact that, though their destinies are tragic, their souls are small, occupied with infinitesimal details of feeling, the slaves of worldly convention, of religious or sentimental formalities. The most striking example of this lack of balance is Clarissa, who is crushed beneath her destiny [1]. Sophia Western, on the contrary, is the true type

---

[1] The panegyric of Clarissa Harlowe by Miss Howe (Letter 150, part V) gives us the portrait of Richardson's ideal young woman, tirelessly reasoning and sermonizing. She writes, sews, paints, and sings better than anyone else, does good works, keeps house, rises early, etc., all on principle, and on Saturday does her moral accounts for the week, making the debit and credit balance : " Once a week, she used to reckon with herself ; when, if within 144 hours, contained in the six days, she had made her account even, she noted it accordingly ; if otherwise, she carried the debit to the next week's account ; as thus : Debtor to the article of benevolent visits, so many hours. And so of the rest."

of a woman made for life, capable of following the way which she has hewn out for herself, and of accomplishing her long and heavy task with energy. So clearsighted a girl must needs develop into a woman with a heart and a head. Let us thank the fate which allowed Fielding to meet such a one, and to appreciate all the wealth and beauty of her soul.

One might hesitate to contrast Tom Jones with Lovelace, because the object of the two authors in painting their heroes, was by no means the same. But here it is different. Sophia, like Clarissa, is a model of conduct. She trusts herself and others, and she does not insist too much upon perfection ; she prefers truth to holiness, and above all she is capable of unmasking a hypocrite, whom she considers the most odious of all men. Take the opposite of all this, and you have a fairly faithful portrait of Clarissa.

A contrast pushed so far cannot be a mere coincidence. Fielding certainly intended it. Even apart from the question at issue between the two authors, we may, with due proportion and reserve, see between them the same sort of parallel as has so often been drawn between Molière and Racine. Mithridate in *Mithridate*, like Harpagon in *L'Avare*, is rival of his own son ; Nero in *Britannicus* hides behind a curtain, and Orgon in *Tartuffe*, under a table ; and so forth. Similarly the pathetic scenes between Clarissa and her family have their corollary in the discussions between Sophia, her father, and her aunt. Richardson and Fielding see the same situation from a different angle, the one as a tragic, the other as a comic writer. Western, who wishes to marry his daughter for his own sake rather than for hers, is as grotesque as Argan and Harpagon and grotesque in the same way. And Sophia, the rebellious daughter, reminds one of Molière's young women, for example, of Henriette in the *Femmes Savantes*. A single detail maliciously added to her portrait, gives the final and characteristic touch : " Her forehead might have been higher without prejudice to her."

TOM JONES

It is impossible to leave Sophia Western [1] without observing Fielding's progress, from one novel to another, in depicting women. *Joseph Andrews* contains nothing more than sketches. Mrs Heartfree in *Jonathan Wild* is already more clearly outlined against a background of humorous female characters. Here, in *Tom Jones*, the manner is the same, but the principal character is fully formed, and stands out in high relief among a mass of minor types. Does Fielding owe his progress to himself and to his own greater maturity? I am not certain that he was not influenced to some extent by Richardson's works and that he did not gain from them a knowledge of certain windings of the feminine soul.

This preoccupation with Richardson is not the only one present in *Tom Jones*. Fielding is no longer the man of a single adversary; and if we have paused over long before Richardson, it is because his very greatness makes it possible to use him as a counterfoil to the figure of our hero. Let us now see how the scope of his effort spreads. Richardson is but the symbol of a vast group of enemies, of all the moral prigs, all the Pharisees, whom Fielding shovels pell-mell into the common grave of ridicule.

Religious, philosophical and literary controversies pullulated in England during the eighteenth century. Three thick volumes were needed by Leslie Stephen to give a brief and accurate summary of them. For all these quacks and their panaceas, Fielding expresses the same scorn, which is professed without exception by all the humourists and best minds of his century. For half a dozen really great thinkers, such as Locke, Berkeley, and Hume, no century has ever seen such swarms of pedants. Hume and Gibbon both avowed their irritation at the ' sceptical fop '. Swift had

[1] Schiller was particularly struck by Fielding's Sophia. In a letter to Wilhelm von Humbold, where he discusses Greek women and Schlegel's idea of them, he reproaches them with a want of femininity. " In Greek antiquity, there is no poetic representation of womanhood. Shakespeare's Juliet and Fielding's Sophia Western are far ahead of the most beautiful feminine portraits of antiquity. (Schiller's *Briefe*, edit. Fritz-Jonas, Vol. IV, p. 355, etc.).

already shut up all ' sages ' in Laputa. Fielding, too, delivers blows on all sides with a fine impartiality : of his two ' thinkers ', Square and Thwackum, he says that they do not sing in the same key, but that the song which they sing is the same ; and he nails theologian and deist to the same pillory. He had already, in true Swiftian style, ridiculed the commonplace refutation of deism in the Ordinary's speech to Jonathan Wild. In *Tom Jones* the hardest blows seem to be reserved for the deist, Square, but his enemy is not spared. On either side of Squire Allworthy, each appears as a pendant to the other, a little after the manner of Pangloss and Martin in *Candide ;* and on every occasion they give opposite justifications for the same pharisaical morality. For such is Fielding's lesson : a mean soul, whatever ideas be presented to it, can only produce meanness. On every occasion Square gives a grotesque repetition of the same phrases, ' the eternal fitness of things,'' the natural beauty of virtue ' ; Thwackum meets him with opposite formulæ ' the divine power of grace ', ' no religion exists independent of honour ' [1]. Both agree in heartily flogging an honest ne'er-do-well like Jones, and in predicting to Mr Allworthy that the scamp will end on the gallows. But the Spirit of Comedy is preparing a series of

[1] " This gentleman (Square) and Mr Thwackum scarce ever met without a disputation ; for their tenets were indeed diametrically opposite to each other. Square held human nature to be the perfection, of all virtues and that vice was a deviation from our nature, in the same manner as deformity of body is. Thwackum, on the contrary, maintained that the human mind, since the fall, was nothing but a sink of iniquity till purified and redeemed by Grace. In one point only they agreed, which was, in all their discourses on morality, never to mention the word goodness. The favourite phrase of the former was the natural beauty of virtue, that of the latter was the divine power of grace. The former measured all actions by the unalterable rule of right, and the eternal fitness of things, etc." III, 3. To stress the continuity of Fielding's thought we should note that Mr Wilson in *Joseph Andrews*, speaks of a society of hypocritical philosophers who have replaced God by the ' rule of right '. Again, letter XXXVII of Sarah Fielding contains a portrait of three pedants, one of whom, Mr Newman, speaks of nothing but ' the nature of things ', another, Mr Smith, swears only ' by experience,' and the third, the sceptical Mr Scrold, holds that ' Incertainty is the only certain thing '.

joyful revenges for us. We shall find a hundred incidents, in the course of the narrative revealing the two parasites in most ignoble postures. One day Tom Jones comes to see Molly Seagrim, and finds the philosopher Square hidden in a corner of the room, in an odd and unseemly attitude. On another occasion Thwackum, seeing Tom disappearing in the distance with Molly, tries to surprise him in *flagrant délit*, and receives from his pupil the soundest thrashing which has ever reddened the back of a pedantic Grundy. Happy is the novelist who can thus distribute blows to antipathetic characters! He gives them no quarter. These detestable, grotesque gluttons, representative of a whole class, are overthrown in the final discomfiture of their protégé Blifil, while their martyr Tom Jones triumphs, thanks to the providential Allworthy.

" Our business is only to report the truth ", proclaims Fielding. And what a plenteous truth it is, how abundant in comic characters. With what immortal ridicule are covered all alike, judge, priest, methodist, quaker, doctor, innkeeper, who seek to hide their ruthless selfishness beneath unctious formulae. We have already drawn attention to this magnificent gallery of characters, individualized by a single touch, laid bare by a word. A comparison between Dame Slipslop, the ' waiting gentlewoman ' in *Joseph Andrews*, and Mrs Honour, her sister in *Tom Jones*, will suffice to show the advance made by Fielding, from one work to another. The second of the two is the richer in psychological detail : her character is a delicious blending of good natural tendencies and a distrust engendered by her profession. Innumerable nuances show her to be superior to Slipslop in birth and education ; and this is as it should be, for Sophia Western could never have had a Slipslop as maid [1]. Beside her, are other equally delightful portraits of women. Consider Bridget, sister of Mr Allworthy, whose old maid's heart cannot resist the conquering moustaches of a military dowry-hunter :

[1] Many points in Mrs Honour's character have been compared with the Nurse in *Romeo and Juliet*.

guessing her hypocritical, sensual, untruthful, and affected, we are not surprised when in the end, for all her brave show of virtue, she turns out to be the long-sought mother of poor Tom Jones.

And so, with all his brilliant verve, Fielding attacks hypocrisy and vanity, whether it be in young or old, rich or poor. He is no respecter of persons, and it is this which Richardson, with his homage to social rank, could never forgive. Here again, however, he distinguishes between those who sin unwittingly and those who are designedly wicked. The former are merely ridiculous, the latter odious.

Western, the charming Sophia's father, must be placed among the ridiculous. I do not know that English literature [1] has produced any other figure as full of life as this country squire, " whose sallies, freaks, unreasonableness, obstinacy, coarseness, roughness, brutal kindness, and love of sport and the bottle, make up as arrant a country gentleman as ever walked the county of Somerset. He is nearly always in the wrong, but with the best faith in the world, and it is a real pleasure to listen to him ". Such is the testimony of a French contemporary of Fielding [2], and nothing could be more complete. Taine, seeking in English literature examples to confirm his thesis, has paused for a long time before Western and traced an admirable portrait of him, highly coloured, vigorous, and alive, but one in which certain characteristics have been very dexterously omitted. On reading the description, one would imagine that Western was a character after Fielding's own heart, and the central figure of the novel. He is, however, nothing of the sort, and there are, on the

---

[1] This type of brutal drunken and ridiculous squire was traditiona in the theatre. It is a feature of Restoration comedy, and Fielding gave a prototype of Squire Western in his Sir Positive Trap (*Love in Several Masques*) and more especially in Squire Badger (*Don Quixote in England*). In all his comedies the country squire is always the town dupe (like Molière's de Pourceaugnac). Fielding adds novelty to the type by making this ridiculous dupe a quarrelsome old man, redeemed by his kind heart.

[2] Clément, *Les Cinq Années Littéraires*, tome II, lettre 50.

contrary, numerous touches, which show that for Fielding himself this rough type of country gentleman was beginning to be, as it were, out of date. He obviously belongs to a generation which has passed, the generation which preceded Tom Jones and Sophia Western, and which has not changed its habits with the times. He is the John Bull of forty years earlier, coarse, rustic, uneducated. Even his taste in music betrays it ; he makes his daughter play him drinking songs and popular airs, whereas Tom and Sophia swear only by Handel. He is a Jacobite, while Tom, on the contrary, enlists to defend the crown of the Hanoverian King. His language is often ignoble and he gets regularly and conscientiously drunk : he shouts and swears with the most insane violence. All these characteristics (as Taine was unwilling to see) scandalize those among whom he moves, even Jones, who is as vigorous and full of life as he is himself, but infinitely better bred. Between them lie forty years of education and the *Spectator*.

Nor does Fielding hide his dislike for Western's behaviour to his daughter. The squire adores his child, but he treats her much as he treated his wife, to whom he was ' a good husband '; that is to say, explains Fielding, " he very seldom swore at her (perhaps not above once a week) and never beat her : she had not the least occasion for jealousy and was perfect mistress of her time ; for she was never interrupted by her husband, who was engaged all the morning in his field exercises, and all the evening with bottle companions. She scarce indeed ever saw him but at meals, where she had the pleasure of carving those dishes which she had before attended at the dressing. From these meals she retired about five minutes after the other servants, having only stayed to drink ' the king over the water '. Such were, it seems, Mr Western's orders ; for it was a maxim with him, that women should come in with the first dish, and go out after the first glass. Obedience to these orders was perhaps no difficult task ; for the conversation (if it may be called so) was seldom such as could entertain a lady. It consisted chiefly of hallooing, singing, relations of sporting adventures, b-d-g, and abuse of women and the Government.

" These, however, were the only seasons when Mr Western saw his wife ; for when he repaired to her bed, he was generally so drunk that he could not see ; and in the sporting season he always rose from her before it was light " (VII, 4).

This brutal squire cannot imagine that marriage may be anything but a business proposition. Devoid of all delicacy of feeling, he treats his beloved daughter with a harshness which is by turns ignoble and grotesque. It is difficult to say which makes the more forcible plea against the ancient dictatorial authority of the father of a family, the tragic horror of Richardson, when he paints the cold ferocity of the Harlowes and the circle of selfish and cowardly beings among whom the weak Clarissa is cast, or the cynical irony of Fielding, showing us a girl left alone to face the ugly brutality of the squire and the irrational absurdities of Aunt Western.

But it is here that Fielding proves the depth of his psychological insight. Sophia Western, ill-treated as she is by a father whom she cannot help loving for his jovial frankness and good heart, is quite ready to fall in love with Tom Jones, another example of the same type of humanity, but less imperfect, improved by the progress in manners and customs of the last forty years, and conforming to the ideal of a younger generation. In him she finds her father, without his brutality, coarseness, and drunkenness, but with sufficient traces remaining for her, to catch the resemblance.

It is on details such as these that the unity and coherence of a book depend. Tom Jones, as opposed to Western, represents the generation of Pitt succeeding that of Walpole [1],

[1] William Pitt and Fielding were at school together at Eton. Pitt was certainly one of Fielding's friends and it is said that he was present at Radway Grange, Sanderson Miller's house, when Fielding gave a reading of some of the chief pages of *Tom Jones* before a number of his admirers. He and Lyttleton gave the novel unreserved praise (cf. Cross, vol. cit., II, p. 115). For a very laudatory allusion to Pitt, cf. *Tom Jones*, XIV, 1.

the modern Englishman, the town-dweller, energetic, tenacious, Christian, taking the place of the old-fashioned type (for so these newcomers see him), coarse, boorish, spending his time in drink and sport, selfish and weak-willed [1], with no respect for the clergy or for women. When Jones thinks that he has lost the woman whom he loves, he prepares to sail for the colonies. When Western loses his daughter, he shouts and curses and rushes in pursuit of her like a madman ; but a hare passes, he forgets his daughter, dashes after the huntsmen, returns to get drunk with them, and ends by making up his mind to go home. In this difference in attitude lies the whole transition from one generation to another.

Yet Fielding does not treat Western harshly. Because the squire is not purposely wicked, he is drawn without hatred, rather with a touch of amused contempt. Fielding appears to have reserved all his hatred for young Blifil. He is the son of Bridget Allworthy's marriage with the aforesaid captain, a military fortune-hunter of more than doubtful repute, taken straight from the pages of any novel of adventure. Blifil, the son, is an English Tartuffe ; and it is perhaps because we know Molière's admirable creation too well, that this character seems insufficient, badly-drawn, in a word, unreal. For Tartuffe does not do evil for pleasure, but from motives of interest ; with Blifil the interest, the turning of his vice to account, only comes later. Fielding shows him doing wrong on the sly, from his earliest childhood, while he is still too young to calculate how he may benefit by his hypocrisy. He has scarcely appeared on the scenes before he opens the door

[1] Western, when he is struck by a lord, does not retaliate. Truth to tell, he is very much out of his element in London ; and he is handier with his fists than with a sword. Henley said of Fielding's portrait of Western : " The novelist literally plays with Western : he knows him ever so intimately, yet his introduction of him seems almost careless : he shows him a tyrant, and a ruffian and a sot ; yet he has ever a kindly, and at the same time a leisurely, half-laughing, half-reticent mastery of his creation, which he never permits to get out of hand ; so that he is able, on occasion, to assent, and to make us assent to such an outrageous familiarity as that of the boxing of Squire Western's ears, by a person unnamed."

of a cage where little Sophia keeps a favourite bird ; he wanted, says he, to give the poor prisoner its liberty ! Throughout his life he continues to do harm, pretending all the while to be actuated by noble motives. He accepts the rôle of Sophia's betrothed, with a view, he piously declares, to doing his share towards weaning her heart and mind from the wretched Jones, who is bound to make her miserable. It is quite natural that he should be the well-loved pupil and ally of Thwackum and Square, whose contradictory theories he has a genius for reconciling. Ignoble interests, and the desire to deprive Jones of his share in the inheritance and of the wealthy Sophia's hand, arise later to reinforce his native wickedness ; but it must not be forgotten that he is vile by nature and from birth, and that he delights in bringing suffering to noble souls, whom he basely envies because of their nobility. Can such a character be described as psycho-ligically false ? He is, at all events, a product of his age. Blifil is the contemporary of that Lovelace who torments Clarissa for his personal pleasure, because she is virtuous and he does not believe in virtue. The aberration is drawn infinitely better in Lovelace than in Blifil, who remains a little stiff and theoretical ; nevertheless, the temperament is similar. Here again let us observe in passing, the extent to which this conception shows Fielding in opposition to Richardson. With Fielding as with Molière, the dangerous character is not the frank, honest libertine, loyal in the vice which he openly parades, but the honey-tongued hypocrite. Besides, what Fielding needed was a background to Tom Jones. Against this sombre setting the portrait of his hero is more brilliantly lighted, and its significant features stand out more clearly. Compared with the rogue who plays the part of an honest man, he is the honest man who seems to play the rogue [1].

[1] La Harpe in his *Lycée* or *Cours de Littérature* (Part III) has an acute comparison between Richardson and Fielding. He adds that " the English . . . are conscious of Richardson's faults and in general prefer Fielding, and I must confess that this time I agree with them. *Joseph Andrews* is too English to appeal to foreigners as much as it

TOM JONES

Whether they be ridiculous or detestable, the same guiding principle enables us to judge all these characters : either their conscience is warped or its voice is muffled. Fielding's irony spares no one ; for even the best are not always exempt from selfishness and vanity. A sort of Nemesis watches over his characters : at the very moment of perfection some little weakness is revealed, some foolishness, some characteristic less fine than the rest. Even a Sophia Western, with her forehead " which might have been higher " does not escape ; and many a passage of delicate, sympathetic mockery corrects what might seem her too great perfection [1].

And Allworthy ? Where is the irony in the portrait of this worthy man, so perfectly perfect, so interminably discursive ? Is not the virtuous Allworthy, the typical retailer of platitudes, so incurably and monotonously right ? Is he not in the same aesthetic class as the Thoroughgood of *George Barnwell*, who precedes, and as the Grandison who follows him ?

Embarrassed as Fielding was in painting his benefactor Allen, the portrait [2], is not devoid of interest. Blifil is

does to those of Fielding's nationality : but, in my opinion, *Tom Jones* is the finest novel in the world. First of all the fundamental moral idea on which the work is based is a stroke of genius. Of the two principal actors who fill the stage, the first always seems to be wrong and the second right ; in the end, the first turns out to be the honest man, and the second the rogue . . . but one is prudent and the other is not. . . This contrast reveals the history of society and no better lesson has ever been taught." He goes on to point out other perfections of *Tom Jones* and concludes " No one has attempted to imitate Fielding. Like Molière he stands alone."

[1] I am sure that certain ridiculous and *useless* accidents (the fall of the horse, the upturned dress, etc.) only happen in order to humiliate her a little. On one occasion she is even slightly vain (VII, 9).

[2] Ralph Allen, postmaster of Bath, settled in 1742 at Prior Park, near Bath. He was very rich and made a point of inviting to his house well-known men, writers, and poets. Pope and Warburton were among those whom he knew. He was one of the best known figures in Bath, where, during the season, there were the most brilliant social gatherings. Allen had acquired a great reputation for philanthropy. According to tradition he often helped Fielding out of pecuniary difficulties. Fielding mentions him with gratitude in *Joseph Andrews* and in the dedication of *Tom Jones*. He dedicates *Amelia* to him. There is no doubt that Allen is the original of Allworthy. After Fielding's death, Allen helped his widow, and left £100 to each of his children.

Allworthy's Tartuffe, but it is because there is a touch of the foolish Orgon about Allworthy. Of course, Fielding, if only out of gratitude, could never have made him as stupid and as easily taken in as Orgon. He makes him a sensible and reasoning man, withal kind and charitable, pious, with a fine, liberal religion accessible, at the same time to the influence of the deist Square and the Anglican Thwackum, and seeking for moral truth in the happy mean. When a girl who repents her sin is brought before him, he is a lenient judge. He adopts the bastard Jones without stopping to consider whether public opinion will accuse him of being the father. Yet he allows himself to be deceived by the hypocrite Blifil, drives Jones from his presence and disinherits him without even giving him a hearing. This is a curious symptom and very acutely observed ; Fielding is ever ready to make his good men play the rôle of dupe. Adams, Heartfree, and Allworthy are quite easily swindled without the reader's thinking any the less of them. The reason is that " England had not yet become, though . . . . she was then in process of becoming, ' the commercial State ' *par excellence.* Hence an irreducible minimum of cuteness in the affairs of life, was not yet regarded as a condition in the absence of which goodness is apt to degenerate into flabbiness [1]."

Fielding was between Scylla and Charybdis and he could not and would not chose either ; on the one hand, Allworthy is too easily duped for us to give him unreserved admiration ; and, on the other, he is represented as so perfect and so intelligent, that he ought not to let himself be so foolishly taken in. Nor is it easy to understand how Allen, a practical business man, could be so enthusiastic at finding his own portrait in the features of this virtuous prig [2]. The point

---

[1] Whittuck *op. cit.* p. 75.

[2] I find only one discordant note in the praises which are sung of Allen, namely, " Ralph Allen . . . had since the year 1720, enjoyed a grant, or farm, of all the by-way or cross-road letters in England and Wales, which grant he possessed till his death in 1764. It is said that this Ralph Allen, of Prior Park, owed much of his large fortune to the result of his practice of opening letters ; and it is added that by opening

of interest for us is to observe that even this portrait of a perfect man has its shadow.

II

Our novelist, who has seen and described men, good, bad or worse, never loses an opportunity of proclaiming that he is a moralist. Yet from all these portraits is it possible to deduce a moral doctrine other than a somewhat negative hatred of hypocrisy ? By what criterion can we replace the bourgeois, Christian traditionalism of Richardson, the Puritanism of Thwackum, or the rationalism of Square ? What is Fielding's moral doctrine ?

Its point of departure is feeling. Feeling has a moral value of its own, independent of its object. The man who feels very keenly is capable of great happiness whether imaginary or real[1]. He feels the joys of others as deeply as he does his own. How then can he reject the happiness which a good action will bring him[2] ? Satisfy your feelings and they will lead you straight to goodness. Speak not of social prejudice nor of what the world thinks ; " the truest honour is goodness ". Can any success or prosperity equal

one of these cross-road letters he gained information of a plot for the Jacobite invasion of England and this information being sent to London, gave to its inhabitants the first news of an impending rebellion." (Doran, *London in the Jacobite Times*, London, 1877, vol. II, p. 97). If Allen's fortune really originated in this way, it is not difficult to understand his pleasure in seeing himself in the character of so naif and worthy a person.

[1] " Reader if thou hast any good wishes towards me, I will fully repay them by wishing thee possessed of this sanguine disposition of mind ; since, after having read much, and considered long on that subject of happiness . . . I am almost inclined to fix it in the possession of this temper ; which puts us, in a manner, out of the reach of fortune. . Indeed the sensations of pleasure it gives are much more constant, as well as much keener than those which the blind lady bestows." (XIII, 6).

[2] " Do not the warm rapturous sensations, which we feel from the consciousness of an honest, noble, generous, benevolent action, convey more delight to the mind than the undeserved praise of millions ? " and elsewhere he speaks of " the very best and truest honour, which is goodness " (XIV, 7).

the intimate joy which comes from the consciousness of having done a good action [1] ? The only way to be happy is to be good. Allworthy adopts a bastard and loves him as much as his own nephew, in spite of his friends' shocked faces. Tom Jones, at the height of his misfortunes, helps a scoundrel who has tried to rob him, because he finds that the poor wretch was stealing in order to feed his children.

In Fielding's novels none of this is entirely new. Some parts of *Joseph Andrews* are sentimental and effusive in much the same way. But in *Tom Jones* there is more method and above all, a new argument, that pleasure is to be experienced *in this world* by doing good. Joseph Andrews was guided by a parson from whom he caught a glimpse of heavenly rewards ; for Tom Jones the reward of the just lies within himself, in the intimate satisfaction which he feels from having done a good action. Observe that believer as he is, to the great scandal of Thwackum, Allworthy refuses to seek absolution when he is in danger of death. Conversely, evil finds its principal punishment in remorse [2]. Tom Jones is so racked by it that Sophia can wish him no further punishment. There are, however, some who are incapable of remorse. What of them ? What of a Blifil, (a Jonathan Wild) ? Such men may be left with their own poor external satisfactions. Tom Jones, in the moment of his greatest distress, does not envy the wicked Blifil's prosperity, any more than Heartfree could have envied Jonathan Wild.

It should be observed, in passing, that this essentially altruistic standard already foreshadows, in more than one

----

[1] Tom Jones proclaims " I had rather enjoy my own mind than the fortune of another man. What is the poor pride arising from a magnificent house, a numerous equipage, a splendid table, and from all the other advantages or appearances of fortune, compared to the warm solid content, the swelling satisfaction, the thrilling transports, and the exulting triumphs, which a good mind enjoys in the contemplation of a generous, virtuous, noble, benevolent action " (XII, 10).

[2] " Poor Jones, whom we have left long enough to do penance for his past offences, which, as is the nature of vice, brought sufficient punishment on him themselves " (XI, 9).

respect, the utilitarianism of forty years later. To try to induce in men a calculating virtue, without reference to the hereafter, to preach that beneficence is the same thing as enlightened self-interest, is to subscribe in advance to the Benthamist formula [1]. The greatest difference, apart from numerous details, is that pure sentiment here holds a much greater place. At the time when Fielding was writing *Tom Jones* it had not yet been abused to satiety.

His is an altruistic doctrine. The difficulty arises when we pass from actions which affect others to those which affect only ourselves ; from the idea of beneficence to that of perfection. The first is derived from the feeling for the existence of others, the second from the feeling for *nature*. Nearly all the characters in *Tom Jones* are country people ; and the pure air of the Somerset fields blows through the whole book. On the other hand disreputable adventures, such as that of Lady Bellaston, or of Lord Fellamar who wants to abduct Sophia and villainously causes the arrest of Jones, are adventures of the town, regarded as an agent of corruption. The country is the haunt of those virtues which move the heart, and to speak of it calls up a vision of the Golden Age [2]. It is already represented as the refuge of those whom life has wounded and who come to it to find a cure for their misanthropy ; the Mr Wilson of *Joseph Andrews* is succeeded in *Tom Jones* by a ' Man of the Hill ', who tells his story at length ; after the turmoils of a town existence, his life in the country is edifying and idyllic. It is among men who live in the bosom of nature, that sentiments are found in their native purity, " the plain, simple workings

---

[1] Certain arguments are almost word for word those of Bentham : " To save several families from misery rather than hang up an extraordinary picture in our houses, is being in some degree epicures : for what could the greatest epicure wish rather than to eat with many mouths instead of one ? which I think may be predicted of anyone who knows that the bread of many is owing to his own largesses " (II, 5).

[2] Chapter 8 of Book XIV contains an idyllic picture of country life. There are many others in *Tom Jones*.

of honest nature " ; a whole moral doctrine is implied in that phrase [1].

But this alone would not be enough. The inspiration of ' nature ', can sometimes be bad, or, at all events, our temperament may lead us to evil, and this is precisely why Fielding, as a good comic writer, delights to show us his hero's failings. One day Jones after a good meal and sufficient wine, lies down near a river and dreams of his beloved Sophia. " Oh," he says," my fond heart is so wrapt in that tender bosom, that the brightest beauties would for me have no charms, nor would a hermit be colder in their embraces. Sophia, Sophia alone shall be mine. What raptures are in that name ! I will engrave it on every tree." Whereupon he rises, has the misfortune to meet not Sophia but the worthless Molly. " The chance, the tender grass, and some devil too [2]. ." Poor Jones ! He does make very frequent claims upon our indulgence. His story is nothing but a long train of weaknesses. Can we take Nature as our only guide, when she so besets our path ' with pitfall and with gin ' ? How are her different commands to be reconciled ?

The truth is that for Fielding, actions have not an absolute value to be mathematically determined [3] ; every deed has

[1] There are obviously many points of similarity between these ideas and the ancient epicurean and stoic moral philosophy, and particularly the synthesis which it suggested to the cynics (Fielding was brought up on Lucian). A comparison with Rabelais is equally appropriate ; cf. his description of the dwellers in Thélème " . . . men that are free, well-born, well-bred, and conversant in honest companies, have naturally an instinct and spur that prompteth them into virtuous actions, and withdraws them from vice, which is called honour. . ." (*Gargantua*, ch. 57, trans. Urquhart and Motteux) ; cf. Fielding's remarks upon honour and goodness quoted above.

[2] cf. La Fontaine, *Les Animaux malades de la Peste.*

[3] In his eyes the compulsory duties are of mediocre importance, the essential duties being those which, morally speaking, are called ' duties of charity ' : " I have told my reader . . . that Mr Allworthy inherited a large fortune ; that he had a good heart, and no family. Hence, doubtless, it will be concluded by many, that he lived like an honest man, owed no one a shilling, took nothing but what was his own, kept a good house, entertained his neighbours with a hearty welcome

to be judged not only by its consequences, but by its motives. It is by this criterion, as we saw, that Sophia judges Tom Jones. Black George, the poacher, comes to help Jones out of his difficulties, but cannot resist the temptation of stealing from him a five-hundred-pound note. Tom thinks only of how great the temptation was for the rascal and is ready to pardon him. Allworthy, however, prevents this : " Such mistaken mercy borders on injustice, and is very pernicious to society, as it encourages vice. The dishonesty of the fellow I might perhaps have pardoned, but never his ingratitude." He goes on to admit that attention should be paid to extenuating circumstances and adds that he himself, when serving on the grand jury, has often recommended a highwayman to mercy " but ", he continues, " when dishonesty is attended by any blacker crime, such as cruelty, murder, ingratitude, or the like, compassion and forgiveness then become faults " (XVIII, 11). Thus ingratitude is placed side by side with murder as an unforgivable crime !

We have here one of the central ideas of the book, to wit, that the moral value of an action is essentially dependent upon the state of mind of the man who has committed it. In the moral teaching of Fielding, feeling holds the first place ; on the one hand happiness does not lie in outward prosperity but in inward contentment ; and in the same way perfection does not consist in the accomplishment of actions which are reputed virtuous, but in the consciousness of a good intention. All Blifil's actions are outwardly virtuous, but Blifil is a rogue ; all Tom Jones's actions appear to be vicious, but Tom Jones is an excellent fellow : " Tommy Jones was an inoffensive lad amidst all his roguery."

Such is the primary, and, one might say, the most frequent

---

at his table, and was charitable to the poor, *i.e.*, to those who had rather beg than work, by giving them the offals from it ; that he died immensely rich and built a hospital.

" And true it is that he did many of these things ; but, had he done nothing more, I should have left him to have recorded his own merit on some fair free stone over the door of that hospital " (I, 3.)

aspect of Fielding's morality, the aspect which best lends itself to an overflow of emotion. It is not yet the romantic motive of sincerity which redeems and passion which purifies ; it is its prelude. I do not think it can often be met with in English literature prior to Fielding (save perhaps, without method, in Steele). In any case, there is no example of it before him in the novel. Richardson is full of feeling, much more so than Fielding, but he is at the same time rigidly Christian and, in his work, there will not be found that justification of feeling as a moral value, from which there will gradually emerge sentimentality, the *douceur de pleurer* (the characters in *Tom Jones* by no means deprive themselves of this pleasure [1]) and the romantic eulogy of sentiment.

Fielding, however, does not stop at this point. Side by side with this emotional aspect of his teaching, there is a rational, one might almost call it a rationalistic aspect. He speaks unhesitatingly of ' natural law ', and ' natural justice ' : terms which show that he, in common with most men of his century, looked upon ' nature ' as synonymous, or nearly so, with ' reason '. The destructive irony of Jonathan Wild troubled us not a little ; we wondered in the name of what moral ideal Fielding dared thus to demolish the accepted standards. I believe that this ideal would be the standpoint of pure intelligence, which can rise to a sufficient height above things to see them whole, and above men to see them all equally small. He expresses a well-founded scorn for exaggerated theories which condemn or absolve wholesale. Sometimes he offers no solution, and presents us with two opposite views of charity, without drawing any conclusion. And he ends upon a smile, for he knows that we are not unacquainted with his personal opinion, which is chary of

---

[1] Here, on the contrary, is the paraphrase used by Col. Morden in *Clarissa Harlowe* when he wishes to confess to weeping : " Nor am I ashamed to own that I could not help giving way to a repeated fit of humanity " (V, Letter 125).

extremes [1]. In a long conversation the optimism of Tom Jones, and the pessimism of a solitary misanthropist are engaged against each other, but no explicit conclusion is drawn from the duel. We are shown the evil duplicity of a quaker (VII, 10), and are told why the vague mysticism of the methodists is pernicious (VIII, 8) ; and the prettiest piece of reasoning demonstrates, once again, that no theory can exempt us from doing good (II, 5).

Such is the double aspect of Fielding's moral teaching. His sentimentalism is never unbridled ; it is always restrained and supported by his intelligence. Even when he attacks the moral standards of his age, his blows are methodically directed by the power of reason.

It is undoubtedly because of its intellectual character that although essentially practical, his morality is not one of worldly prudence. A bare trace of this may be observed here and there ; more than once Fielding advises his reader to look to his reputation. He says, explicitly, that to be a good man is not enough, one must also think of the opinion which the world will have of one's actions [2]. May we not recognize in this rather *terre à terre* advice the experience of a man too heedless of calumny, who allowed his enemies to blacken him at will ?

It is because he approaches everything from the stand-point of intelligence, that he sees all mankind as equal, men

---

[1] cf. XIII, 8. Elsewhere he asserts, through the mouth of Allworthy that charity " is an indispensable duty enjoined both by the Christian law, and by the law of nature itself ", and adds a little later this very characteristic phrase, which shows the sort of excess with which he is in equal disagreement : " Nothing less than a persuasion of universal depravity can lock up the charity of a good man ; and this persuasion must lead him, I think, either into *atheism*, or *enthusiasm* " (II, 6).

[2] " Prudence and circumspection are necessary even to the best of men . . . it is not enough that your designs, nay that your actions, are intrinsically good ; you must take care they shall appear so, etc. . ." (III, 7). Balzac, too, wrote in his *Médecin de campagne*, ch. II : " It is by no means enough to be a good man, one must also appear so. Society does not only live on moral ideas ; to subsist, it needs actions in harmony with these ideas."

THE NOVELS OF FIELDING

and women, rich and poor [1]. He does not in any way fall a victim to that demagogic exaggeration which thinks that virtue can only be found among the lowly. Stupidity and wickedness seem to him vulgar wheresoever he may meet them, and he defines ' the mob ' in a way which would have rejoiced the heart of Flaubert, that arch-enemy of the bourgeois in whatever social class he showed his face [2].

I will not dwell for long upon Fielding's liberalism. He pleads earnestly for a certain number of reforms ; and as befits a jurist he pays particular attention to legal reforms. The game [3] and bastardy [4] laws are foolish and cruel ; prisons can do nothing but corrupt their wretched occupants and it is wrong to send first offenders there [5]. The law is too hard ; the rights of the accused are but seldom respected by the court [6]. The justices of the peace are too often ignorant ; they should always have at hand a clerk of the court, acquainted with jurisprudence, so that they may be prevented from condemning or acquitting haphazard.

This list of practical reforms might be prolonged. Indeed, the object of Fielding is always the same ; whether he be concerned with personal or with social morality, his efforts are always directed against hypocrisy and selfishness, and towards truth and equity, which two qualities are indeed

[1] He protests (IV, 11) because they are not treated in the same way in prison. Molly is taken " to that house where the inferior sort of people may learn one good lesson, *viz.*, respect and deference to their superiors ; since it must show them the wide distinction Fortune intends between those persons who are to be corrected for their faults, and those who are not."

[2] " Whenever this word occurs in our writings, it intends persons without virtue or sense, in all stations ; and many of the highest rank are often meant by it " (I, 9). "A liberality of spirit : which last quality I myself have scarce ever seen in men of low birth and education " (IX, 1).

[3] cf. III, 2.

[4] " . . . a base born infant to which all charity is condemned by law as irreligious." (I,5).

[5] " . . many women have become abandoned . . . by being unable to retrieve the first slip " (I, 9).

[6] cf. VIII, 12, for a very fine description of a trial in which everyone is against the accused. And, again, the jest " Justiceship (for it was indeed a syllable more than justice) " (VII, 9).

intellectual necessities. But if we carry our analysis a little further, shall we not end by finding that the morality of a Fielding could not be otherwise ? Comedy must of necessity be founded upon the most universal standard of morality, which appeals to ' natural ' reason, and to common-sense ; for it sets all men to judge the absurdity of one man. Doubtless this is the reason that the great masters of universal laughter, an Aristophanes, a Cervantes, a Rabelais, a Molière, are from the moral point of view ' naturalists '. Fielding founds his moral theory on pure sentiment. But it is the sentiment of " nature ", the sense of " natural reason ", in short, commonsense, which has been called " the best shared thing in the world ".

Fielding's morality and his art coincide in yet another respect. By its very elasticity and indulgence, this doctrine of moderation, which knows no hero [1], and opposes all supernatural excesses of virtue or of vice, is a code of morality for sinners, or rather (since every moral code is in one sense a code for sinners) for venial sinners. It permits a long scale of more or less pardonable faults, in which category are all those of Tom Jones. Knowing that he is at heart a very good fellow and that he wishes no harm to anyone, we can laugh heartily at his mistakes, tremble at his imprudences, rejoice at his escapades (and Fielding's moral code allows him many). This is the reason why the book is such a marvellous and inexhaustible treasure-house.

Finally, by allowing people to be classified distinctly as good and bad, according to their inward dispositions (as revealed by the author), this code of morality adds to those which preceded it a precious element of artistic success. It fits into the general scheme of the work. The sympathetic people can remain so, without being condemned to an irksome perfection, their faults and imprudences can contribute

---

[1] Speaking of ' philosophers ' he says : " for though such great beings think much better and more wisely, they always act exactly like other men " (V, 5).

towards the arrest or suspension of the action. Hence the construction gains infinitely in suppleness ; we have not, on the one hand, a hero advancing towards the *dénouement*, and on the other, a villain preventing him from reaching it ; numerous agents, by stupidity, awkwardness or evil intent, suddenly suspend the plot, and the most frequent obstacle is the hero himself. There is, moreover, no need to point out how such a theory enriches everyday observation, how subtle is the appreciation of values which it engenders, and how wide the range of moral and psychological shades which it reveals. It opens for the artist an inexhaustible vein of ridicule. With such an instrument in his power the comic novelist can strike a thousand different chords of laughter.

III

If I have thought it necessary to insist here upon the moral teaching of Fielding, it is because it is developed throughout *Tom Jones* with a sureness of touch and a method not to be found in any of his other works. Here, everything is to the point. What gives this novel its greatness and its classical character is quite definitely the perfect relation of all the moral, psychological and artistic elements to the whole. Let us try to see how this harmony is obtained, and to distinguish something of the mysterious agencies which make it possible.

The primary factor is the concision and clearness of the construction. Whereas Defoe and Richardson desire to give and do give, the impression of a story which is telling itself without the interposition of the author between the reader and the facts, Fielding never for one instant ceases to pull the strings which make his characters move. He is a man telling a story, a man who will not let himself be forgotten, and who sometimes interrupts the thread of his narrative to give us his own impressions and comments. He holds the floor, so to speak, and he intends to use his right and even to abuse it, should it please him to digress [1]. Yet this constant intervention of the author which, after Fielding, was to become one of the traditions of the English novel, does not yet encroach upon the narrative ; Fielding is usually prudent enough to confine it to a special chapter which acts as a preface to each book. These chapters have been diversely appreciated. George Eliot adored those sections of the novel where the author " seems to bring his armchair to the proscenium and chat with us in all the lusty ease of his fine English [2]." Some of these prefaces contain very interesting literary ideas, and it might even be said that the moral and artistic purpose of the work is in them defined and set forth. The great objection to them is that the author has not always something to say ; thus the preliminary chapters of the last four books are somewhat empty. This, however, is but a passing characteristic of his novels which establishes the importance of *Tom Jones* as a profession of the author's faith. *Amelia* has no prefatory chapters.

Fielding then, conducts his story himself. Coleridge has compared the plot of *Tom Jones* with that of *Oedipus Tyrannus* [3]. It will not do, however, to press a comparison which is not literally exact, since the secret of Tom Jones's birth is not unveiled progressively. But the English novel certainly moves as surely and inevitably to its end as does the Greek drama, and whoever, knowing *Tom Jones*, re-reads

---

[1] " Reader, I think proper before we proceed any farther together, to acquaint thee, that I intend to digress, through this whole history as often as I see occasion : of which I am myself a better judge than any pitiful critic whatever " (I, 2). Digression, then, was the rule. Congreve, in his *Incognita* justifies himself in just as impertinent a manner, he warns his reader that " when I digress I am at that time writing to please myself ; when I continue the thread of the story, I write to please him." cf. Swift, *A Tale of a Tub*, Section XI, for an equally amusing justification for his digressions.

[2] George Eliot, *Middlemarch*, Bk. II, ch. 15.

[3] " Upon my word, I think the *Oedipus Tyrannus*, *The Alchemist*, and *Tom Jones*, the three most perfect plots ever planned " (Table Talk, July 5th, 1834).

THE NOVELS OF FIELDING

it with this idea in mind, cannot fail to be amazed at the clearness of the construction [1]. It would be impossible to take this immense frame to pieces. We will merely note the most important sections.

First of all there is the exposition, some fifty pages which should be read at leisure, which bring the characters in turn on the stage. There is no confusion ; first we are shown Mr Allworthy, then his servant, Mrs Wilkins, who finds the child, then his sister Bridget, and then young Jenny Jones, whom everyone is soon to take for Tom's mother (I, 1-9). The stage is cleared and there appears another group, which gravitates round Captain Blifil, the only characters common to each group being Allworthy and his sister Bridget. In the second book the Jones group encounters the Blifil group ; this results in the first attack on Tom Jones, which once

---

[1] One cannot sum up *Tom Jones*. The following is the order in which the books appear ; it will be seen with what vigorous method they follow one another :

I	Tom is found. Bridget Allworthy marries Captain Blifil.
II	First attack on Tom. Partridge, suspected of being his father, refuses to confess and is punished. Death of Captain Blifil.
III	Encounters between young Blifil and young Jones. Comparison between the two.
IV	Sophia Western. She falls in love with Jones.
V	The Sophia-Jones passion put to the first test (Molly Seagrim), which it withstands.
VI	Sophia refuses Blifil. Tom Jones is turned out of doors.
VII	Sophia is threatened and flees. An accident to Tom prevents them from meeting.
VIII	Tom meets Partridge (another obstacle in the way of his reunion with Sophia). The action is suspended while the ' Man of the Hill ' tells his story.
IX & X	At the Upton inn all the characters of the story meet without knowing it. Battles.
XI	Sophia goes straight to London.
XII	Tom likewise.
XIII	They meet at Lady Bellaston's. Each of them lies.
XIV	Numerous adventures. Arrival of Western.
XV	Tom leaves Lady Bellaston. Mr Allworthy arrives in London.
XVI	Tom wounds an enemy in a duel, is arrested, and receives a letter from Sophia breaking off relations between them.
XVII	Nightingale, Mrs Miller, Mrs Waters, all under an obligation to Jones, work for him.
XVIII	*Dénouement.* All secrets revealed. Tom marries Sophia.

again clears the stage of several people. Jenny Jones and Partridge, the supposed parents of Tom, go to fulfil their destiny elsewhere ; Captain Blifil dies and is buried, and we are ready for the third book which leaves young Blifil and young Jones face to face with each other, and shows us what those among whom they move, particularly their masters, Square and Thwackum, think of them. And thus the novel pursues its even course ; so even that books IX and X, situated, mathematically speaking, in the middle of the work, also mark the central point of the action. Here we may observe Fielding's technical skill at work. Tom Jones and his servant Partridge arrive at the Upton inn, escorting a certain Mrs Waters whom Tom has just rescued from a highwayman. Now in the preceding chapters, the points have been set for all the *dramatis personae* in the two ' pursuits ' (Sophia after Jones, and Western after Sophia) in such a way that they must, every one, pass the night at this same inn, and several other comic characters, whom we do not yet know, will come to join them there. There follows all through the night a string, nay a torrent of misunderstandings and droll deceptions, such as might well rouse the jealousy of the most ingenious writer of vaudeville. But observe that the agents thereof are invariably acting according to nature ; if Jones succumbs to the encouraging glances of Mrs Waters, and thus loses his fair Sophia, it is because Jones, as we have already been aware for some time, is very weak when faced with temptations of this sort. If the whole inn is very soon cognizant of his success and can inform the unfortunate Sophia of it a little later, it is because Partridge is an incorrigible gossip and likes to appear well-informed in the kitchen. Can we really exclaim at the unlikelihood of these meetings ? After all, it is not surprising that people who run after one another should end by finding one another. Was it not even less astonishing in the eighteenth century than it would be to-day ? Critics who have expressed disapproval of these coincidences, frequent in the novels of the time, do not remember that the action of *Tom Jones* takes place in a limited space, that in those days communications were not as rapid as they are to-day ; roads were few and travellers by them were less frequent and could easily be followed from relay to relay, and from inn to inn. If each one of us, even with all the complications of modern life, can call to mind innumerable coincidences, how many more must the men of the eighteenth century have experienced, and with much less surprise ?

Truth to tell, in the Upton scene, Fielding seems to have piled them up at will. Here, more than anywhere else, one has the impression that he is amusing himself by inventing incidents step by step as he writes. Thus after a quasi-homeric battle has set all the characters by the ears, a young lady and her maid arrive at the inn : " Hither they were obliged to pass through the field of battle, which they did with the utmost haste, covering their faces with their hanker-chiefs, as desirous to avoid the notice of anyone. Indeed their precaution was quite unnecessary. . ." for both Jones and Partridge were fully occupied and did not think of looking at them. Why were they so anxious to avoid being seen, if indeed, as we are carefully told later, the two ladies were unknown to Jones and Partridge ? I can only think of one explanation of this ; when writing this page Fielding may possibly have intended the two ladies to be Sophia and her maid, Mrs Honour, and it is only while he is writing that he thinks of a new complication : the lady becomes Mrs Fitzpatrick, who in her turn is being pursued by a ridiculous husband, and the latter thinking to surprise his wife, finds Jones and Mrs Waters ! Fielding cannot resist the pleasure of adding another amusing incident to a list which is already long. And the mistakes and misunderstandings bound and rebound off one another with all the hurly-burly of a carnival.

We must not, however, imagine that all these incidents are used merely for decorative purposes. They introduce new characters, but these characters, Mrs Fitzpatrick, her husband, and even her servant, are forthwith caught up into the action of the story [1]. The maddest of these truculent scenes at Upton are also among the most important in the novel. They are the culminating point after which the action subsides again towards its *dénouement*. Supreme irony ! The two lovers meet there for the first time since they separated swearing to be true, and they do not see one another. Sophia, vexed that Jones should prove unworthy, flees, taking the road to London. The second part of the novel finds her being pursued, in her turn. With a sudden twist the plot changes front and proceeds towards its logical conclusion [2].

It is but rarely that one fails to notice in Fielding the shrewd eye of the dramatist, ever conscious of the general action. We have already seen with what care he always seeks to explain and show why such and such a character is on the stage and what he is about to do, why Allworthy cannot do otherwise than believe the bad reports which he receives of Tom Jones, why Square, the philosopher, lets himself be surprised with his sweetheart Molly, why young Blifil, who knows the secret of Tom's birth, does not reveal it to anyone, why a beggar who finds Sophia's pocket-book, confides it to Tom Jones and no other. Always this care for verisimilitude ; always this careful smoothing of the way before our feet, lest any unevenness should make us stumble. Observe, however, that this does not in any way prevent our being taken by surprise ; the essential is not that the actions of the characters should fail to astonish us (on the

[1] " We warn thee not too hastily to condemn any of the incidents, in this our history, as impertinent and foreign to our main design, because thou dost not immediately conceive in what manner such an incident may conduce to that design. This work, may indeed be considered as a great creation of our own ; and for a little reptile of a critic to presume to find fault with any of its parts, without knowing the manner in which the whole is connected, and before he comes to the final catastrophe, is a most presumptuous absurdity." This notice comes in Chapter I of book X, in the very middle of the Upton scenes.

[2] By considering them from another standpoint, one could divide the eighteen books into three equal parts : six chapters of life in the country, six of adventures in the highways, and six of London life.

contrary, the comedy of their actions lies often in their unexpectedness), but that, being first of all astonished, we should on reflection feel that they are legitimate and logically in character. The whole of the Bellaston incident, which has scandalized so many readers of *Tom Jones*, may be explained thus [1].

"*Quandoque bonus dormitat Homerus.*" Tom Jones, one fine day, finds in his path the dwelling place of a solitary misanthrope, who is known as the Man of the Hill. This hermit tells him, at great length, the story of his life. No one can dispute the fact that this story is tedious ; it is an almost exact reproduction of the biography of Mr Wilson, given in *Joseph Andrews,* and these moral tales are even less supportable on a second than on a first hearing. We will not linger either to justify or condemn this digression, the survival of a fashion already out-worn. *Don Quixote* and *Gil Blas* set the unfortunate example, and Fielding is by no means the last to make use of it [2]. The Man of the Hill is a blot upon *Tom*

---

[1] I can imagine Fielding answering : " Yes, it is true that what passes between Tom and Lady Bellaston is not strictly honourable, but what have *I* to do with it ? It is in the text." The literary quality of the *unexpected* in dramatic action and its type have been excellently expressed by Mr Galsworthy : " True dramatic action is what characters do, at once contrary, as it were, to expectation and yet because they have already done other things. No dramatist should let his audience know what is coming ; but neither should he suffer his characters to act without making his audience feel that those actions are in harmony with temperament, and arise from previous known actions, together with the temperaments and previous known actions of the other characters in the play. The dramatist who hangs his characters to his plot, instead of hanging his plot to his characters, is guilty of cardinal sin."

[2] Dickens, on the subject of Miss Wade's story which he introduced into *Little Dorrit* (Ch. XXI of the second part) compares his purpose with that of Fielding, and expresses the following opinion on the subject of the Man of the Hill. " I have no doubt that a great part of Fielding's reason for the introduced story . . . was, that it is sometimes really impossible to present, in a full book, the idea it contains . . . without supposing the reader to be possessed of almost as much romantic allowance as would put him on a level with the writer." (*Life of Ch. Dickens* by John Forster, p. 688). In this way the story of the Man of the Hill would be a glance at the destiny reserved for a Tom Jones, and, as it were, a condensation of the moral lessons taught by the novel.

TOM JONES

Jones, because he is, perhaps, the only character of some importance who does not play an active part in the book.

Those who, at first sight, may appear uselessly comic are often most indispensable to the action. Partridge, a sort of English Sancho Panza, is not merely Tom's confidant. Sophia having left her father, would soon find her lover and the novel would end, were it not that Tom at this moment meets Partridge, Partridge the barber, schoolmaster, and surgeon, foolish yet at the same time cunning, a coward and a worthy man, vain of his three or four Latin words, of which he is none too sure. His foolishness is disarmingly well-meaning ; ten times his babbling brings his master within an ace of ruin ; still Jones always forgives him, because it is impossible to be angry with a good fellow like Partridge. But, and this is the important point, Partridge's stupidities could never be attributed to anyone else. Each character in the book is specific, each has its own part to play, from Aunt Western, whose political ideas come just in time to prevent Squire Western from tyrannizing over his daughter and allow the girl to escape, to Mrs Honour, the waiting-woman of comedy, whose very defects make her invaluable to the separated lovers.

All this is done almost too well. A critical reader might sometimes have the impression that things are too carefully arranged. When the end of the novel is at hand, Tom Jones does good turns to several people, to his friend, Mrs Waters, to a highwayman, to his landlady, Mrs Miller, to young Nightingale ; not one of these good deeds will be lost, and eventually all these characters will help in getting him out of his difficulties. The book is a vast and living organism, in which the actors are like organs, each one of which plays its part in its own place, and performs its function in the general progress of the whole. No novelist before Fielding had paid such attention to rigorous construction [1].

[1] Mr W. L. Cross, who has examined with the utmost care, the construction and time-scheme of *Tom Jones*, going so far as to refer to the almanacks of 1745, concludes that " Fielding in his aim to give a perfect air of reality to *Tom Jones*, actually consulted an almanack

Rigorous, however, does not mean rigid. It is only by carefully picking the book to pieces and resolving it into its essential parts that one gets the impression of a mechanism. In reality nothing could be less like a work written according to a theory than *Tom Jones*. The author himself says that it is not a system but a history. One might almost say 'It is history' for Fielding uses the words ' a history ' and not ' a story '

To be true to his principle, which was to fasten his plot on to his characters, and to be true to it without being monotonous, Fielding needed an extraordinarily rich gallery of characters. A work such as *Tom Jones* literally devours them. Where, then, are they to be found ? Certainly not in society, where uniformity of manners is the ideal ; and thus the stage puts a great obstacle in its own path when it limits itself to depicting fools of rank ; " Vanbrugh and Congreve copied nature : but they who copy them draw as unlike the present age as Hogarth would do if he was to paint a rout or a drum in the dresses of Titian and of Van Dyck." And how and where can one observe the aristocracy, if one is not an aristocrat oneself ? No, this inexhaustible mine of comic characters is to be found well within reach, in ' low life '. " The various callings in lower spheres produce the great variety of humorous characters [1]." It is these small people,

---

for his sun and moon ; he constructed the dramatic action throughout on a time-scheme as carefully prepared as if he were writing a play." (*The History of Henry Fielding*, II, 190). For some of Fielding's errors, see the *Gentleman's Magazine* of May, 1791, and *Notes and Queries*, May 30th, 1863. The question of these mistakes, and some others, is raised and discussed by Mr. Cross.

[1] "To let my reader into a secret, this knowledge of upper life,though very necessary for preventing mistakes, is no very great resource to a writer whose province is comedy, or that kind of novels which, like this I am writing, is of the comic class.

"What the Pope says of woman is very applicable to most of this station, who are indeed so entirely made up of form and affectation that they have no character at all, at least, none which appears. I will venture to say, the highest life is much the dullest, and affords very little humour or entertainment. The various callings in lower spheres produce the great variety of humorous characters ; whereas here, except among the few who are engaged in the pursuit of ambition, and the fewer still who have a relish for pleasure, all is vanity and servile imitation " (XIV, 1).

who give vent so ingenuously to their natural passions, whom he likes to paint. And he takes them from anywhere and everywhere, whenever chance brings them across his path.

In this respect more than in any other *Tom Jones* realizes, definitely and completely, Fielding's conception of ' a comic epic poem in prose '. We must not however use the word ' epic ' loosely. A modern definition of the word would hardly proceed by the same method as that of the classical critics. Their principal object was to delimit a type, and so they defined it according to its external characteristics. We all know how lamentable was the result and how many the failures of poets, who wished to make an epic according to theory. To-day, after these painful experiences, no one would dare confine the epic within the limits of a set form. Rather than speak of *epics* we would use the term epic works, the reading of which give an impression *sui generis*, that no other work can produce. And if we try to analyse this impression rather more closely, we shall find that the common character- istic of all the works which are usually called, and deserve to be called, ' Epics ' is that they express, at a given moment, the soul of a generation, in all its fullness and all its depth, perhaps in all the dimness of its hidden dream. The theatre does not admit of the epic ; its forms are too closely defined, too narrow, it is too partial. A work is epic when it is the complete expression of a moment of collective life, a fragment of the legend of the centuries. As soon as the epic appears with an Æschylus or a Shakespeare, it overflows and submerges the theatre. In this sense alone can impersonality be called one of the conditions of an epic ; the individuality of the author is drowned in a sort of mass-personality ; the voice of a whole people speaks through his voice. His *ego*, far from disappearing, is magnified. Can it be said that Milton, Dante, or Virgil are absent from their poems ? No, they remain incomparably and forever present, but they are more than themselves, for their individuality is living one moment of universal life. And this moment, through them, remains fixed forever in the history of humanity.

The novel, being the least limited of all forms (who will be bold enough to define it ?) is also that which can most easily assume an epic character. No one could deny this character to works such as *Gargantua* or *Don Quixote*. In them, too, the personality of the author is exalted in the broad, vast personality of his epoch. By laughter, Rabelais plunges suddenly to the very depths of those subterranean, imperishable springs of the race, and it is of this divine water that we drink when we raise the joyous cup of Pantagruel to our lips.

In this sense *Tom Jones* often gives the impression of an epic. It is a picture of all England that we find there [1], and a picture of England at a moment when, suspended between her great past and her prodigious future, she was most limpidly herself. *Joseph Andrews* had not as yet given, and *Amelia* was not to give again this impression of a complete picture. *Tom Jones* is the England of the time. Rare have been the English who owned it and who confessed to their portraits, and they are still rare ; *Tom Jones* still raises a furore, less because of a few somewhat improper scenes than because of the frank and faithful picture which it gives of that trivial life, lived without ideals, from day to day, in perfect self-satisfaction, which was the life led by long generations of Britons. *Tom Jones* is a ' common ' book and is proud of the fact. It is the work of a man who paid no attention to social conventions and marks of respectability, but saw his compatriots as they were and told all he saw. His *mea culpa* is their *mea culpa*. He will never be forgiven, and the majority of his countrymen will always, like Richardson, bring against him that charge of vulgarity, which so often irritated when it did not amuse him [2].

[1] " Oh, if we had but a *Tom Jones* of the time of Augustus " was the frequent cry of Dr Arnold, of Rugby (quoted in an article in *Frazer's Magazine*, 1858).
[2] During his controversy with Bowles regarding Pope, Byron tries to define what is meant by ' vulgarity ', the vulgarity which he

TOM JONES

The characters in *Tom Jones* are epic, in another sense of
the word, by reason of the number of enormous mishaps
which befall them and which they overcome, and the fullness
of life which results therefrom ; a fullness which is all the
more apparent because the connection between the different
planes on which the figures move is so admirably maintained.
Just as in the *Iliad* or the *Odyssey* the protagonists are thrown
in high relief against a background of figures which
are virtually anonymous, just as they are ' great '
in comparison with the mass of humanity, the innumerable
soldiers, servants, charioteers, and companions, so the
important figures of Tom Jones, Western, and Sophia grow
tall by comparison with the crowd of minor characters, which
swarms about them on a lower plane.

Where does Fielding find his people ? Like Molière, that
other great artist of whom we are always reminded when we
think of Fielding, ' *il prend son bien où il le trouve* '. Partridge
was taken from Cervantes, and the conversations between
this barber and Tom Jones often recall those between Don
Quixote and Sancho [1] ; Molière's *L'Amour Médecin* suggested
the discussion between the doctors [2] ; *L'Avare*, the misunderstanding by which two speakers find themselves in
agreement, while really speaking of different persons [3] ; and
the *Malade Imaginaire*, the pretentious medical gibberish [4].
Elsewhere he confesses to getting direct inspiration from the

denounces in the cockney poets of Hunt's school: "I do not mean that
they are coarse, but ' shabby-genteel ', as it is termed. A man may be
coarse and yet not vulgar, and the reverse. Burns is often coarse, but
never vulgar. Chatterton is never vulgar, nor Wordsworth, nor the
higher of the Lake School, though they treat of low life in all its branches
It is in their *finery* that the new under-school are most vulgar, and they
may be known by this at once, as what we called at Harrow ' a Sunday
blood ' might be easily distinguished from a gentleman, although his
clothes might be the better cut, etc. . . Vulgarity . . . does not
depend upon low themes, or even low language, for Fielding revels in
both—but is he ever *vulgar* ? No. You see the man of education, the
gentleman, and the scholar, sporting with his subject—its master,
not its slave. Your vulgar writer is always most vulgar, the higher
his subject. (Loc. cit., p. 591).

[1] VIII, 9.   [2] II, 9.   [3] VI, 5.   [4] VII, 13.

pictures of his friend Hogarth [1]. He also drew upon Shakespeare, Le Sage, Marivaux, and Scarron, the pleasing titles of whose chapters attracted him. But he profited above all by his own observation of contemporary reality. Why should he seek out Molière's doctors, when every year he had those of Bath before his eyes ? At Bath, too, he must have met his gamesters, his Fitzpatrick, the brisk rogue and fortune hunter [2]. A little English village certainly gave birth to the scandal about Jones the bastard, and all the tittle-tattle at the barber's and the grocer's which was caused by Allworthy's adoption of the child ; in some such village this or that country conversation must have been heard :

" Jones . . . inquired . . . whether they were in the road to Bristol.

' Whence did you come ? ' cries the fellow.

' No matter,' says Jones, a little hastily, ' I want to know if this be the road to Bristol ? '

' The road to Bristol ! ' cries the fellow, scratching his head, ' why, measter, I believe you will hardly get to Bristol this way to-night.'

' Prithee, friend, then ', answered Jones, ' do tell us which is the way.'

' Why, measter ', cries the fellow ' you must be come out of your road the Lord knows whither ; for thick way goeth to Gloucester.'

' Well, and which way goes to Bristol ? ' said Jones.

' Why, you be going away from Bristol ', answered the fellow.

' Then ', said Jones, ' we must go back again ? '

' Ay, you must ', said the fellow.

' Well, and when we come back to the top of the hill, which way must we take ? '

' Why, you must keep the straight road.'

---

[1] I, 11 ; II, 3 ; III, 4 ; of Thwackum : " The pedagogue did in countenance very nearly resemble that gentleman who, in the Harlot's Progress, is seen correcting the ladies in Bridewell."

[2] cf. Barbeau, *op. cit.*, p. 95-7.

TOM JONES

' But I remember there are two roads, one to the right and the other to the left.'

' Why, you must keep the right-hand road, and then go straight forwards ; only remember to turn vurst to your right, then to your left again, and then to your right, and that brings you to the squire's ; and then you must keep straight vorwards, and turn to the left.'

Another fellow now came up and asked which way the gentlemen were going ; of which being informed by Jones, he just scratched his head, and then leaning upon a pole he had in his hand, began to tell him, ' That he must keep the right-hand road for about a mile, or a mile and a half, or such a matter, then he must turn short to the left, which would bring him round by Measter Jin Bearnes's.' ' But which is Mr John Bearnes's ? ' says Jones. ' O Lord ! ' cries the fellow, ' why, don't you know Measter Jin Bearnes ? Whence, then, did you come ? ' " (VII, 10).

Elsewhere we recognize the village school and its master, Partridge, who at the same time fulfils the functions of barber and clerk : " His scholars were divided into two classes : in the upper of which was a young gentleman, the son of a neighbouring squire, who, at the age of seventeen, was just entered into his Syntaxis ; and in the lower was a second son of the same gentleman who, together with seven parish-boys, was learning to read and write." Poor Partridge " among his other treasures, had a wife, whom he had married out of Mr Allworthy's kitchen for her fortune, viz., twenty pounds " (II, 3).

Allworthy has a garden which is described. Here we get a glimpse of Fielding's method ; like all great realists, he does not make a servile copy of reality, but interprets it by weeding out everything which is not essential. Allworthy's garden, the obvious model of which is to be found in Allen's estate at Prior Park, does not conform in every detail to this pattern ; but it is ' truer to life ' than if it had been minutely copied, for it resembles the Harlowes' garden, whose most characteristic details such as the water-fall, the ruined tower overgrown with ivy, etc., have been reproduced. It is not *a* garden, it is *the* garden of the day.

Fielding amuses himself by putting all his friends into his great novel, sometimes mentioning them by name and sometimes disguising their personalities under so thin a veil that no one was deceived ; his kindred, his wife, and even himself, all go in. *Clarissa* gives hardly a single portrait of contemporary English society ; there are no judges, no inns, no coaches nor postillions, no lawyers, shopkeepers nor peasants, nothing, or almost nothing, but a subtle analysis of complicated spiritual conditions—the picture of an external environment is as utterly lacking there as it is in Racine. Fielding, on the contrary, draws a social *ensemble*. The whole of eighteenth century English society, organized by squires for squires, passes before us in the pages of *Tom Jones*, with its struggles and battles, its gross gaiety and heavy communicative *joie de vivre*.

For this epic of Fielding is above all things comic. So far we have been mainly concerned to observe how truly comic it is in the highest sense of the word, the sense in which it is used by a Meredith, to express the intellectual contemplation of reality by a man who remains captain of his own soul. Let us try to carry our analysis a little further.

Fielding's comedy attains in *Tom Jones* its perfect equilibrium. Its most sure characteristic is sanity. More even than that of Molière, his gaiety leaves an impression of complete satisfaction and well-being. Perhaps the secret of this lies in the fact that in *Tom Jones* he is careful never to poke fun at one absurdity without also poking fun at its opposite. He jeers at Square but also at Thwackum. If Blifil is odious, Tom Jones is ridiculous. Here, Fielding's laughter is no longer the slave of a formula. His wide and fluid morality allows him to pardon all men, but also, by a natural corollary, commands him to laugh at them all. Neither the perfect Allworthy nor the author himself can always escape a gentle mockery [1].

We should certainly not escape it ourselves, were we to seek with pedantic pen to label and catalogue the divers examples of Fielding's comic genius. Laughter has wings, and we must watch Fielding's jests flying in the bright sunlight of his work, for pinned in a glass-case, they would lose their changing lustre and all the soft bloom of their delicate hues. We may, however, say that here again we frequently find that epic plentitude which is the general note of *Tom Jones*. *Joseph Andrews* and *Jonathan Wild* are at two extremes and Fielding's comic art moves, so to speak, between them. The first was essentially a work of humour, the second of irony : Adams is sympathetically ridiculous ; Wild odiously ridiculous. *Tom Jones* unites and combines these two aspects of the comic genius. The broadly humorous portrait of Tom balances the caustically ironical sketch of Blifil. And this comic harmony is not the least of the factors which contribute to give this work its character of completeness. Besides being the complete expression of an epoch, *Tom Jones* is the complete expression of Fielding's genius.

The comic element is present in every page. It has settled indeed in the very centre of the work, in the fundamental contrast between the two principal figures, and it is found again, in the tone which the author adopts towards his characters : ' Wait ', he says at some point ' I am going to introduce my heroine : but you must not think that she is an ordinary heroine, etc.' (IV, 1). Then this human puppet becomes useless, is thrown aside, and lies as it has fallen, in a droll attitude in the corner of the stage, until the

---

[1] For example, the chapter in which Allworthy lectures Jenny Jones at great length, on the subject of chastity is presented under the following title : " Containing such grave matter that the reader cannot laugh once through the whole chapter, unless peradventure he should laugh at the author " (I, 7). One can imagine Fielding smiling in his sleeve at the thought of the author of *Joseph Andrews* praising chastity.

showman's hand needs it once again, picks it up, and once more endows it for an hour or so with life.

There is also comedy in the nice arrangement of events. Providence is frequently kind to the author; and as he admits it himself and is amused by it, we cannot do otherwise than laugh with him. From the general structure of the work it descends to every detail; sometimes, as we have observed, it takes a moral or philosophical direction, but sometimes, and more frequently, it is a disinterested comedy, pure laughter, frank delight in incongruous sights. The author himself laughs, he is visibly amused [1], and little by little we are won by his laughter; by reading of so many joyous adventures which end well we acquire that "gaiety of spirit conceived in scorn of fortuitous event [2]" which is the essential of Pantagruelism. And, indeed, to live as he lived and to keep that exuberant good humour, our novelist must have swallowed a very strong dose of that Rabelaisian herb known as 'pantagruelion'.

Sometimes we get the full-throated laughter of a battle between husband and wife (II, 4) or the amusing homeric struggle so often quoted (IV, 8):

" Molly, having endeavoured in vain to make a handsome retreat, faced about; and laying hold of ragged Bess, who advanced in the front of the enemy, she at one blow felled her to the ground. The whole army of the enemy (though near a hundred in number), seeing the fate of their general, gave back many paces, and retired behind a new-dug grave; for the churchyard was the field of battle, where there was to be a funeral that very evening. Molly pursued her victory and catching up a skull which lay on the side of the grave, discharged it with such fury, that having hit a Tailor on the head, the two skulls sent equally forth a hollow sound at their meeting, and the Tailor took presently measure of his

[1] I am convinced I never make my reader laugh heartily, but where I have laughed before him " (IX, 1).
[2] " *gaité d'esprit confite en mépris des choses fortuites.*" (Rabelais).

length on the ground, where the skulls lay side by side, and it was doubtful which was the more valuable of the two. Molly then taking a thigh-bone in her hand, fell in among the flying ranks, and dealing her blows with great liberality on either side, overthrew the carcase of many a mighty hero and heroine.

" Recount, O Muse, the names of those who fell on this fatal day. First, Jemmy Tweedle fell on his hinder head the direful bone. Him the pleasant banks of sweetly winding Stour had nourished, where he first learnt the vocal art, with which, wandering up and down at wakes and fairs, he cheered the rural nymphs and swains, when upon the green they interweaved the sprightly dance ; while he himself stood fiddling and jumping to his own music. How little now avails his fiddle ! He thumps the verdant floor with his carcase. Next, old Echepole, the sowgelder, received a blow in his forehead from our Amazonian heroine, and immediately fell to the ground. He was a swinging fat fellow, and fell with almost as much noise as a house. His tobacco-box dropped at the same time from his pocket, which Molly took up as lawful spoils. Then Kate of the Mill tumbled unfortunately over a tombstone, which catching hold of her ungartered stocking, inverted the order of nature, and gave her heels the superiority to her head. Betty Pippin with young Roger, her lover, fell both to the ground ; where, oh, perverse fate ! she salutes the earth and he the sky. Tom Freckle, the smith's son was the next victim to her rage. He was an ingenious workman, and made excellent pattens ; nay, the very patten with which he was knocked down was his own workmanship. Had he been at that time singing psalms in the church, he would have avoided a broken head. Miss Crow, the daughter of a farmer ; John Giddish, himself a farmer ; Nan Slouch, Esther Codling, Will Spray, Tom Bennet ; the three Misses Potter, whose father keeps the sign of the Red Lion ; Betty Chambermaid, Jack Ostler, and many others of inferior note lay rolling among the graves.

" Not that the strenuous arm of Molly reached all these :
for many of them in their flight overthrew each other.

" But now Fortune, fearing she had acted out of character,
and had inclined too long to the same side, especially as it
was the right, hastily turned about : for now Goody Brown
whom Zekiel Brown caressed in his arms ; nor he alone, but
half the parish besides ; so famous was she in the fields of
Venus, nor indeed less in those of Mars. . . Goody Brown
no longer bore the shameful flight of her party. She stopped
short, and calling aloud to all who fled, spoke as follows :
' Ye Somersetshire men, or rather, ye Somersetshire women,
are ye not ashamed thus to fly from a single woman ? But,
if no other will oppose her, I myself and Joan Top here, will
have the honour of the victory.' Having thus said, she flew
at Molly Seagrim."

Elsewhere Fielding seeks a more learned form of comedy [1].
He often obtains amusing results through a surprise or misunderstanding [2]. Finally, one of his most frequent and most
personal touches is the sudden contradiction between the
deeds and words of one of his characters ; the philosopher
Square, after a high-flown discourse, bites his tongue and
fails to stifle a curse.

This broad merriment is to be found throughout *Tom
Jones*. But in many passages there also sounds a wittier and
more delicate gaiety. The whole of Book II, which describes
the marriage and death of Captain Blifil, is an example of
this. It is written in a clear, sober style, but the sparks fly
as though from dried wood and remind one of the Voltaire

---

[1] Mr Square "was deeply read in the ancients, and a professed master
of all the works of Plato and Aristotle. . . In morals he was a professed
Platonist, and in religion he inclined to be an Aristotelian. But though
he had, as we have said, formed his morals on the Platonic model, yet
he perfectly agreed with the opinion of Aristotle, in considering that
great man rather in the quality of a philosopher or a speculatist, than
as a legislator. This sentiment he carried a great way ; indeed, so far
as to regard all virtue as matter of theory only " (II, 3).

[2] For instance, when Sophia and her Aunt Western respectively
sing the praises of Jones and of Blifil while each thinks the other is
speaking of the same man (VI, 5).

of the *Romans* at his best. We would cite especially Chapter 8, where the captain complacently builds castles in the air, founded in anticipation of Allworthy's death. The recital swells and mounts in an even flight of full phrases ; and suddenly the period breaks and falls at the words : " in short . . . he died of an apoplexy." Everything that follows, everything that surrounds the captain's death up to his magnificent epitaph, is a masterpiece of light irony. Let us take a few other phrases at random. Western, we are told, " was fonder of Sophia than of any other human creature ". Nothing is underlined ; but consider that it is Western who is being described and that his hounds are not ' human creatures '. Elsewhere the two young men, Jones and Blifil, are mentioned : " The preference which Sophia gave the former of these, would often appear so plainly that a lad of more passionate turn than Master Blifil was, might have shown some displeasure at it." A great deal lies in the word ' shown ', placed there so innocently, when we remember that Blifil is a hypocrite. Again, one day Tom comes to Molly's room, and, in the midst of a quarrel, a curtain falls and discloses the objects behind it ; " among *other* female utensils appeared—the philosopher Square." One could multiply examples such as these.

These are but the least qualities of one of the truest prose-artists that England has ever known. An examination of the variants in the different editions shows with what care Fielding wrote and corrected his work. He confides to us that he worked ' thousands of hours, in composing *Tom Jones*, and he would certainly never have reached this absolute perfection without the most assiduous labour. Such a chapter as the invocation to fame (XIII, 1) is written throughout in a style of firm and regular beauty, which recalls the great Latin prose writers. But what he most frequently offers us is a sudden ' slice of life ' such as the greatest modern realists give us, for example, a dialogue at an inn, a conversation with a surgeon (VII, 13), a servant's remonstrance with her master (I, 3). Above all I would indicate the amusing chapter in which Tom Jones and Partridge are present at a performance of *Hamlet* by Garrick. I do not think anything could surpass the worthy Partridge's comments on the candle-lighter, the ghost, Hamlet, the king, or the grave-digger :

" ' But I never saw in my life a worse grave digger. I had a sexton, when I was a clerk, that should have dug three graves while he is digging one. The fellow handles a spade as if it was the first time he had ever had one in his hand. Ay, ay, you may sing. You had rather sing than work, I believe.' " On leaving the theatre Jones asks him which of the actors he likes best. " To this he answered with some appearance of indignation at the question, ' The king, without doubt.' ' Indeed, Mr Partridge ', says Mrs Miller, ' you are not of the same opinion with the town ; for they are all agreed, that Hamlet is acted by the best player who ever was on the stage.' ' He, the best player ! ' cries Partridge, with a contemptuous sneer, ' why I could act as well as he, myself, I am sure, if I had seen a ghost, I should have looked in the very same manner, and done just as he did. And then, to be sure, in that scene as you called it, between him and his mother, where you told me he acted so fine, why, Lord help me, any man, that is any good man, that had such a mother, would have done exactly the same. I know you are only joking with me ; but, indeed, Madam, though I never was at a play in London, yet I have seen acting before in the country ; and the king for my money ; he speaks all his words distinctly, half as loud again as the other. Anybody may see he is an actor [1] ' (XVI, 5).

[1] Fielding is here giving a helping hand to his friend Garrick, who was, at that time, Quin's rival. Quin was the representative of the old declamatory school, while Garrick pleaded that acting should be as natural as possible. In 1747 Garrick who had been playing for several seasons at Covent Garden under the direction of Rich, became stage-manager of Drury Lane, where he took with him, Mrs Clive, Mrs Woffington, Macklin, etc. In the autumn of 1749, the two theatres opened simultaneously with *Romeo and Juliet*. The struggle, then, was at its liveliest when *Tom Jones* appeared.

TOM JONES

It is also impossible to resist the pleasure of quoting a delightful piece of realism, which suddenly enlivens that dull story of the Man of the Hill. Once again we are indebted to Partridge for it.

"In the parish where I was born, there lived a farmer whose name was Bridle, and he had a son named Francis, a good, hopeful young fellow : I was at the grammar school with him, where I remember he was got into Ovid's Epistles, and he could construe you three lines together sometimes without looking into a dictionary. Besides all this he was a very good lad, never missed church o' Sundays, and was reckoned one of the best psalm-singers in the whole parish. He would, indeed, now and then, take a cup too much, and that was the only fault he had.' ' Well, but, come to the ghost ', cries Jones. ' Never fear, sir, I shall come to him soon enough ', answered Partridge, ' You must know, then, that Farmer Bridle lost a mare, a sorrel one, to the best of my remembrance ; and so it fell out that this young Francis shortly afterward being at a fair at Hindon, and as I think it was on, ——, I can't remember the day ; and being as he was, what should he happen to meet but a man upon his father's mare. Frank called out presently, ' Stop thief ' ; and it being in the middle of the fair, it was impossible, you know, for the man to make his escape. So they apprehended him and carried him before the justice : I remember it was Justice Willoughby, of Foyle, a very worthy, good gentleman ; and he committed him to prison, and bound Frank in a recognizance I think they call it—a hard word, compounded of *re* and *cognosco* ; but it differs in its meaning from the use of the simple, as many other compounds do. Well, at last, down came my Lord Justice Page to hold the assizes ; and so the fellow was had up and Frank was had up for a witness. To be sure I shall never forget the face of the judge, when he began to ask him what he had to say against the prisoner. He made poor Frank tremble and shake in his shoes. ' Well you fellow ', says my Lord, ' what have you to say ? Don't stand humming and hawing but speak out.' But, however, he soon turned altogether as civil as Frank, and began to thunder at the fellow ; and when he asked him if he had anything to say for himself, the fellow said he had found the horse. ' Ay ! ' answered the judge, ' thou art a lucky fellow : I have travelled the circuit these forty years, and never found a horse in my life : but I'll tell thee what, friend, thou wast more lucky than thou didst know of ; for thou didst not only find a horse but a halter too, I promise thee.' To be sure, I shall never forget the word. Upon which, everybody fell a-laughing, as how could they help it ? Nay, and twenty other jests he made which I can't remember. There was something about his skill in horse-flesh which made all the folks laugh. To be certain, the judge must have been a very brave man, as well as a man of much learning. It is indeed charming sport to hear trials for life and death. One thing, I own, I thought a little hard, that the prisoner's counsel was not suffered to speak for him, though he desired only to be heard one very short word, but my Lord would not hearken to him, though he suffered a counsellor to talk against him for above half an hour. I thought it hard, I own, that there should be so many of them ; my Lord, and the court, and the jury, and the counsellors, and the witnesses, all upon one poor man, and he too in chains. Well, the fellow was hanged, as, to be sure, it could be no otherwise, and poor Frank could never be easy about it. He never was in the dark alone but he fancied he saw the fellow's spirit.' ' Well and is this thy story ? ' cries Jones. ' No, no ', answered Partridge, ' Oh Lord have mercy upon me ! I am just now coming to the matter ; for one night, coming from the ale-house, in a long, narrow, dark lane, there he ran directly up against him ; and the spirit was all in white, and fell upon Frank ; and Frank, who is a sturdy lad, fell upon the spirit again, and there they had a tussel together, and poor Frank was dread-fully beat : indeed he made a shift at last to crawl home ; but what with the beating and what with the fright, he lay ill above a fortnight ; and all this is most certainly true, and the whole parish will bear witness to it.'

The stranger smiled at this story, and Jones burst into a loud fit of laughter ; upon which Partridge cried, ' Ay, you may laugh, Sir ; and so did some others, particularly a squire who is thought to be no better than an atheist ; who, forsooth, because there was a calf with a white face found dead in the same lane next morning, would fain have it that the battle was between Frank and that, as if a calf would set upon a man. Besides, Frank told me he knew it to be a spirit, and could swear to him in any court in Christiandom ; and he had not drank above a quart or two, or such a matter of liquor at the time. Lord have mercy upon us, and keep us all from dipping our hands in blood, I say ! "

I have thought it worth while to quote this episode in full because an analysis of it will reveal almost all the qualities of Fielding's originality : a copy at once minute and sober of reality, social criticism, couched in a tone of veiled but pitiless irony, a poignant sympathy for the poor wretch crushed by justice ; and finally the comic ring of the conclusion ; this normal explanation, presented as though it were something absurd which only an atheist could believe ; all this and especially his particular way of raising laughter, so to speak from behind the scenes, give the narrative its peculiar flavour. Certain readers, made no doubt of a metal on which the chords of Fielding can awake no harmonies, have said that they lack *tone*. We shall return to these critics, who are rare. Fielding's genius clearly reached its zenith in *Tom Jones*, and his contemporaries themselves felt that they had been present at the birth of a masterpiece [1].

[1] In a letter dated May 18th, 1749, Horace Walpole says that Tom Jones was selling so well that Miller, the publisher, added another £100 to the £600 contracted for. The account of the editions, shows that at least 10,000 copies must have been sold during the course of the first year (cf. Cross, *op. cit.*, II, 126). Fielding's political enemies evidently attacked it violently. But the degree of its success can be measured by the clamour which it raised in Richardson's circle. Richardson's anger, expressed in his letters, was unbridled. Even

his women admirers did not manage to hide that they had their share in *Tom Jones's* success. Lady Bradshaigh informed him that " As to *Tom Jones* I am fatigued with the name, having lately fallen into the company of several young ladies, who had each a Tom Jones in some part of the world, for all so call their favourites, etc." Richardson implicitly recognized this superior success when he wrote in *Grandison :* " The French only are proud of sentiments at this day : the English cannot bear them ; story, story, story, is what they hunt after, whether sense or nonsense, probable or improbable."

CHAPTER V

AMELIA

One of Fielding's plays, performed in 1732 and entitled *The Modern Husband*, depicts among several other ' modern ' households, that of a couple called Bellamant. Mrs Bellamant, a woman of honour, opposes every advance made by a dissolute lord who thinks he can seduce her by employing his customary tactics. Mr Bellamant is a kind-hearted man, but weak and incapable of resisting temptation. His wife, who remains obstinately virtuous, finally forgives her husband when he has betrayed her [1].

Fielding makes use of this same canvas for the adventures of the Booth couple. Captain Booth who has been flung into prison through a misunderstanding, meets there a certain Miss Matthews whom he has not seen since his youth, and who has become ' no better than she should be '. Do they

---

[1] In *The Modern Husband* Fielding seems to have wanted to do something new. He writes to Lady Mary : " I hope your Ladyship will honour the scenes which I presume to lay before you with your perusal. As they are written on a model I never yet attempted ", etc., and in his Prologue he declares that he wishes to
" Restore the sinking honour of the stage :
The stage, which was not for low farce design'd
But to divert, instruct and mend mankind."
The Modern Husband contains also a rather biting comedy of manners, which shows us in Mr and Mrs Modern, a husband trading upon his wife's shame. Its success was unequal to the pains expended on it by Fielding, who kept and doubtless worked upon his play for a year before he produced it. On this subject see above, pp. 10-11.

remember Dido and Æneas ? The author, at any rate, remembers for them [1]. Miss Matthews-Dido gives the Captain a lengthy account of her misfortunes. Booth-Æneas replies by a copious recital of his own, adding a eulogy of Amelia, his lady, the virtuous, tender wife whom he loves better than anything in the world. *Sunt lacrymae rerum.* The two speakers are overcome by emotion, and the embarrassed historian has only just time to draw a veil over this very loving husband's lapse. A few days later, Amelia arrives at the very moment when Miss Matthews, thanks to the money received from an adorer, has furnished the captain with bail. We are not told, at the time, whether Mrs Booth has discovered her husband's fault. But it never ceases to act upon his destiny. On the one hand, his remorse is henceforth one of the chief *motifs* of the novel, on the other Miss Matthews, the disappointed mistress, makes several attempts to win back the man who has once yielded to her charms. Meanwhile a certain lord tries long and cunningly to seduce Amelia ; but Amelia has the good fortune to meet a Mrs Bennet who was once the victim of similar manoeuvres. Mrs Bennet tells her her story, and Amelia thus forewarned, is better able to defend her honour. But she has scarcely been rescued from one enemy before another takes his place. Colonel James, her husband's friend, also tries to seduce her ; again Amelia escapes. The disappointed lord and colonel avenge themselves on the husband for the wife's disdain. Miss Matthews joins the Booths' persecutors, their protector, Dr Harrison, deceived by false reports and misleading appearances, himself persecutes them for a time, Amelia's mother disinherits her, Booth is put on half-pay. This unfortunate couple has to struggle against terrible financial difficulties, and Booth's enemies imprison him several times for debt. Indeed, one

---

[1] He states it clearly in the *Covent Garden Journal* when he is passing judgment on *Amelia* : " Neither Homer nor Virgil pursued them [the Rules] with greater care than myself, and the candid and learned reader will see that the latter was the noble model which I made use of in this occasion (*Covent Garden Journal, January* 25*th*, 1752).

really cannot see how the poor wretches will avoid dishonour
and ruin, if Providence does not intervene on their behalf.
And so it comes about. A repentant thief confesses on his
death-bed that Amelia has been disinherited by a false will [1].
A good judge straightens out the affair. The wicked sister
is punished and Booth has only to apply to himself the advice
which Mercury gave to Rabelais' wood-cutter : " Behold
thou art rich : be good ! "

In this book we must not look for the fine organic movement
which carried *Tom Jones* along so vigorously. *Tom Jones*
gave us an action, *Amelia* presents plots. We cannot think
of giving this work the detailed analysis which we applied to
Tom Jones. But if its general structure is less clear, its
' joining ' is, on the other hand, just as finished and the
adjustment and combination of the various parts, just as
perfect in craftsmanship. An attentive reader will have no
trouble in seeing how the Matthews' plot fits in with the
James plot, and how the latter is, in turn, connected with the
Bennet plot. All this detail is very carefully, almost too
carefully managed ; more than once one feels its artificiality.

The reason for this is that in *Amelia* Fielding is impeded
by the very nature of his subject ; this married life, described
from day to day, runs the risk of appearing very insipid, and,

---

[1] Sarah Fielding's *David Simple* tells a very similar story. In it
there are two brothers, David and Daniel Simple, one of whom is
perfect and the other a cunning hypocrite. Daniel, with the help of
a maid-servant and her lover, has a false will made. David, whom he
has turned out of doors, nearly dies of poverty and illness. The false
witness John finally confesses his crime. The theme in *Amelia* is the
same, but in this case there are two sisters, one of whom devises a false
will to deprive Amelia of the fortune which has been bequeathed to
her. Here, too, the remorse of an accomplice discloses the truth.
Did Fielding borrow the story from his sister Sarah, or is it based upon
some experience which they had in common ?

The drawing of the characters, absurdities and pictures of town-
life in *Amelia* suggests other comparisons, particularly of tone—with
the works of Sarah Fielding. There is no doubt that Fielding remembered his sister when he was describing Amelia, and particularly Amelia's
adventures. See in *David Simple* the story of Cynthia, where numerous
touches which have an autobiographical appearance, recall the story
of Amelia.

in Jules Laforgue's penetrating epigram, too ' daily '[1]. In order to avoid the threatened monotony, the author has multiplied the surprises, the sudden and providential arrivals of people who unravel or further complicate a tangled situation, the recognitions, misunderstandings, mistakes, and accidents ; in particular, he often succeeds in creating suspense by leaving his reader in ignorance of some essential detail. At the end of each book in *Amelia* [2] one might almost employ the classic formula of the vaudevilles in the fifth act, the magic phrase ' all is now explained ', which suddenly comes to calm a bewildered spectator.

But tactics such as these become wearisome with too frequent use. One grows hardened to these cracks of the whip whereby the author seeks to lash life into the flagging action. Certainly you are conscious that the circumstantial details of Miss Matthews' story will be necessary to the narrative and, indeed, you often find, some chapters further on, that some minute point, which seemed to you superfluous, is, on the contrary, essential [3]. Nevertheless that first feeling of tedium persists. It is good that a reader should have confidence in his author, but this should not be too often put to the test. " I wonder at your patience ", says Booth when he is telling his story, and the admission is dangerous. More

---

[1] ' *Dieu, que la vie est quotidienne !* '

[2] After a whole chapter of explanations given after the event, but given (for once) at the beginning of the following book, Fielding concludes : " These were several matters of which we thought necessary our reader should be informed ; for, besides that it conduces greatly to a perfect understanding of all history, there is no exercise of the mind of a sensible reader more pleasant than the tracing the several small and almost imperceptible links of every chain of events by which all the great actions of the world are produced " (XII, 1).

[3] In Book VI, chapter 3, Mrs Ellison, Amelia's landlady, shows her " by chance " a letter from Mrs Bennet. Thanks to this apparently trifling detail, Amelia is able in chapter 9, to recognize the handwriting of Mrs Bennet in a mysterious anonymous communication. She immediately wishes to go and see her, and it happens that " by the greatest luck in the world she told me yesterday where her lodgings were ". This dovetailing of details is a characteristic feature of *Amelia*.

dangerous still is the paragraph which Fielding has inserted at the end of Chapter I, Book 3 : " We shall place this scene in a chapter by itself which we desire all our readers who do not love, or who perhaps do not know the pleasure of tenderness, to pass over ; since they may do this without prejudice to the thread of the narrative." Too many hasty readers will allow themselves to be tempted by this invitation.

II

They will make a great mistake. This book is very different from those which preceded it, and its interest lies not in the string of adventures, but in something else.

In one of his letters, R. L. Stevenson speaks of a novel which he is contemplating : " The fact is, I blush to own it, but *Sophia* is a regular novel ; heroine and hero, and false accusation, and love and marriage and all the rest of it. . . The problem is exactly a Balzac one, and I wish I had his fist, for I have already a better method, the Kinetic, whereas he continually allowed himself to be led into the static. But, then, he had the fist, and the most I can hope for is to get out of it with a modicum of grace and energy, but for sure without the strong impression, the full, dark brush [1]." I am fain to borrow this comparison from Stevenson in order to speak of *Amelia*. Truly the method employed in *Tom Jones* might be called Kinetic, and its unity a unity of movements ; the method adopted in *Amelia* is, on the contrary, static. Fielding is here describing a situation, the situation of the Booths in the face of life. The work may not possess the dramatic concentration of *Tom Jones* but it has, nevertheless, a real unity, or rather an artistic harmony which is all its own, and which is, of its kind, one of the most remarkable literary successes that I know.

[1] *Vailima Letters*, January 31st, 1892.

THE NOVELS OF FIELDING

Just as in a Tintoretto all the lines, the direction of the gestures, the play of light and colour are composed round a single figure or group, so here this entire work is arranged about the person of Amelia. All the other characters live only in relation to her, derive from her, lead up to her, and have no value or interest apart from her. Already, long before her first appearance on the scene, she is the sole subject of conversation. Miss Matthews' story is directed insidiously against her and is intended to eclipse her in the eyes of Booth, the naif listener; all Booth's comments and exclamations indicate that he has fallen into the trap and is making comparisons; only he makes them to the advantage of Amelia. When he begins his own story it is one long panegyric on his Amelia, so deep and so sincere that Miss Matthews, who has to listen to it, can hardly hide her impatience. And if afterwards Booth's fault seems so revolting, we are not concerned on general moral grounds, but on account of Amelia [1].

So the first quarter of the novel is unfolded without the presence of the heroine in person; but her virtues are extolled, and she is in the thoughts of the principal characters, who speak of no one but her [1]. At length she appears. And the first characteristic which she displays is her profound love for this husband who has just shown himself so weak, a love so utter and complete that it stays to count no cost and has time for no refinements and subtleties and no self-analysis, but bravely faces all the sacrifices which life may demand of it.

Fielding repeatedly declares that his object has been to paint a model of feminine virtue. His Amelia, the antithesis of Richardson's neurotic heroines, shall typify the good English wife and mother, honest, courageous, and sane. It has

[1] "To say the truth we are much more concerned for the behaviour of the gentleman than of the lady, not only for his sake but for the sake of the best woman in the world, whom we should be sorry to consider as yoked to a man of no worth nor honour " (IV, 1).
[2] It will be remembered that Molière employs the same device in Tartuffe.

200

often been said, and not without reason, that she is the Sophia of *Tom Jones*, married ; it will not be necessary to set her in the midst of wildly romantic complications, that the heroism of her character may be thrown into relief. The profound pathos of the novel lies, on the contrary, in the fact that an innocent woman is persecuted and brought to bay, not through the action of criminals, but through the weakness of her good-hearted husband. Here, possibly, is the first authentic appearance in a novel, of the ' *tragique quotidien* '. Poverty is their great enemy. Money here begins to play the important part which it was to retain in the modern works of our realists, money visible or hidden, is the mainspring of the action, and gives rise to all its most agonizing turns. Because her husband is under an obligation to Colonel James and a lord, both of whom are rich, Amelia must tolerate and humour them. Because she declines to carry her affability as far as dishonour, they have their revenge. Even the law comes to their aid. Fielding's novel clearly sets forth the power with which society endows wealth and how difficult it is to be proud and virtuous when one is poor ; even Amelia when she is rid of her persecutor, is unable to return the presents which he has given her.

Already the note of Balzac seems to sound in Fielding's novel, with his insight into the fatality of poverty and the tyranny of all-corrupting money. If ' Milord ' wishes to seduce Amelia he has only to remember that she is very poor and he very rich. We are far now from the romantic brutalities and Machiavelian arts of Lovelace. The details of this attempt at seduction must be read in the original [1]; the growing intimacy between Amelia and her landlady, Mrs Ellison, who is his lordship's procuress, Milord's attempts to approach Amelia, his flattery, the presents which he brings for the children, the atmosphere of good breeding, of compliments and elegance with which he seeks to intoxicate his

[1] cf. *Amelia*, VII, 7.

victim ; and the real, heart-rending details given by his first victim, Mrs Bennet, should likewise be read in the text. Think how few women have ever to defend themselves against an attempt as theatrical as that of Lovelace ! Amelia, on the contrary, is exposed to what every young woman who is poor meets on each step of her way—that insidious seduction, which is all the more dangerous because disguised under a veil of charm. It is just because the events are so ordinary that Fielding's story teaches a lesson which is of value.

But Amelia escapes from these dangers. What, then, is the secret of her strength ? It should probably be found in the simplicity of her sentiments. She has but three or four, pure and unalloyed, and she does not complicate them, even by self-analysis. The first is a deep and unwearied love for her husband. Booth is by no means worthy of it ; he is a poor, weak creature, easily led, and powerless against the attractions of a clever courtesan or a gaming-table. He has inherited many of Tom Jones's characteristics, but he is less energetic, more nervous, and more sensitive, he often weeps, and is very voluble. In depicting him Fielding may sometimes have been thinking of his father, the brave soldier and impenitent gambler.

To the historian of manners and customs, however, Booth is interesting from another standpoint ; he belongs to a period when a gentleman can still only choose between a small number of professions. He cannot imagine being anything but a soldier or a country landowner. When these two occupations fail him, he is plunged into irremediable distress, and he relies on nothing but the help of his friends to extricate him. If he thinks at one time of adopting a trade, he very soon finds some pretext for abandoning the idea. Indolently and easily he slips into the rôle of a social parasite, accepting everything from everyone, even from a Miss Matthews ; we are not told that he ever gave her back her money [1].

[1] In this particular, it is impossible not to notice a resemblance to the Bellaston episode in *Tom Jones*.

Such is the man whom Amelia loves, for whom and through whom she tastes the bitter joys of sacrifice. She does not *wish* to see his imperfections, least of all to make use of them in order to rule him. One day when he reproaches her unjustly she refuses to quarrel with him, saying that they will not discuss the matter further and that she will wait until he is calmer. At last the time comes when, weary of the burden of his remorse, weary of the difficulties with which this secret fault has complicated his married life, Booth decides to confess and to ask her pardon : " . . . I cannot now forgive you the fault you have confessed (she answers), and my reason is—because I have forgiven it long ago."

One is often moved to amazement by the unwearied goodness of this woman of brain and heart towards a man so obviously faulty. It must, however, be remembered that Amelia sees Booth with the eyes of her time, which looked upon gamblers and ' rakes ' with greater indulgence than we do. A contemporary French writer, after reading *Amelia*, judges Booth " a most gallant man, the best creature and the best husband in the world [1] " and concludes that Booth would be a very good fellow if he were not so weak in the face of temptation. We know how indulgent Fielding is with those who are good-hearted, and it is not Booth's heart which is at fault.

Amelia forgives him. Hers is the supreme abnegation of a woman who will not see the weaknesses of the man whom she loves, and who, she knows, loves her. Already her indulgent wisdom is to be found in embryo in the curious words of Sophia Western to Mrs Fitzpatrick : " I think . . . I shall never marry a man in whose understanding I see any defects before marriage ; and I promise you I would rather give up my own than see any such afterwards." And Mrs Fitzpatrick, continuing her story, during the course of which she is warned by a friend that her husband (whom she no

[1] Clément, *Les cinq années littéraires* : " le plus galant homme, la meilleure créature, le meilleur mari du monde ".

longer loves) is keeping a mistress, wonders whether it is egoism or vanity which makes her so distressed at the news. "What think you, Sophia?" "I don't know, indeed", answered Sophia, "I have never troubled myself with any of these deep contemplations; but I think the lady did very ill in communicating to you such a secret [1]." Was it wise of Amelia to have married Booth? She refuses to ask herself the question. Her husband's very weaknesses, his incapacity to combat circumstances for which he, a soldier, was not made, arouse in Amelia the maternal instinct which is hidden in the heart of every good wife. She loves her husband all the more for feeling that he needs her [2].

Amelia is a 'positive' woman who looks life in the face and seeks the best means of extracting happiness from it. As a mother she adores her children; and we owe to this maternal love some exquisite scenes of domestic tenderness. Here again, are we not indebted to Fielding for a new note in the English novel? This love of children, care for their future and familiar intimacy between them and their parents, carries us far from the manners painted by Richardson, from the 'respect' of Clarissa who is highly 'honoured' when she is, one day, permitted to share her mother's bed. There is here a new gentleness in family relations which already foreshadows the author of the *Vicar of Wakefield*. Up to now this century had paid but little heed to children.

The daily heroism of a mother shines out from every page of *Amelia*. I give a very well-known passage as an example of it, which is, at the same time, an example of deep and restrained pathos:

"It was about seven when Booth left her to walk in the park; from this time till past eight she was employed with

---

[1] *Tom Jones*, XI, 7.

[2] For an extremely intelligent interpretation of Amelia's character I refer the reader to an article by Miss Clara Thomson, *A Note on Fielding's Amelia* (*Westminster Review*, November, 1899). Miss Thomson is the author of a very acute study of Richardson which I have often found useful.

her children, in playing with them, in giving them their supper, and in putting them to bed.

When these offices were performed, she employed herself another hour in cooking up a little supper for her husband, this being, as we have already observed, his favourite meal, as indeed it was hers. . . It now grew dark, and her hashed mutton was ready for the table, but no Booth appeared. Having waited, therefore, for him a full hour, she gave him over for that evening ; nor was she much alarmed at his absence, as she knew he was in a night or two to be at the tavern with some brother-officers ; she concluded, therefore, they had met in the park, and had agreed to spend this evening together.

At ten then she sat down to supper by herself. . . And here we cannot help relating a little incident, however trivial it may appear to some. Having sat some time alone, reflecting on their distressed situation, her spirits grew very low ; and she was once or twice going to ring the bell to send her maid for half-a-pint of white wine, but checked her inclination in order to save the little sum of sixpence, which she did the more resolutely as she had before refused to gratify her children with tarts for their supper from the same motive. And this self-denial she was very probably practising to save sixpence, while her husband was paying a debt of several guineas incurred by the ace of trumps being in the hands of his adversary " (X, 5).

Is not this picture of a woman, tied to an inferior man, as it were, an implicit vindication of woman's right to be considered a moral person ? The appearance of a Clarissa Harlowe and an Amelia certainly bears witness to an evolution of social manners. Swift, Pope, and even Addison look upon woman as an inferior, and even when they pay her homage, it is as though to a weaker being, charming but frail, both intellectually and morally. In the work of Richardson, as well as in that of Fielding [1], women appear, on the contrary,

---

[1] In a conversation between Booth and his friend, Col. James, Fielding has contrasted very neatly the old and the new points of view.

THE NOVELS OF FIELDING

as being more sensitive and less coarse than men, superior to them in the wealth of their psychological or moral life. A woman like Amelia even possesses the virile qualities which are lacking in her husband.

I have already mentioned the central position which the character of Amelia occupies in Fielding's novel. This is the strong and, at the same time, the weak point of the book inasmuch as Booth, the hero of the various incidents, is not the character who holds our interest. We should not feel the least concern about him, if we did not know that his fate reacts immediately upon that of Amelia. " How will his wife get him out of this new difficulty ? " is the question we ask when his stupidity has once again involved him in a fresh embarrassment. And, in the end, it is through his wife's fortune that he will find peace and prosperity.

Thus the centre of interest is not always the centre of action. The result is a certain awkwardness, a slight lack of balance, as it were, in the construction. But for this lack of balance—if the expression be not too strong—the reader who studies the novel closely is compensated by its admirable psychological construction. The movement of the action is replaced by the evolution of the characters ; Amelia and Booth are, in the end, far from being what they were at the beginning. Experience gradually shapes their souls and teaches them that Art of Life, Fielding's conception of which we shall try to define later. I need not here emphasize, since I have done so elsewhere, the masterly drawing of the secondary characters. Amelia, Mrs Bennet, Miss Matthews, and Mrs Ellison live with the same intensity and the same fullness as the minor personages in *Tom Jones*. There is even a marked progress here, for the direct description of the *dramatis personae* has now almost entirely disappeared ; they

"I don't know how it is, Will, but you know women better than I." "Perhaps, Colonel", answered Booth, "I have studied their minds more." "I don't, however, much envy you your knowledge ", replied the other, "for I never think their minds worth considering." (IV, 6).

are no longer analysed, we see them before us acting, speaking, putting on and taking off their masks. If the author shows us a hypocrite, like Mrs Ellison, and a gentlemanly rogue, like Trent, he intends that we ourselves shall be taken in at first and shall only discover their vice by degrees. Other characters, like Colonel James, are sometimes friends, sometimes enemies. In no other work have I found so deep a pleasure in divining the secret motives of actions, in feeling how much a writer of genius can suggest without expressing it at length. The book sticks to life strictly but intelligently.

There are manifold examples of this psychological realism. I would refer the reader, in particular, to conversations, where, beneath the smooth surface of a quiet dialogue, he may feel the movement, the swell, as it were, of a hidden current of sentiments ; above all, to a certain interview between husband and wife, in which Booth's *arrière pensées*, his preoccupations and remorse, reveal themselves by a scarcely perceptible ripple on the surface (VI, 6)[1]. I should also like to draw attention to a profound and painful scene (X, 6) in which Booth seeks a quarrel with his wife in order to try to humiliate her at the very moment when he feels that she is about to despise him. *Amelia*, more frequently than any other work of Fielding, gives the impression of creatures independent of the author and of the reader, of personal beings endowed with all the unforeseen spontaneities of life.

The chief and the deep beauty of this novel lies in its psychological realism. Doubtless this perfection can be explained by Fielding's age and the greater maturity of his experience, and also by the opportunity, which his profession as justice had given him, of observing the human heart. These explanations, however, are most true of the secondary characters which swarm round the chief couple. For the Booths themselves, there is something else. With the art of

[1] See also, in Book X, chaps. 7 and 8, two parallel scenes, one between Booth and Trent, and the other between Amelia and Mrs Atkinson. We are shown how far the curse of poverty can carry them but also where the sentiment of honour draws the line.

a great realist, Fielding has certainly transposed into them memories of his own life. It has often been pointed out that Amelia resembles his first wife, and he has taken pains to fix the resemblance by inserting a particular detail, the accident to Amelia's nose, on which critics have so idly insisted [1]. But if we readily admit that Amelia is the first Mrs Fielding, must we also believe that Fielding has described himself in Booth ? The portrait would be neither flattering nor true.

Now, autobiography is one thing and the artistic transposition of a psychological theme, is another. The *motif*, here, is the conjugal relationship as seen by Fielding several years after the death of a passionately loved wife. (When he wrote *Amelia*, he had just passed through a moral and religious crisis of which we shall speak later.) Christian moralist, as he now was, he could not reflect without remorse upon the laxity of his youth, which distance, possibly, led him to exaggerate. So now he lives again through the first years of his married life ; doubtless his second wife has much to tell him of the daily heroism of his first, whose faithful servant she had been. He realizes all the secret sufferings which his carelessness must have caused in the past. After this, is it surprising that Booth is drawn with a somewhat brutal touch ?

It would be as slanderous to say that the weak Booth is an exact portrait of Fielding, as it would be flattering to describe the saintly Amelia, as the living image of his wife. But the Booths are a sort of symphonic variation on the theme of the Fieldings. Among our novelist's books *Amelia* plays, to some extent, the same part as, for instance, *L'Education Sentimentale* plays in the work of Flaubert. Both are their

---

[1] In his first edition Fielding forgot to mention that Amelia's nose after being broken, was cured. His critics did not fail to notice the omission and Johnson went so far as to say " that vile broken nose never cured, ruined the sale of perhaps the only book which being printed off betimes one morning, a new edition was called for before night," (Mrs Piozzi, *Anecdotes of Dr Johnson*).

authors' favourite creations [1], the works into which have
gone, by a subtle psychological transmission, the inmost
secrets of their own lives. Fielding and Flaubert are not there
in person, but here and there an accent or a trembling of the
voice make us aware that more than once they have
recognized themselves in their characters.

We spoke just now of variations on a theme. And it is
from the language of music that we must borrow our images,
if we desire to give the true impression left upon our minds
by *Amelia* ; for this work is in truth a symphony of sentiment,
a psychological score. In it each character has his theme.
At first one hears only a few notes, a few phrases in the midst
of some other development. Then the little phrase disappears
for several chapters, to reappear from time to time, with
growing frequency ; and each repetition makes it richer and
fuller, the theme at first only outlined, becomes a *motif*, ample,
sonorous, and expressive. Then the different *motifs* meet
and unite, are lost and found again, until at last the
triumphant themes are heard in unison, vanquishing their
counter-themes. Many a time has the author of *Amelia*
reminded me of his contemporary Handel.

If an example be needed, we may select Sergeant Atkinson.
He loves Amelia, secretly, with the love of a faithful dog,

[1] Fielding has confessed his preference, more than once, particularly
in some articles in the *Covent Garden Journal* of which we shall speak
later. It is well known that in *L'Education Sentimentale* Flaubert is
remembering a great and unavowed love of his youth. He seems to
have loved this melancholy book, into which he poured all his dis-
illusions, more than any other (cf. *L'Education Sentimentale*, Conard's
edition, Introduction). M. Henry Céard describes how one day he
went to see Flaubert and told him of his admiration for *L'Education
Sentimentale*. . . " No matter ", continued Flaubert, " the book,
my good friend, is damned, because it doesn't do this ", and joining
his long hands, so fine in their strength, he simulated a pyramid. " The
public wants a book which exalts their illusions, while *L'Education
Sentimentale* . . ." He dropped his great hands and made a gesture
as though all the fallen dreams were plunging into a great pit of
despair ; I suspected that he was very much moved by my meagre
praise." cf. M. Henry Céard, *Le Nouvel élu du grenier*, *Mercure
France*, 16.5.1918, p. 277. *Amelia* too, is a book that ' doesn't do
this '.

and is ready to do anything for her, though she suspects nothing. The appearances, rare at first, then more and more frequent, of this poor timid heart, this obscure hero who ends by playing a rôle of the first importance in the book, are indeed in the full psychological harmony of the narrative, like the muffled beat of a minor chord in the accompaniment. At last, one day this good man, lying on the point of death, humbly declares his love to Amelia. And then " that heart . . . which all the treasures of the universe could not have purchased, was yet a little softened by the plain, honest, modest, involuntary, delicate, heroic passion of this poor and humble swain ; for whom, in spite of herself, she felt a momentary tenderness and complacence, at which Booth, if he had known it, would perhaps have been displeased."

In this picture of a poor dumb love, and in this softening of the impeccable Amelia, there is a touch of moral delicacy which we were not accustomed to find in the author of *Tom Jones*.

III

No moral theory can be sound unless it be supported by the psychological analysis of motives and intentions. And to this truth must be added the corollary that all coherent psychology demands in the end a moral conclusion. In the chapter which Fielding uses as an exordium to his *Amelia*, we can observe the passage from one to the other :

" To speak a bold truth, I am after much mature delibera- tion inclined to suspect that the public voice hath, in all ages, done much injustice to Fortune, and hath convicted her of many facts in which she had not the least concern. I question much whether we may not, by natural means, account for the success of knaves, the calamities of fools, with all the miseries in which men of sense sometimes involve themselves, by quitting the directions of Prudence and following the blind guidance of a predominant passion ; in short, for all the ordinary phenomena which are imputed to fortune, whom, perhaps men accuse with no less absurdity in life, than a bad player complains of ill-luck at the game of chess.

But if men are sometimes guilty of laying improper blame on this imaginary being, they are altogether as apt to make her amends by ascribing to her honours which she as little deserves. To retrieve the ill-consequences of a foolish conduct, and by struggling manfully with distress, to subdue it, is one of the noblest efforts of wisdom and virtue. Whoever, therefore, calls such a man fortunate, is guilty of no less impropriety in speech than he would be who should call the statuary or the poet fortunate who carved a Venus or who writ an *Iliad*.

Life may as properly be called an art as any other ; and the great incidents in it are no more to be considered as mere accidents than the several members of a fine statue or a noble poem . . . By examining carefully the several gradations which conduce to bring every model to perfection, we learn truly to know that science in which the model is formed : as histories of this kind, therefore, may properly be called models of Human Life, so, by observing minutely the several incidents which tend to the catastrophe or completion of the whole, and the minute causes whence those incidents are produced, we shall best be instructed in this most useful of all arts, which I call the *Art of Life*."

This is the first time that Fielding sets forth his moral aim so clearly and so explicitly. What then is this *Art of Life* ?

We have already had occasion to indicate its main rules in discussing *Tom Jones*. The evolution of Fielding's code of morality continues in *Amelia* and ends in a conclusion which might, indeed, have been anticipated in the preceding work. All that we have said in our chapter on *Tom Jones*, concerning the appreciation of moral values, the primordial importance of sentiment [1], the essential part played by remorse [2], the idea that doing good is better than being perfect [3], all that we have added on the part played by the ideas of Nature and Reason [4] in his ethics, is here confirmed in almost identical terms and it would be tedious to repeat it. In *Amelia*, however, Fielding adds a new element, which is now, for the first time, set forth clearly in his work, to wit the Christian element.

It is true that we have already discerned numerous traces of an evangelical christianity in the homilies of good Parson Adams ; and Tom Jones did not fail to declare that he was, on the whole, a good Christian. But between these simple

[1] I could cite many examples, of which the following are two : ' good minds, that is to say, minds capable of compassion " (IV, 9). " He had a tenderness of heart which is rarely found among men ; for which I know no other reason, than that true goodness is rarely found among them ; for I am firmly persuaded, that the latter never possessed any human mind in any degree, without being attended by as large a portion of the former " (IX, 4).

[2] " In fact, if we regard this world only, it is the interest of every man to be either perfectly good or completely bad. He had better destroy his conscience, than greatly wound it. The many bitter reflections which every bad action costs a mind in which there are any remains of goodness, are not to be compensated by the highest pleasures which such an action can produce " (IV, 2) ; cf. the whole of Chapter XI, 8, showing Booth's remorse.

[3] " But, sir ", cries the young one, " a clergyman is a man as well as another ; and if such perfect purity be expected. . ." " I do not expect it ", cries the doctor, " and I hope it will not be expected of us. The Scripture itself gives us this hope, where the best of us are said to fall twenty times a day. But sure we may not allow the practice of any of those grosser crimes which contaminate the whole mind. We may expect an obedience to the ten commandments, and an abstinence from such notorious vices, as, in the first place, Avarice, etc." To Avarice he adds Ambition and Pride. The conversation is on the subject of ministers of religion and the example which they ought to set to other men (IX, 10).

[4] " Indeed, my dear Sir, I begin to grow entirely sick of it ", cried Amelia, " for sure, all mankind almost are villains in their hearts."
" Fie, child ", cries the Doctor. " Do not make a conclusion so much to the dishonour of the great Creator. The nature of man is far from being in itself evil. . . Bad education, bad habits, and bad customs, debauch our nature, and drive it headlong as it were into vice," etc. (IX, 5).

indications and the serious teaching of *Amelia*, there is the same difference as between Adams and the logician whom we now meet, Dr Harrison, an active doer of good, and, at the same time, a frequent preacher of the divine word. During the last years of his life, Fielding was converted ; or preferably, since the word ' converted ' may seem somewhat strong, not to say unsuited to a man who had never been hostile, he carried to its conclusion the evolution which was leading him to a more and more convinced Christianity. We know that he was preparing to write a great apologia in which death interrupted him [1]. An examination of the catalogue of his library shows a striking number of books dealing with religious exegesis and controversy [2]. And I found the clearest clue to this conversion when I was comparing the two editions of *Jonathan Wild*. In the 1743 edition Fielding makes Heartfree say : " If the proofs of a Supreme Being be as strong as I imagine them, surely enough may be deduced from that ground only to comfort and support ", etc. while in the 1754 text these words are replaced by " If the proofs of Christianity be as strong ", etc. Even for a believer the correction is assuredly not indispensable ; it is, therefore, all the more eloquent. Between 1743 and 1754, honest Heartfree passes from deism to Christianity ; and the writer whose moral ideal he is expressing, is at the same time undergoing a similar religious transformation. And this is why Booth, whose ideas are at first a subject of some anxiety

[1] Murphy says : " The interests of virtue and religion he never betrayed ; the former is amiably enforced in his works ; and for the defence of the latter, he had projected a laborious answer to the posthumous philosophy of Bolingbroke ; and the preparation he had made for it of long extracts and arguments from the Fathers and the most eminent writers of controversy, is still extant in the hands of his brother, Sir John Fielding."

[2] We may cite among others : South, *Sermons*, 6 vols ; *Deism Revealed*, 2 vols ; Collins, *Grounds and Reasons of Religion* ; Chandler, *Vindication of Christianity* ; Toland, *Christianity not Mysterious* ; *Life of St Francis Xavier* ; Hume, *Sacred Succession, or Priesthood by Divine Right* ; Reynolds on *God's Revenge against Murther* ; *A Defence of Natural and Revealed Religion*, 3 vols. ; Locke's, Tillotson's. Clarke's, Boyle's, Bacon's works ; the *Pensées* of Pascal, etc.

THE NOVELS OF FIELDING

to his wife [1], is converted in prison, after reading the sermons of Barrow, that ' great and good man ' whose pen must surely have been guided by an angel [2]. This too is the reason why Dr Harrison is inflicted upon us at such length, with his somewhat pedantic joviality, pugnacious Christianity, and assiduous sermons. He is a sort of synthesis of the moral cynicism to be found in Lucian, and of the evangelical teaching to be found almost everywhere. All the same his Christianity is still very broad, and is more than ever hostile to the austerity and formalism of sects. If a methodist appears in the novel, he is an arrant hypocrite, an odious rascal beneath a sanctimonious exterior. Tolerance is still one of the essential virtues of a good man, but it must be a Christian tolerance. Henceforward religion is the guiding principle of Fielding's moral doctrine.

At this point I must, however, in sincerity confess that I am not very much impressed by Booth's conversion ; as long as he is in distress, he doubts Providence [3] ; as soon as he becomes rich he believes in it. Doubtless this is all very human, but it is not very philosophical.

The reason may be that Fielding now cared less than ever for pure philosophy. His attitude at this period of his life, when he was engaged in an active struggle against evil, reminds me of the saying of a modern philosopher. " Ethics are peace, but applied ethics are a field of war [4]." Fielding,

[1] " ' I have often wished, my dear ', cries Amelia, ' to hear you converse with Dr Harrison on this subject ; for I am sure he would convince you, though I can't, that there are really such things as religion and virtue.'
This was not the first hint of this kind which Amelia had given ; for she sometimes apprehended from his discourse, that he was little better than an atheist : a consideration which did not diminish her affection for him, but gave her great uneasiness." (X, 9).
[2] " If ever an angel might be thought to guide the pen of a writer, surely the pen of that great and good man had such an assistant " (XII, 5). These words are said by Booth.
[3] " I never was a rash disbeliever ; my chief doubt was founded on this, that as men appeared to me to act entirely from their passions " etc. (X. 9).
[4] " La morale est la paix ; la morale appliquée a pour champ la guerre." (Renouvier).

the Justice, was working with all his might in this field of applied ethics. At Bow Street, he came into daily contact with the rogues who were brought before him, and was led to a conclusion which he frequently expresses in the *Covent Garden Journal*, soon after the publication of *Amelia*. The increase of crime is " as we have observed before, principally to be attributed to the declension of religion among the common people [1]."

If the number of crimes was to be diminished, religion must be restored, and for this end Fielding worked his hardest. In 1752, he published a piece of work about which he had been thinking " for some time ", a pamphlet entitled *Examples of the Interposition of Providence in the Detection and Punishment of Murder* [2]. The announcement describes this pamphlet as " very proper to be given to all the inferior kind of people, and particularly to the youth of both sexes, whose natural love of stories will lead them to read with attention what cannot fail of infusing into their tender minds an early dread

---

[1] He had published in January, 1751, *An Enquiry into the causes of the late increase of robbers, etc., with some proposals for remedying this growing evil*. In this he proposed certain remedies, some of which were almost immediately adopted by legislation. But much remained to be done and Fielding urged moral as well as judicial reform. For allusions to religious reform see the *Covent Garden Journal*, February, *passim*. On March 3rd, he wrote in this journal : " More murders and horrid barbarities have been committed within the last twelve months than during many preceding years. This, as we have before observed, is principally to be attributed to the declension of religion among the common people."

[2] Full title : *Examples of the Interposition of Providence in the Detection and Punishment of Murder. Containing above thirty cases, in which this dreadful crime has been brought to light, in the most extraordinary and miraculous manner ; collected from various authors, ancient and modern, with an introduction and conclusion both written by Henry Fielding, Esq.* The work is dedicated " to the Right Rev. Father in God, Isaac Lord Bishop of Worcester." In *Tom Jones*, there was already the curious phrase : " Here an incident happened of a very extraordinary kind : one, indeed, of those strange chances, whence very good and grave men have concluded that Providence often interposes in the discovery of the most secret villainy, in order to caution men from quitting the paths of honesty, however warily they tread in those of vice." (*Tom Jones*, XVIII, 3). So he really had been thinking of the subject " for some time."

and abhorrence of staining their hands with the blood of their fellow-creatures."

While duly observing the differences between two works of such unequal literary merit, we must not forget that they were composed at the same time and by the same author. It is the very Providence of the *Examples* which appears at the end of *Amelia* to punish so 'miraculously' (the same word is used) the forgers and criminals. To reverse the phrase which we used just now, we might almost say that the argument is perhaps not very philosophical but that it is, after all, human. This is what the Bow Street Justice wants. He is speaking to men, and men are not philosophers.

Now, in every page of *Amelia* Fielding's moral reasoning takes more and more this practical—I had almost said pragmatical—turn. This realist even introduced realism into his ethics. He boldly attacks the daily life of his contemporaries and seeks to evolve the many reforms which will enable him to purify it. His book abounds henceforth in disputes and arguments on all the questions of the day, from the education of women to the re-organization of the police. He demands better laws for the suppression of criminal offences,[1] of receivers of stolen goods, and of adultery. In him there grows plainer the movement of opinion which eventually rid modern England of the duel, by killing it with ridicule [2]. As Booth is a military man we are often told

[1] For a good example see I, 4, concerning the complications of bail granted for perjury and refused for felony, and the note " By removing ", etc. Also XI, 7, where the judge complains that the prosecution of a receiver of stolen goods is made almost impossible by the law : " as to this offence, to say the truth, I am almost weary of prosecuting it ; for such are the difficulties laid in the way of this prosecution, that it is almost impossible to convict anyone of it."

[2] V, 6 ; IX, 3 ; XII, 3, where the religious argument is principally used : " Honour ! nonsense ! Can honour dictate to him to disobey the express commands of his Maker, in compliance with a custom established by a set of blockheads, founded on false principles of virtue, in direct opposition to the plain and positive precepts of religion ", etc. Grandison, too, has to consider the question of duelling.

about the army, in which the officers are badly paid [1] and too far removed from their men, and where young men with influence are too often promoted at the expense of those who have been longer in the service [2]. Above all, the book contains a ruthless indictment of the stupidity of an obsolete jurisprudence, of bad judges [3], and of the abominable prison system made to encourage crime by completing the corruption of the criminals.

But above all these practical reforms, there is one which Fielding urges with calm, impressive gravity, the reform of political morality. A dialogue between Dr Harrison and a peer, whom he has visited in order to recommend Booth, is a profound and severe analysis of the evil suffered by England through corrupt politics and irreligion [4] : " The same periods

[1] " How is it possible that without running in debt, any persons should maintain the dress and appearance of a gentleman, whose income is not half as good as that of a porter ? It is true that this allowance, small as it is, is a great expense to the public ; but if several more unnecessary charges were spared, the public might, perhaps, bear a little increase of this, without much feeling it " (IV, 8).

[2] " Atkinson now returned to his guard and went directly to his officer to acquaint him with the soldier's inhumanity ; but he who was about fifteen years of age, gave the sergeant a great curse, and said the soldier had done very well " (IV, 7). It is obvious that Fielding knew about the grievances of the officers through his father.

[3] I, 2, contains an extremely severe description of an ignorant judge. Judge Thrusher " who was never indifferent in a cause but when he could get nothing on either side ", is shown carrying out his duties. He either refuses to hear witnesses or commits them to jail, and examples are given of three or four condemnations as grotesque as they are odious.

Other passages recall Fielding's *Inquiry* ; cf. in this same Chapter 2, the protest against the advanced age of the London watchmen.

For prisons, see, in particular, I. 3.

[4] We ought to quote the whole of XI, 2, " Do you not know, Doctor, that this is as corrupt a nation as ever existed under the sun ? And would you think of governing such a people by the strict principles of honesty, and morality ? "

" If it be so corrupt ", said the doctor, " I think it is high time to amend it ; or else it is easy to foresee that Roman and British liberty will have the same fate ; for corruption in the body politic as naturally tends to dissolution as in the natural body." To which the peer replies that the evil is more serious. The country dies of old age and the picture which he paints is so sad that the doctor replies : " This is a

happen to every great kingdom as to the natural body. In its youth it rises by arts and arms to power and prosperity. This it enjoys and flourishes with a while ; and then it may be said to be in the vigour of its age, enriched at home with all the emoluments and blessings of peace, and formidable abroad with all the terrors of war. At length this very prosperity introduces corruption, and then comes on its old age. Virtue and learning, art and industry, decay by degrees. The people sink into sloth and luxury and prostitution. It is enervated at home—becomes contemptible abroad ; and such indeed is its misery and wretchedness, that it resembles a man in the last decrepit stage of life, who looks with unconcern at his approaching dissolution." The peer who paints so black a picture of England, thinks that this decadence is irremediable and declares that even if a Minister were found sufficiently idealistic to undertake the cleaning of these Augean stables, he would not have the confidence of his contemporaries who have been fooled too often. " Do you imagine ", he asks, " that if any Minister were really as good as you would have him, that the people in general would believe that he was so ? " To which Dr Harrison replies that they would be justified in distrusting him ; " but", he adds, " doth your Lordship believe that the people of Greenland, when they see the light of the sun and feel his warmth, after so long a season of cold and darkness, will really be persuaded that he shines upon them ? "

What discouragement and bitterness, what pessimism is here ! We are far now from *Tom Jones* (XIV, 1), where, it will be remembered, Fielding holds, doubtless in opposition to Richardson, that the England of his time is less vicious than frivolous, and less dissolute than vain. The atmosphere of

melancholy picture indeed ; and if the latter part of it can be applied to our case, I see nothing but religion [which would have prevented this decrepit state of the constitution] should prevent a man of spirit from hanging himself out of the way of so wretched a contemplation. The words in brackets were added in the final edition of *Amelia*, made, we are told, from a copy corrected by Fielding's own hand. They are important in that they accentuate Fielding's conversion.

crime and moral decadence in which his profession had since forced him to live, succeeded in leaving its mark upon him. Hence this sadness [1] which reminds us irresistibly of Chesterfield's cry of despair some years later. " We are no longer a nation." In 1750 and the years which followed, a wave of pessimism passed over England. It came finally to a head in 1757 with Brown's *Estimate,* which so rudely awakened the public conscience. But the man who really restored her energy to England was Pitt—Pitt the faithful friend and admirer of Fielding. " I want ", he says, " to call England out of that enervate state in which twenty thousand men of France can shake her." The epithet ' enervate ' is also used by Fielding [2]. It is strange that this despairing sadness should so often recur on the very eve of England's prodigious triumph. All the historians have observed this sort of collective neurasthenia which was to be followed by the victorious awakening of the Seven Years War.

Fielding is clearly conscious of the evil, but he seems to think that religion is the best remedy. *Amelia* is purposely a moral novel, and its morality is Christian. " The following book is sincerely designed to promote the cause of virtue ", states the dedication to Ralph Allen, in terms which would not have been disowned by Richardson. And, however different their manner of serving " the cause of virtue ", it is obvious that in *Amelia,* Fielding's method came more near to that of the writer whom he now calls ' the ingenious author of Clarissa '. Amelia Booth is more sensitive and tender than Sophia Western ; she is less virile, has the ' vapours ', faints, and weeps copiously on the slightest pretext. Laughter for laughter's sake, disinterested comedy, has almost disappeared from this work. It is replaced, on the one hand, by a satire on " the most glaring evils, as well public as private, which

---

[1] Compare what we have said of the second edition of *Jonathan Wild,* the plot in the prison and the " speech of the grave man ". This second edition is two years later than *Amelia.*

[2] " It is enervated at home, becomes contemptible abroad ", wrote Fielding (*loc. cit.*).

at present infest the country[1] ", and, on the other, by an ever-encroaching sentimentality, moving descriptions inserted with the avowed intention of bringing tears to the eyes of the sentimental public[2], real *scènes de mouchoirs* which sometimes give the book a false air of belonging to the tribe of plaintive and tear-provoking tales.

If we need evidence, clearer still than our own impressions, of this change in Fielding's ideas, we shall find it in a curious page of the *Covent Garden Journal* (February 4th, 1752). Taking as his text Richardson's opinion that comedy can only be the means to a higher end and must confine itself to being a " vehicle of moral instruction ", our author undertakes to enumerate the masters of comedy. It is not surprising to find him citing Lucian, Cervantes, and Swift as the three greatest. He adds Shakespeare and Molière, and several other writers who, endowed with the same gifts, have employed them to the same end. " There are some, however, who, though not void of these talents, have made so wretched a use of them, that had the consecration of their labours been committed to the hands of the hangman, no good man would have regretted their loss ; nor am I afraid to mention Rabelais, and Aristophanes himself in this number. For, if I may speak my opinion freely of these two last writers, and of their works, their design appears to me very plainly to have been to ridicule all sobriety, modesty, decency, virtue, and religion, out of the world."

How far we have drifted from *Tom Jones* and his invocation

---

[1] The first sentence of the dedication to Ralph Allen is : " Sir, the following book is sincerely designed to promote the cause of virtue, and to expose some of the most glaring evils, as well public as private, which at present infest the country."

[2] The dedication also says : " The good-natured reader, if his heart should be here affected, will be inclined to pardon many faults for the pleasure he will receive from a tender sensation." Better still, or worse, in announcing a tender scene Fielding writes : " We shall . ... place this scene in a chapter by itself, which we desire all our readers who do not love, or who perhaps do not know the pleasure of tenderness, to pass over ; since they may do this without any prejudice to the thread of the narrative " (III, 1).

to the gods of laughter, among whom this same Aristophanes, this same Rabelais were set in a place of honour. Why have they now been condemned ? The answer is that in passing from *Tom Jones* to *Amelia*, we have passed from sentiment to sentimentality, from the moral to the moralizing novel. His contact as a magistrate with the daily realities of crime seems, little by little, to have made Fielding understand the practical usefulness of that bourgeois morality at which he used to scoff. Rabelais and Aristophanes now seem dangerous ; as a judge, charged with the defence of public morality, he would consign their works to the hangman. And thus bit by bit the magistrate in him was killing the artist.

IV

Having duly expressed my admiration for the new beauty of psychological analysis in *Amelia*, I am now emboldened to confess that I feel a certain indulgence towards those who, in spite of all its qualities, have found this book a little long.

His contemporaries expected much from the author of *Tom Jones*, and this eager expectation of *Amelia* explains the initial success of the sale. The book had to be reprinted on the very day of publication [1]. But its readers were a little disappointed. Evidence of this is not only found in the correspondence of Richardson, whose judgment is obviously suspect, but also in contemporary reviews. All Fielding's political enemies, all the newspaper-writers whom he had attacked, now took their revenge. Fielding himself confesses

[1] The testimony of Dr Johnson quoted on p. 208 note 1, shows that the first edition was exhausted on the first day. It contained 5,000 copies. The second impression of 3,000 copies was published in January, 1752 ; and a third was not needed until the edition of *Complete Works* in 1762, such was the success of the first impression and the failure of the second ; cf. Paul de Castro, *Notes and Queries* November, 1917.

his disappointment at this disputed success when he sets up, in his *Covent Garden Journal* (January 25th) a " Court of Censorial Inquiry " before which *Amelia* is summoned, to defend herself against a charge of " Dullness ". The first accusation that Counsellor Town brings against her is that of being " very sad stuff " [1]. Amelia is " a low character ", " a fool ", " a milksop ". Her adversary reproaches her with her weakness, her frequent faints, her servile habits, such, for instance, as herself dressing the children and doing the cooking ; he finally asserts that " she is too apt to forgive the faults of her husband ". The Counsellor finds that the book contains " no wit, humour, knowledge of human nature, or of the world, and is in fact, thoroughly bad ". But a " grave man " comes into the witness-box and confesses that he is the father of the accused who, he says, is his favourite child. " If you, Mr Censor, are yourself a parent, you will view me with compassion when I declare that I am the father of this poor girl, the prisoner at the bar ; nay, when I go further and avow, that of all my offspring she is my favourite child. I can truly say that I bestowed more than ordinary pains in her education ; in which I will venture to affirm, I followed the rules of all those who are acknowledged to have writ best on the subject ; and if her conduct be fairly examined she will be found to deviate very little from the observation of all those rules : neither Homer nor Virgil pursued them with greater care than myself, and the candid and learned reader will see that the latter was the noble model, which I made use of on this occasion.

I do not think my child is entirely free from faults. I know nothing human that is so ; but surely she doth not deserve the rancour with which she hath been treated by the public.

---

[1] Fielding reproduces *verbatim* the reproaches made by the critics. Shortly after the publication of *Amelia*, Mrs Carter wrote to Miss Talbot : " Methinks I long to engage you on the side of this unfortunate book, which I am told the fine folk are unanimous in pronouncing to be very sad stuff." *Letters between Mrs Elizabeth Carter and Miss Catherine Talbot*, 1809, Vol. II, p. 71.

However, it is not my intention, at present, to make any defence ; but I shall submit to a compromise, which hath been always allowed in the court in all prosecutions for dullness. I do, therefore, solemnly declare to you, Mr Censor, that I will trouble the world no more with any children of mine by the same Muse [1] "

Now, however much the irony in this be emphasized, it is nevertheless very different from the combative tone of the prefaces in *Tom Jones* or of the apostrophes in *Joseph Andrews*. Fielding seems to have aged [2], to have grown weary of the struggle, weary of forever replying to the same ceaseless accusations. About this time his sister, Sarah Fielding, defends him in her curious novel, *The Cry*. " Comic authors ", she writes, " have difficulty in escaping from their prison. The public desires nothing but laughter and jests from them. Let them paint the most agreeable images of human nature, let them ever so accurately search the inmost recesses of the human heart, there is a general outcry up against them, that they are spiritless and dull [3]." This valuable confidence, this

---

[1] Richardson rejoices to note his adversary's confession. On February 22nd, 1752, he writes to Mrs Donnellan : " Mr Fielding has over-written himself, or rather under-written ; and in his own journal seems ashamed of his last piece ; and has promised that the same muse shall write no more for him. The piece, in short, is as dead as if it had been written forty years ago, as to sale." He continues with a few phrases which reveal him in all the blindness of his hatred : " You guess that I have not read *Amelia*. Indeed, I have read but the first volume. I had intended to go through with it ; but I found the characters and situations so wretchedly low and dirty, that I imagined I could not be interested in any one of them."

[2] He was at the time, only forty-four years of age but he speaks of himself in the " trial " of *Amelia*, as an old man.

[3] cf. *The Cry*, a novel by Sarah Fielding and Miss Collier, pp. 169-70. There can be no possible doubt that this passage reproduces Fielding's ideas on Adams and, at the same time, contains an allusion to the half-success of *Amelia*. " That strong and beautiful representation of human nature, exhibited in Don Quixote's madness in one point, and extraordinary good sense in every other, is indeed very much thrown away on such readers as consider him only the object of their mirth. Nor less *understood* (*sic*, but doubtless *misunderstood* is meant) is the character of Parson Adams in *Joseph Andrews*, by those people who, fixing their thoughts on . . . some oddnesses in his behaviour, and

confession of a new intention justifies our having seen in Fielding's last work, something more than a feebler repetition of the themes used in *Tom Jones*. There is no longer any suggestion of the ' comic epic poem in prose '. *Amelia* is a psychological novel in the most modern sense of the term. And if it be sometimes heavy with moral, religious, or social propaganda, if the hand which has painted the characters has lingered over its task so as sometimes to delay the action, we may regret it, but we cannot accuse Fielding of not having accomplished what he set out to do. Perhaps *Amelia* did not find the public which it deserved. The depth and pathos of its analysis have not always been discerned by readers of its own day or of ours. I must ask mine to forgive me, if I have not made them feel these things as deeply as I could have wished [1].

peculiarities in his dress, think proper to overlook the noble simplicity of his mind, with the other innumerable beauties of his character. . . That the ridiculers of Parson Adams are designed to be the proper objects of ridicule (and not that innocent man himself) is a truth which the author hath in many places set in the most glaring light. . .

We are very apt to do as manifest an injury to comic writers, as we do to the characters they represent ; and because they here and there properly embellish their pictures with visible figures, we want to turn the whole into farce, by desiring to see nothing but the grotesque : we expect in every page to meet with such jests as shall distort our features into a broad grin."

[1] I do not know of any contemporary whose judgment of *Amelia* was clearer, whose tone more just (save in a few instances) than Clément, author of *Cinq Années Littéraires* (Letter 91, dated London, January 1st, 1752). His long examination of this work contains a remark on the supposed vulgarity of Fielding which might well be taken as the motto for a study of his genius. " *Rien n'est trop bas dans la nature pour un être vraiment noble.*"

CHAPTER VI

CONCLUSION : FIELDING'S CONCEPTION OF THE NOVEL

In the life of every man there comes a time when he is most fully and powerfully *himself*. When this flowering of the consciousness coincides with an equal maturity of his conscience, of his intelligence and of his artistic sense, the man is ready, if circumstances be favourable, to produce his greatest creation.

Fielding attained this rare and beautiful equilibrium during the ten years of his life which saw the publication of his four great novels. All the richness of his personality is expressed in their diversity : and now that I have analysed these works, I should like to try to examine as a whole that period of his psychological life and literary experience, of which they are the living witnesses.

While passing from one novel to another we have been able to observe a more and more distinct evolution. We may, if we wish to define it straightway by its two extremes, say that Fielding began with a work of intellectual criticism, *Jonathan Wild,* and ended with one of sentiment, *Amelia.*

We do not, strictly speaking, know the exact point at which this evolution started. The plays, which might have enlightened us, are too impersonal an expression, too much governed both by an imperative literary tradition and by the frivolous taste of the paying public, to be regarded as a real confession. Even a paper like *The Champion* cannot be of much use in this respect. It is too much warped by

225

ephemeral political passion, too anxious, moreover, to please those who financed it, to have much value as a human document. On the other hand, I think I have shown that the first version of *Jonathan Wild* would have possessed this psychological value. I have discussed this work at length and have tried to imagine it in its primitive form, before it had been toned down and sentimentalized, in 1743 by the man who wrote *Joseph Andrews*, in 1754 by the author of *Amelia*. And I think I have proved that we may imagine the first version to have been a work of irony, acid and unalloyed ; even in the softened form in which it has reached us, *Jonathan Wild* remains one of the greatest works of irony which have ever been written.

Now, this irony, this play of the intelligence, is to be found yet again in *Joseph Andrews*. But the note is there less marked ; the parody, less profound, no longer attacks an odious character, the corrupt minister, but a ridiculous pedant, the virtuous prig. Finally, with the character of Adams, sentimental comedy makes an entry into Fielding's novels.

We have seen that *Tom Jones* marks the perfect equilibrium between the two extremes of Fielding's comedy. Though still ironical when he is speaking of a Blifil, a Thwackum, or a Square, the author allows sentiment to colour his portraits of Tom, of Sophia, and even of Western. One of the reasons for this is that henceforward his characters are, so to speak, seen and painted from within. More and more do their actions show us, or allow us to guess, the intentions which they hide more often than reveal. More and more often are the motives which prompt the various characters explained to us. But does not this tend, little by little, to do away altogether with comedy ? We can scarcely laugh any more at a comic hero when we understand the deep reasons which have made him commit an apparently ridiculous action. The more we *feel* as he does, the less easy is it for us to assume a detached attitude of amusement. Tom Jones or Sophia

Western, being psychologically richer than Joseph Andrews or Fanny, move us to far more sympathy; but " the greatest foe of laughter is emotion ". One result is that in *Tom Jones* laughter draws further and further away from the protagonists to take refuge among the secondary characters.

The evolution is completed in *Amelia*, the novel of sentimental analysis, the touching story of a real couple embroiled in the complications of a difficult existence. Here, laughter has completely ceased to be the centre of the work; it is no more than one of its ornaments.

Properly speaking, however complete an evolution may be, it can only transform existing elements; St Augustine would never have sought for God if he had not already found him. Thus the last Fielding, the Fielding of the *Examples of the Intervention of Providence* already exists in embryo in the historian of *Jonathan Wild* and his progress to the gallows; similarly, the author of *Amelia* takes up again a subject attempted by the dramatist of *The Modern Husband*. These are proofs of a singular continuity : the point of view alone, has changed from one work to another. Which of these two, the ironical Fielding of the beginning, or the sentimental Fielding of the end, is the *real* Fielding ? Who would dare to say ? Least of all perhaps Fielding himself. At the beginning ' reason ' and at the end ' sentiment ' takes the lead in his psychological life. But both elements are always present, and we have seen how vain it would be to try to separate them.

Yet this evolution of a soul acquires a peculiar importance from the fact that it lies at the very heart of its age. Fielding is, as it were, the deep and explicit conscience of his generation. He has lived with it, better still, he has lived in it.

Let us observe, to begin with, that he has a close, and, one might almost say, a personal acquaintance with all classes of English society. While young and still little more than a child, he is matured by family quarrels and so learns to observe and distrust, and not to rely too much upon others. His residence in Leyden, his visits to London, where doubtless

227

his father introduces him to life, his frequent journeys in the country, his profession as lawyer, his trades as pamphleteer, dramatist and theatrical manager, and finally his post as a magistrate, all these furnish him with the most diverse human documents. Need we add in addition that his birth and education as a gentleman (who remains a gentleman) permit him to *dominate* all this experience. However mediocre the sphere in which a hostile fate may sometimes oblige him to dwell, he can never feel one with his surroundings, as a writer risen from the ranks might have done.   He is Henry Fielding *Esquire ;* is proud of it, proclaims it (and so is never forgiven by his enemies in Grub Street). Richardson who is not a gentleman, in the old sense of the word [1], avenges himself by calling Fielding ' common '. But, on the contrary, it is precisely this which is perhaps one of the secrets of Fielding's greatness. He never allows himself to be overcome by the life which he is observing ; he is the opposite of Richardson who is completely absorbed in the bourgeois existence which he describes. Fielding is detached, like a lawyer or a physician ; he observes and judges life, his own and that of others [2]. With what penetration he scans it, and with what mastery, with what admirable and pathetic lucidity he reproduces it, we have already seen throughout his work, which is crowned by the cruel examination of conscience in *Amelia*.

Fielding is so steeped in his own generation that his personal progress is but an expression of its internal evolution [3].   It has often been said that in the eighteenth

[1] Mr Saintsbury, speaking of Richardson, says a little severely but justly, " unlike Fielding, he was not a ' gentleman ' ".

[2] " Fielding's talent was observation not meditation." (Coleridge, *Anima Poetae*, p. 166, London, Heineman).

[3] Leslie Stephen defined this representative character of Fielding in the following terms : " A complete criticism of the English artistic literature of the eighteenth century would place Fielding at the centre, and measure the completeness of other representatives pretty much as they recede from or approach to his work. Others, as Addison or Goldsmith, may show finer qualities of workmanship and more delicate sentiment ; but Fielding, more than anyone, gives the essential, the very form and pressure of the time." (*English Thought in the Eighteenth Century*, II, p. 380).

century England (and France also) [1] passed from the reign of reason to the reign of sentiment. Summary as it may appear, the statement is both exact and expressive. M. Cazamian [2] has analysed, with a fullness which is here impossible, the swing which carries the English soul during this period from classicism to romanticism, from an ' intellectual ' to an ' imaginative or emotional ' phase, emotional (or sentimental) at first and imaginative later. Launched at the beginning of the century this movement, which was to end in romanticism, hurled itself in turn against the opposition of Addison, Pope, and Johnson, all champions of the threatened discipline. M. Cazamian does well, in my opinion, not to separate their three classic efforts, which are all efforts to check an advancing movement.

This movement which can be just felt at the beginning of the century, becomes decisive towards the middle. It does not, indeed, produce a sudden ' moulting ' in the English soul ; but these years, which almost coincide with the great period of Fielding's genius, are marked by a general growth of the sentimental forces about to regenerate England.

In politics, after the period of scepticism and corruption presided over by Walpole, a series of obscure convulsions prepared the way for the magnificent revival of patriotism which was incarnate in the person of Pitt. In religion this era saw the birth of the great emotion of Methodism, the influence of which among its partisans was as incalculable as

---

[1] Sainte-Beuve, writing of the quarrel between Mme. du Deffand and Mlle de Lespinasse, says very justly : "No union could possibly have lasted between these two women, however sincerely each had sought to preserve it . . . Their generations differed too greatly. Madame du Deffand stood for the century before Jean-Jacques, before the exaltation of the romantic ; her maxim was that ' the note of romance is to passion what copper is to gold '. And Mlle de Lespinasse belonged to that last half of the century, into which romance was entering in full swing."

[2] cf. L. Cazamian, *L'évolution psychologique et la litterature en Angleterre*, Chap. VI. M. Cazamian there defines " le passage du ton rationnel au ton sentimental du moi " which is characteristic of the psychological history of the eighteenth century in England.

was its contagion even among its enemies, for it really decided the form taken by English religious mentality of our own day. Fielding who calls the Methodists ' enthusiasts' (which is as much as to say ' lunatics ') is nevertheless led by the very proximity of this profound faith to examine himself and to return to the more direct, less dogmatic forms of primitive Christianity. The end of the century sees no more of those rationalistic controversies on religion which marked its first half. Arguments can no longer be conducted on ' rational ' lines ; it is possible to discuss with people whose beliefs are founded on reason, but what intellectual reasoning can have any hold on sentiment ? So the old laws, the old religion no longer satisfy. The time has come for patriotic sentiment, in the guise of Pitt, to remake that national unity which the old despised authority was powerless to re-establish [1]; religious sentiment, thanks to Methodism and the renewed sensibilities which it brings with it, creates once again that spirit of religion which had been almost destroyed by the controversy for and against the Deists.

The revival is equally marked in the sphere of ethics, which cannot for that matter be separated from religion. And here the victory of sentiment was all the more easy, since its ethics are always the weak point of every intellectualist system. What moral ideal had the intellectual age of Congreve or even of Pope ? Richardson writes *Pamela*, and Fielding makes abundant fun of him in *Joseph Andrews*. But what moral standard does he propose to put in its place ? We have tried to define it in speaking of *Tom Jones* ; altruism, the feeling of goodness, an ingenious blend of stoicism and Christianity, in which the moral standard of Christ, which is a sentimental standard, will play (in *Amelia*) a more and more preponderant part. So Fielding himself preaches a morality based upon sentiment, upon religious sentiment.

It is remarkable how universal the movement is at this

---

[1] Fielding's papers did much to encourage this revival of patriotic sentiment.

period and how much circumstances help to determine it. Fielding is not completely absorbed by it until he writes *Amelia*; that is to say, he is not completely carried away by the new current, until the day when his experience as a magistrate enables him to plumb to the depths the demoralization of a society, which he had up to the present thought rather frivolous than vicious. When the Bow Street justice becomes aware that the intellectual criticism which destroys institutions and beliefs has shaken the very bedrock of society, he feels the urgent need for a reform which, if it is to act rapidly in the spheres which it ought to reach first, must be a *sentimental* reform ; hence his *Examples*, hence certain pages of *Amelia*. Nothing could show, more clearly than this conversion brought about by Fielding's experience, the extent to which social and political conditions have made the will to reform imperative, towards the middle of the century. It is like sap rising from all sides to regenerate the old rotten tree.

But the agents of this reform are not all pure sentimentalists. Fielding, Hogarth, Garrick, and Handel, whom I am fain to associate with them, accept and employ sentiment, but they have no desire to escape the intellectual discipline of art. In the course of the eighteenth century, two literary generations tried in turn to preserve the classical order. Pope's generation succeeded in keeping the traditional forms intact. Nor did that of Johnson modify them, but it saw the magnificent success of a new literary genre, more supple and better adapted to sensibilities impatient for reform, it saw the modern novel, the artistic transposition of daily reality.

Again Fielding's career is as eminently ' representative ' of this purely literary evolution as it was of the psychological and moral transformation of his contemporaries. He, too, like the writers of the age of Pope, has sought at first to express himself in the classical forms, the Poem (epistle or satire), the Essay and, above all, the Drama, in which he seems for some time to think that he has found his medium. But in none of them can he incarnate his genius, because these classical forms are now sterile and outworn, and only live on the memories of a past glory. And now circumstances having driven Fielding from the theatre, set him on the path of a new form of art wherein the free flight of his inspiration will be hampered by no obsolete tradition. No doubt he was not responsible for the birth of the novel. Neither Fielding, nor anyone else, is the ' Father of the English Novel '. It existed already ; it has always existed since men existed, who loved to hear stories. But it had not yet produced in England any of those masterpieces which bow posterity beneath the weight of their prestige. For masters Fielding has to go back to Lucian, to the *Æneid*, to the *Odyssey*. Here lay his great opportunity : Dryden and Pope, who expressed themselves in artistic forms which were already under sentence of death, are to-day very nearly dead to modern readers. Fielding, on the contrary, had the good fortune to enter upon an almost new *genre*, and having once encountered it, immediately imposed his laws upon it.

Although a very clear psychological and moral evolution may be observed from *Jonathan Wild* to *Amelia*, Fielding's works are all nevertheless closely related. Their profound unity is a unity of art. For all the shades and differences which we have observed in their due time, there is a certain conception of the novel which is specifically Fielding's, or at least a particular note which is heard in one work after another, and which is the authentic mark of his own genius.

Its essence does not lie in his subjects, nor in the incidents worked into his plot. " The fellow has no invention ", said Richardson disdainfully ; and indeed, the basis of these incidents is often borrowed from the common stock of the picaresque novelists or from contemporary life. But it is in the regrouping of these elements that Fielding's mastery is so brilliantly manifest. A little clumsy in *Jonathan Wild*, which still resembles the usual ' biographies ', he finds his method in *Joseph Andrews* when he decides to construct his novel according to the principles of dramatic action. The plot of *Tom Jones* is directed on these principles, with a perfection which is almost too severe ; and in *Amelia*, under an influence derived from Virgil, this severity at last becomes more flexible.

Properly speaking, and to use the terms of its inventor, the novel of Fielding is a comic epic poem in prose. And I believe that Fielding invented it quite consciously, using, on the one hand, his dramatic experience, and, on the other, his classical education and the rules of the epic as interpreted by the critics, and, above all, by the French critics. It is significant that he often quotes Le Bossu and always with the greatest respect. Whoever has the curiosity to re-read this worthy abbé's *Traité du Poème Epique* cannot fail to notice an interesting kinship between his ideas and those which Fielding expresses whenever he speaks of the theory of his art [1]. I fear that literary historians have not given serious

[1] Sarah Fielding likewise quotes Le Bossu and quotes him in French. The *Treatise of the Epic Poem* was an eighteenth century classic, which had often been translated into English. The following passages afford some interesting comparisons with Fielding. After defining the Epic Le Bossu adds, " If a man were to write an epic in prose would it be the same thing as an epic poem ? I think not, for a poem is a discourse in *verse. But this would not prevent it from being an epic nevertheless.*" Elsewhere we see the dawn of the theory of the ' vulgar ' novel. " The commonalty are as subject as are great lords to lose their estates and ruin their families by their wrath and divisions, and by the negligence and little care they have of their business. They have as great need of Homer's lessons as have kings and are as capable of profiting by them." Here again is an observation which is applied to the letter in *Tom Jones*. " These three parts of a single whole are denoted in a very vague and general manner by the terms beginning, middle, and end. We may interpret them more precisely and say that the causes and designs which lead one to do an Action are the beginning of that Action ; that the effects of these causes and the difficulties which are met with in the execution of these designs are the middle thereof, and that the unravelling and resolution of these difficulties is the end of the Action. This unravelling and end may come about in different ways.... For sometimes the Action ends with the recognition of some person who was unknown before. Sometimes, without any such recognition, some person undergoes a great change of fortune, etc." (p. 145). Again the following, on the subject of happy endings : " Our poets have given us no examples of a hero who remains unfortunate and succumbs. Sad endings are proper for tragedy, but these

enough consideration to the epic-novel as expounded, if not invented, by Fielding. He seems to me really to have tried by this to give the novel its classical letters patent, to establish it once for all as a literary *genre* ; and he himself in practice observes the ' laws ' of the epic with increasing fidelity. Here again as in his psychological or moral evolution, we recognize in him the universal effort of Johnson's generation to make new demands harmonize with traditional rules.

A criticism so well-considered and an attempt so lucid would suffice to place Fielding far above not only the novelists of adventure but also Richardson, who was content to use the

reasons will not serve for the Epic, since it serves less to purge the passions than *to make men leave off evil habits and take on good ones* " (pp. 193-4). It will be remembered that Fielding advised Richardson to give *Clarissa* a happy ending ; would that we knew his arguments. " But ", writes Le Bossu elsewhere, " care must likewise be taken that no Action or Adventure of any length be described, without persons who are interested therein." Almost all Fielding's narratives are interrupted by an amused or moved audience. One is reminded too of what Fielding wrote in *Jonathan Wild*, in which he wished to write a biography which should be truer than nature, by recounting therein all that his hero might or ought to have done. Here is Le Bossu on the subject : " Homer, Virgil, and the rest have made no scruple in disregarding History, in order to make their Fables seem more real. Aristotle seems to confirm this doctrine when he teaches that a poet, unlike an historian, does not set down what Alcibiades was, what he did, or what he said in this or that encounter ; but only what with the most probability he should have said or done " (p. 251).
One remembers how Fielding wrote of his different landladies. This also is in accordance with Father Le Bossu's teaching, " . . . for valour in general must be distinguished from the valour of Achilles, neither must that be confounded with the valour of Æneas " (p. 389)
Finally this is how he speaks of the ' bad examples ' which may be given by the epic. It is the same argument often used by Fielding to defend himself from the charge of having described bad characters : " These reflections are not designed to exclude from Poetry all that is condemned by Morality. A Poet should never set a bad example, but there is a great difference between a bad example and the example of a bad action or of a wicked person " (p. 389).
All this is obviously a little pedantic, but the pedantry would not strike contemporaries who were accustomed to this sort of criticism, in the same way as it strikes a modern reader. Fielding was, I am convinced, perfectly sincere when he tried to write his comic epic poem in prose, and Adams's appreciation of Homer in *Joseph Andrews* is not a mere *trait* in the picture of an old scholar. There is something more behind it.

epistolary novel without change [1]. In fact, as Mr Saintsbury remarks, Fielding's literary creation is so rich that " almost every kind of novel exists potentially in his Four ", from the social novel or ' slice of life ' to the novel of psychological analysis, of which certain pages of *Amelia* are a perfect example.

The personal method of the author makes this diversity one and individual. Were I asked to define Fielding's great contribution to the history of the English novel I should be inclined to find it in this. For the first time in reading his novels one has the impression of a man who is the master of his narrative. From the very first page he knows where he is going and how to get there. No more adventures flung down helter-skelter, no more heroes tossed about by the hazards of life, until the end shall consign them to death. Smollett, who has perhaps an even greater wealth of imagination than Fielding, was to show his inferiority by returning to a less artistic conception of the novel as a chain of adventures loosely linked together by the life of the central hero [2].

But Fielding is like the master of a house who is showing his visitors round ; he takes them only where he wishes, and he has made a personal choice of what he is going to let them see. With this sovereign artist we are always brought back to the idea of a personal synthesis of different elements. The sources of his inspiration are innumerable, but they are all transmuted into Fielding.

[1] For example, *The Letters of a Portuguese Nun* or *The Letters of a Turkish Spy*, which were so popular during the whole of the eighteenth century ; cf. C. E. Morgan, *The Rise of the Novel of Manners*.

[2] In his preface to *Ferdinand, Count Fathom*, Smollett thus defines the novel : " A novel is a large diffused picture, comprehending the characters of life, disposed in different groups and exhibited in various attitudes, for the purposes of a uniform plan and general occurrence, to which every individual figure is subservient. But this plan cannot be executed with propriety, probability, or success, without a principal personage to attract the attention, unite the incidents, unwind the clue of the labyrinth, and at last close the scene, by virtue of his own importance." This is to return to Le Sage's method, and to the grouping of incidents round a biography.

He observes the whole of reality, shutting his eyes to no part of it. He then selects a few characteristics, which he considers the most expressive. But before making his choice, he has looked at everything, and we feel it. This again places him at the very antipodes of Richardson, who only sees one half of the moral realities and is not even curious about the other half. Fielding discriminates. Our discussion of the four novels has drawn attention to the meticulous perfection with which he collects the most significant material details. The whole of contemporary England lives in them with an accuracy of information which we can control by historical documents or memoirs. For instance I open at random the *Journal* in which Mrs Calderwood describes a journey made in 1756, two years after Fielding's death. Her description of English roads conforms word for word with the one in *Tom Jones*[1]. It is always so with Fielding. He takes everything from life ; for his main ' sources ' you would have to go to the reports of news in the gazettes of his time. But which of these episodes does he retain ? Partial, like all historians, who only retain the facts which they deem 'significant', how does this historian portray his epoch ?

[1] For example Mrs Calderwood describes how between Doncaster and Bantry a suspicious-looking horseman came riding up to their coach. In order to send him away " John Ratty pretended to make a quarrel with the post-boy, and let him know so loud as to be heard by the other, that he kept good powder and ball to keep such folks as him in order ; upon which the fellow scampered off 'cross the common. Upon our coming to Bantry, we were told that a gentleman was robbed there some days before by a man whose description answered to the one we saw " (*Letters and Journals of Mrs Calderwood*, Edinburgh, 1884, p. 5). At Stilton the inn is good but the linen " as perfect rags as ever I saw, plain linen with fifty holes in each towel " (p. 7). She makes this amusing reflection on the " waiting gentlewomen " dear to Fielding : " June 9th, from Stilton we dined at Hatfield, where there was a great many coaches in the courtyard with company leaving London, and every family had a coach full of abigalls (*sic*) who held a most prodigious chattering and scolding at not having proper attendance given them " (p. 7). This is the true Fielding touch.

She writes at Spa : " All Richison's (*sic*) books are translated and much admired abroad : but for Fielding's the foreigners have no notion of them and do not understand them as the manners are so utterly English " (p. 208). This, however, is only a hasty generalization after a conversation.

His first care is for truth ; but if you want to attain truth in art your portrayal must often be made too true. Hence his occasional appearance of exaggeration ; one thinks that he is forcing a note, when he is really only isolating it, or setting it against a contrast. It is possible that this may be due to the influence of contemporary caricature, and one may even find in it a relic of his sojourn in Holland, the cradle of this art [1]. Be this as it may, although in the preface of *Joseph Andrews* he is careful to distinguish *character* from *caricature*, Fielding, who claims to have the same ideas on the subject as his friend Hogarth, is at pains, with a skill worthy of that great artist, to isolate the individual character-istic and engrave it on the memory by repetition : ' the rule of right ' and ' the eternal fitness of things ' of Thwackum and Square are instances of this. He sets before us types of the England of his time, which is about to disappear for ever, the England of the *Marriage à la Mode*, *The Harlot's Progress*, and *The Rake's Progress* : the England of just before the industrial revolution, the England of coaches, squires, inn-keepers, and barber-surgeons, the England of the country and village, a little scandalized at London. Neither he nor his contemporaries had any premonition of the imminent economic transformation, the growth of big towns, nor the approaching turbulence of a conscious democracy. He still belongs to an epoch when the poor can be depicted without too much

---

[1] The English caricature of the eighteenth century seems to have come from Holland with the artists who followed William of Orange. The Italian word ' caricatura ' was introduced into England in the first half of the eighteenth century. In 1742 Gray wrote to his friend Mr Chute, who was in Florence, " The wit of the times consists in satyrical prints ; I believe there have been some hundreds within this month. If you have any hopeful young designer of caricaturas, that has a political turn, he may pick up a pretty subsistence here : *let him pass through Holland to improve his taste* by the way " (cf. Paston, *Social Caricature in the XVIIIth Century*).

Hogarth has an engraving entitled ' Characters and caricatures ', dated 1743. He comments " For a further explanation of the differ-ence betwixt character and caricature, see the Preface to *Joseph Andrews*." The engraving represents a quantity of heads, some of which are ' characters ' and the others ' caricatures '.

bitterness, for he still most often paints the poor of the country side, where poverty is less pitiless. It is only towards the end of his life that he comes into contact with the submerged classes of London, and they make a deep impression upon him. All his earlier work shows us a picture of merry England, which went to *The Beggar's Opera* and rolled with laughter at its thieves.

The frank gaiety of his realism (which is already becoming a little tearful in *Amelia*), is one of the elements which gives it its peculiar quality. There are others, among the most characteristic of which is perhaps the recurrence from one novel to another of certain themes, and favourite features, which he regards as more particularly true. It is to details such as these that Fielding's novels owe their special atmosphere and their individual shade of feeling. A poor wretch in need of help is universally repulsed, and in the end receives it from someone more miserable than himself ; an innkeeper, amiable to begin with, swiftly changes front when he discovers that his client is poor ; a worthy but imprudent man is persecuted because appearances are against him ; an over-shrewd man arrives after a long process of deduction, to logical conclusions which are immediately disproved by facts ; a fond lover speaks enthusiastically of his lady, but almost immediately betrays her with a casual acquaintance. One might multiply these themes, each of which, framed in different circumstances, reappears several times in Fielding's work.

Now, most of these incidents are there for something more than a momentary amusement. They are philosophical. At the bottom of each is a realism even more penetrating than the realism of material detail, a psychological realism, which laughs to see fine theories shattered by the vulgar truth of daily life.

The essential thing about Fielding is his effort to plumb deep and reach the truth. Try, he seems to say, to see into yourself, do not stop at the moral or immoral appearance of an action : the prudish Pamela may be an artful little minx, the virtuous Blifil a rogue, and Square, the moralist, a hypocrite. Go deeper than words and judge deeds ; go deeper than deeds and judge intentions, which are the immediate expression of the soul ; go deeper even than *conscious* intentions. Whoever has made an impartial self-analysis knows how difficult it is to recognize, even in himself, the actual beneath the apparent motives for an action [1].

To this striving after psychological realism which is even more profound than the realism of concrete details we owe some of the most beautiful of Fielding's pages. It is the very foundation of his comedy, contrasting the rigidity of our illusions (about ourselves and others), with the unforeseen changefulness of life [2].

It is not to be expected that I should seek here to cabin and confine in a few formulae this comedy of Fielding, so modulated and varied from one novel to another. To define it exactly would be like an attempt to put into words that *nescio quid individuum* in every human being, which escapes the most subtle analysis. His comedy is himself ; it is his, Henry Fielding's judgment upon the men and things of his time, and upon himself.

We said just now that he was undoubtedly the first novelist in the history of English literature to give the impression of dominating his narrative. This domination is also to be found in his comedy, and rises here to greater heights ; from being artistic it becomes philosophical. Through the spirit of comedy Fielding dominates the characters whom he creates.

As early as his preface to *Joseph Andrews* he carefully distinguishes his own laughter from that of burlesque or

---

[1] cf. F. Paulhan, *Les Mensonges du caractère*, Alcan, Paris. This is where Richardson is so inferior to Fielding. He is taken in by Pamela. He does not see through her or Clarissa. He does not unmask them.

[2] An example of this contrast in its simplest form is Adams's display of vanity just after his sermon against it, or Square's biting his tongue and swearing in the midst of a lecture to Tom on despising pain.

caricature, which he leaves to the picaresque school. Behind
Swift, Molière, and Cervantes, he seeks to reach the hand of
Lucian ; and the philosophy which we have traced in his
own work is indeed analogous to that of the great cynic. His
laughter (and this is one of the chief complaints which
compatriots made and still make against him) upsets conventions, or rather does not even notice them. He cares little
whether a hero be aristocratic or ' low ' ; the essential thing
is that he should be comic, that is to say, he should lend himself to the contrasts born of that psychological realism which
we have mentioned. He cares little, too, if those contrasts
shock the traditions of decency, or morality ; Tom Jones is
for some time afraid that he has been his mother's lover,
and Joseph Andrews that he has been betrothed to his sister.
It is obvious that Fielding finds these errors ' comic '. So
completely unfettered is his mind. When pure from any
mixture, this detachment from the contingencies and
associations of traditional ideas is the point of view of the
mind judging in the absolute. Usually, however, and with
increasing success as his work advances, Fielding tempers and
softens this too severe comedy with a gentle mockery. We
have often had occasion to compare his attitude and method
with those of Molière [1]. He follows Molière's imitators of the
Restoration Theatre, translates him, and is frequently,
sometimes literally, inspired by him. This emigration of
Molière's laughter [2]. is a very curious thing ; this ' virile

---

[1] Some of his contemporaries noticed the relationship. The
Correspondance littéraire of Grimm and Diderot, written after *Amelia*,
describes Fielding as " a very original author, a great artist, always
truthful and sometimes as sublime as Molière " (Aug. 1st, 1753).

[2] It would perhaps be better to say that Fielding takes up again
from Molière a comedy which is universal. It is also curious to see
Fielding's conception of the comic analysed in advance by *Descartes* in
his *Traité des Passions*. " Derision or scorn is a sort of joy mingled
with hatred, which proceeds from our perceiving some small evil in
a person whom we consider to be deserving of it ; and when that
comes upon us unexpectedly, the surprise of wonder is the cause of our
bursting into laughter in accordance with what has been said above
on the nature of laughter. [*i.e.*, a physiological explanation of laughter]
... But this evil must be small, for if it is great, we cannot believe that

CONCEPTION OF THE NOVEL

gaiety [1] of which there is only a passing echo in the French
novel, now passes into the English novel through the medium
of a dramatist expelled from the stage.

For Fielding's laughter *has* remained in the English novel.
He obliged it to continue as a *comic* novel, or, if a less general
term be preferred, a humorous novel : and by that I mean a
novel of *personal* comedy.

I do not, by any means, wish to suggest that his influence
extends no further. He gave the example, the formula of a
more exacting method of building up the plot, which never
quite disappeared after him. In 1749, a critic in *The London
Magazine*, defining as a classic type Fielding's conception of
the novel, describes it as " a novel or prose epic composition "
which " like all such good compositions, consists of a principal
history and a great many episodes or incidents ; all of which
arise naturally from the subject and contribute towards
carrying on the chief plot or design, etc." [2] In point of fact

he who has it is deserving of it, unless when we are of a very evil nature
to bear much hatred towards him." (Descartes, *Traité des Passions*,
Art. 178, Trans. Elizabeth S. Haldane and G. R. T. Ross). The date
of the *Treatise* in 1646-9.
These remarks could be illustrated by examples from Fielding whose
Comedy varies according as he is dealing with a sympathetic Tom
Jones, or a Blifil towards whom one " bears 'much hatred ". See,
too, Art. 189 of the same *Treatise*.
Fielding's ideas may also be compared with those of a French
critic, Abbé (Morvan de) Bellegarde, whom he frequently quotes and
whose *Réflections sur le Ridicucle* was very successful. The translation,
*Reflextions upon Ridicule ; or what it is that makes a man ridiculous
and the means to avoid it*, etc., had reached its fifth edition in 1739.
It is also obvious that Fielding owes a great deal to Shaftesbury's
Characteristics.
[1] *mâle gaité* (Musset).
[2] *The London Magazine and Monthly Intelligencer* of Feb. 1749
devotes its leading article to a résumé of *Tom Jones*, " being a novel
or prose epic compostion, and calculated to recommend religion and
virtue, to show the bad consequences of indiscretion, and to set several
kinds of vice in their most deformed and shocking light. This piece
like all such good compositions, consists of a principal history and a
great many episodes or incidents : all of which arise naturally from the
subject and contribute towards carrying on the chief plot or design.
Through the whole the reader's attention is always kept awake by
some new surprising accident, and his curiosity upon the stretch, to
discover the effects of that accident ; so that after one has begun to
read, it is difficult to leave off before having read the whole."

241

Fielding's successors have too often failed to see behind these episodes, the profound unity and inward movement of his works. We have already mentioned Smollett. Numerous are the incidents and adventures which he has borrowed from Fielding [1]. On the other hand, there is a very close relationship between Parson Adams and Goldsmith's *Vicar of Wakefield*. But these are great writers. With lesser writers the imitation of the outward aspect of the domestic novel had become so common that, even in Fielding's time, readers had begun to weary of it. In 1754 the novelist's sister, Sarah, and her friend, Miss Collier, wrote in the preface to their novel, *The Cry*: " Stories and novels have flowed in such abundance for these last ten years that we would wish, if possible, to strike a little out of a road already so much beaten ", and they conclude with a sentence in which it is tempting to trace the influence of our dramatist turned novelist : " The nearer things are brought to dramatic representation, the more are you acquainted with the personages, and interested in the event of the story " (p. 11) [2].

---

[1] There was a Smollett-Fielding controversy, but its interest is almost purely anecdotal. Smollett was apparently jealous of Fielding Incidentally, *Roderick Random* borrows numerous episodes from *Joseph Andrews*. *Ferdinand Count Fathom* is often reminiscent of *Jonathan Wild* and the *Adventures of an Atom* more than once recalls *The Journey from this World to the Next*. In the first edition of *Peregrine Pickle* Smollett painted Fielding under the name of ' Mr Spondy ' and alluded to his second marriage. The passage was deleted from the later editions but after Fielding had spoken jestingly of ' Roderick Random ' and ' Peregrine Pickle ' in his *Covent Garden Journal*, Smollett published in January, 1752 a coarse and violent pamphlet entitled : *A faithful narrative of the base and inhuman arts that were practised upon the brains of Habbakuk Hilding, Justice, Dealer and Chapman.*

[2] " Our intention in the following pages is not to amuse with a number of surprising incidents and adventures, but rather to paint the inward mind " (p. 7). The following also suggests Fielding : " Let it be remembered that human nature is the picture we intend to paint " (p. 10).
For the swarm of novels after Fielding and Richardson, cf. Chandler, *The Literature of Roguery*, p. 328. George Colman wrote a farce entitled *Polly Honeycomb* (1760) in which he jeered at novel-readers and gave in his preface a list of 182 works which had appeared in ten years. cf. Dobson, *Eighteenth Century Vignettes*, 3rd series.

All these imitators copied only the form. The soul escaped them. When once the novel of adventure *à la* Fielding, had ceased to be fashionable, this medley of imitations fell into oblivion while the fame of their original steadily increased. Is it not a singularly eloquent fact that an edition of his ' complete ' works (as the term was then understood) furnished with notes and a biography, was published in 1762, eight years after his death, and reprinted in 1770 ? Richardson had to wait until 1811 for such an edition of his works.

Fielding was just as successful with the French public. An American critic, Mr F. S. Dickson, has recently counted the editions of Fielding in France and on the continent during the course of the eighteenth century and has compared the result with the number of editions of Richardson. The comparison is distinctly to Fielding's advantage [1]. In spite of translators who were mediocre or worse (*Tom Jones* has never been put into good French) the editor of *L'année littéraire* [2] described Fielding as having " achieved immortality through his novels *Tom Jones* and *Joseph Andrews* ", adding " to-day we worship the very ground on which he trod." Perhaps it is not too late to hope that one day a good French version will be published of one of these great classics of humanity.

But infinitely more interesting than the commercial success of his work is the deep and personal influence exercised by his genius. For it is in this that the real life of a work lies. Up to the time of Meredith and our most recent contemporaries, the English novel has followed Fielding's law : it is a domestic novel, interrupted or accompanied, more or less explicitly, by the humorous comments of the author. It is true that Sir Walter Scott is more particularly struck by the ample, sure construction of *Tom Jones* and of *Amelia,* of which he speaks interestingly in the introduction

[1] cf. F. S. Dickson, *Notes and Queries*, Jan. 6th, 1917.
[2] *L   'e littéraire,* 1763, II. p. 26.

to *The Fortunes of Nigel*[1]. While if Jane Austen, too, may be said to borrow from Fielding her descriptions of daily life and manners, they are like miniatures of his great pictures [2].

But with the two great Victorian novelists the vein of Fielding's inspiration reappears in all its wealth. Dickens, who was, perhaps, more attracted by Smollett, nevertheless confesses the extent of his debt to Fielding [3]. And Thackeray, so irritating when he pronounces judgment on him from his pinnacle, so unjust when he criticizes him, even he tries in all good faith to be a ' better ' Fielding. Is there much difference at bottom between the vanity and affectation which Fielding recognized as the two great sources of his comic and the snobbery against which Thackeray wages war ? Thackeray certainly draws a more complicated society and his cynicism, which awoke deeper echoes in a more analytical generation, may, at first sight, seem more philosophical than that of his spiritual ancestor. But one has only to observe them at grips with an analogous subject in order to feel the superiority of the master. *The Memoirs of Barry Lyndon* transcribes the *History of Mr Jonathan Wild the Great* for the respectable readers of the Victorian age. The sober, pungent irony of the old author is diluted into a gossiping and facile drawing-room philosophy. " They cry fie now upon men engaged in

[1] " Fielding had high notions of the dignity of an art which he may be considered as having founded. He challenges a comparison between the Novel and the Epic. Smollett, Le Sage, and others, emancipating themselves from the strictness of the rules he has laid down, have written rather a history of the miscellaneous adventures which befall an individual in the course of his life than the plot of a regular and connected epopeia, where every step brings us a point nearer to the final catastrophe " (*The Fortunes of Nigel. Introductory Epistle*). The mistake about Le Sage who, in fact, wrote before Fielding, need not be enlarged upon.

[2] cf. Horne, *Technique of the Novel*, p. 154, for a very acute analysis of the points of resemblance between Miss Austen and Fielding.

[3] cf. particularly Gissing, *Charles Dickens*, p. 26, where he shows us the child Dickens " with a head full of Partridge, Strap, and Tom Pipes, and Sancho Panza . . Smollett, Fielding. . when eight or nine years old Charles Dickens read them rapturously, all but got them by heart." etc. See Frank Wilson, *Dickens in Seinen Beziehungen zu den Humoristen, Fielding und Smollett*, Leipzig, 1894.

play ; but I should like to know how much more honourable their modes of livelihood are than ours. The broker of the exchange who bulls and bears, and buys and sells, and dabbles with lying loans, and trades on state-secrets, what is he but a gamester ? The merchant, etc.[1] " For a whole page this brilliant talker goes on about the banker, the doctor, or the lawyer, talking, talking, talking. When we remember the pitiless irony of *Jonathan Wild*, so brutal and so direct, *Barry Lyndon* gives the impression of a Hogarth adapted for the bourgeois readers of *Punch*, just as *Pendennis* often gives the effect of being a *Tom Jones ad usum Victoriae* [2].

I would not have it thought that I am attempting here to form a more or less exact estimate of Fielding's influence, or to trace its curve with the aid of elements which must always be insufficient. In literature more than in anything else ' the letter kills ', and actual instances of borrowing do not always prove the depth of an influence so clearly as some other less evident symptom. It was Fielding's *tone* which imposed itself upon the English novel of the nineteenth century ; and perhaps the surest and least expected witness to this is to be found in certain passages of Meredith, at which I defy any reader of *Tom Jones* not to prick up his ears as though at the sound of a well-known voice [3].

[1] *Barry Lyndon*, IX. Thackeray made the great mistake there of writing memoirs instead of a ' history '. The use of the first person deprives the ironical passages of much of their naturalness : a rogue would not speak of himself in this way. Fielding speaking of Jonathan Wild as an ' historian ' retains the mastery of his subject.

Bulwer Lytton's *Paul Clifford* was also influenced to a great extent by *Jonathan Wild*.

[2] Even the title *The History of Pendennis, his Fortunes and Misfortunes, his Friends and his greatest Enemy* (this enemy being himself) reminds us of *Tom Jones*, who, Fielding tells us, is " nobody's enemy but his own ".

[3] I quote one passage, among many, from *Evan Harrington*. A brilliant cricketer is being described. " But there were reasons for Nick's rare display of skill. That woman may have the credit due to her (and, as there never was a contest at which she did not sit at the springs, so is she source of all superhuman efforts exhibited by men), be it told that Polly Wheedle is on the field ; Polly, one of the upper

THE NOVELS OF FIELDING

This is not the place to discuss whether the English novel will ever free itself from the imperious tradition of humour which was imposed upon it ' for better for worse ' the day that *Joseph Andrews* appeared. But we need not be surprised if Fielding is sometimes attacked by the ' moderns '. If one dislikes the classical novel it is logical enough to strike at the head of the line [1].

Fielding has other enemies. The most numerous are readers who through indolence or lack of psychological acumen, are unable to appreciate all the wealth and delicate shading of his pictures. Such people may perhaps find *Joseph Andrews* mediocre and *Tom Jones* commonplace. Others who have never yet rid themselves of the conventions of a more or less pharasaïcal respectability are prone to look upon Fielding as an immoral novelist, particularly dangerous for the young. And we are still far from the day, desired by John Oliver

housemaids of Beckley Court ; Polly, eagerly courted by Fred Linnington, humbly desired by Nick Frim—a pert and blooming maiden—who, while her suitors combat hotly for an undivided smile, improves her holiday by instilling similar unselfish aspirations into the breasts of others " (Ch. XII, p. 131).

cf. also this, at the end of a chapter : " For the present I pause, in observance of those rules which demand that after an exhibition of consummate deeds, time be given to the spectator to digest what has passed before him " (Ch. XXXII).

[1] Take, for example, an article by Mr James Stephens which appeared in the *English Review* of April, 1914, entitled *An Essay in Cubes* : " The masters of fiction have seldom risen above the level of an after-dinner speaker. The thought of these men does not often rise above banality, etc. A notable example of the after-dinner writer who has attained to fame is Fielding . . . he will say (pleasantly, I admit) what every other after-dinner speaker would have said upon the same incentive." and calls " a glorified mediocrity ". Humour " may be defined as the last refuge of the intellectually destitute ". It is the most accessible form of wit. Novelists judging one another, have ended by forming " a standard of value . . . which is the present classical novel ", and this classical novel is impregnated with humour.

All writers of ' Comedy ' might just as easily be reproached with mediocrity : it is all too evident that they are not thinkers. But it would be just as unfair to say, for example, of Kant that " he could not tell a story ", and to make it a reproach against him.

Hobbes, when *Tom Jones* and *Amelia* will be given to every girl on her eighteenth birthday [1].

Yet the fame of Fielding grows. He sought passionately and anxiously for the truth alone, and so he rallies round him all those who seek it with a soul as honest as his.

Careful biographers have already wiped out most of the calumnies which for so long stained his memory. All who are stopped by such minor issues of glory and who cannot admire a work if they do not also admire the private life of its author may henceforth read *Tom Jones* without any scruples of conscience. But Fielding's real intimates had never any need of such a rehabilitation. It is through his work and in his work that they love him, because they have felt the living pulse of genius beating in it, forever young.

---

[1] " The epics of *Tom Jones* and *Amelia* ought to be given to every girl on her eighteenth birthday . . . carefully read and taken to heart, they would save women from innumerable mistakes and tears." This article of John Oliver Hobbes (Mrs Craigie), in defence of Fielding, appeared in *The Academy*, July 16, 1904. See also, as an indication of an interesting tendency, an article in the *Journal of Education*, July, 1897 on *Tom Jones as a safe novel*. Lastly, there are some curious passages on *Tom Jones* in Jerome K. Jerome's book, *They and I*.

BIBLIOGRAPHICAL NOTES

In Wilbur L. Cross, *The History of Henry Fielding* (3 vols., Yale University Press, 1918) there is a very complete *Bibliography* under the following headings : (1) *Fielding's Published Works* ; (2) *Uncertain or Doubtful Authorship* ; (3) *Works erroneously attributed to Fielding* ; (4) *Dramas on Fielding or his works* ; (5) *Letters and manuscripts*. This bibliography is admirably done.

The FIRST EDITIONS OF THE NOVELS are all in the British Museum and in the Bibliothèque Nationale.

MODERN EDITIONS OF THE NOVELS are numerous, but it is difficult to recommend one rather than another. The text generally used is that of Murphy, which is far from being faultless. It would be better to have reprinted the text of each work according to the last edition published during the life of the author, and to note the variants since the first edition. In this case *Jonathan Wild* would be reprinted from the text of 1754 ; and *Amelia* from the text set up by Murphy from a copy corrected by Fielding's own hand.

The text of *Tom Jones*, as it has come down to us, seems to me subject to special caution. For example, the second edition has considerably curtailed the regrettable digression of " The Man of the Hill ". The third and later editions revert to the text of the first, which is inferior. This may possibly be due to a printer's error. In any case *Tom Jones* stands in particular need of a critical edition, and this would be no light task.

THE NOVELS OF FIELDING

The following is a list of the principal FRENCH TRANS-LATIONS. The greater number are adaptations rather than translations, and many passages have been deleted :

Les Adventures de Joseph Andrews, etc., traduction de Desfontaines 1743 ; Nouvelle traduction par Lumnier 1807.

Histoire de Jonathan Wild le Grand, trad. Ch. Picquet, London, 1763.

Julien l'Apostat (Voyage de notre monde en l'autre), Rheims, 1754 ; and (trad. Kaufmann) 1768.

Histoire de Tom Jones, trad. de la Place, Amsterdam, 1750 ; other editions, Paris, 1751 (3rd), 1767, 1783, 1784.

Later translations by Le citoyen Davaux, Paris an IV (1796) ; by Chéron, 1804 ; by de la Bédoyère, Paris, 1833 ; and by Defaucoupret, Paris, 1833.

Amélie, trad. Mme. Riccoboni, Paris, 1762 ; trad. Philippe Flount des Ruisieux, Geneva, 1782.

Several dramatic adaptations of *Tom Jones* have been attempted in France.

(1) *Tom Jones* : lyrical comedy in three acts, performed for the first time February 27th, 1765, by the Comédiens Italiens du Roy. Music by A. D. Philidor and words by Poinsinet.

(2) *Tom Jones à Londres* : comedy in 5 acts in verse, performed for the first time October 22nd, 1782 ; by Desforges.

(3) *Tom Jones et Fellamar*, continuation of *Tom Jones à Londres* : comedy in 5 acts, in verse, performed for the first time April 17th, 1787. Same author as the preceding.

(4) Mr Cross also mentions a play in manuscript (in five acts), which is in the Yale University Library, entitled *Tom Jones, Comédie*.

(5) *Le portrait de Fielding* : play in one act, containing vaudevilles by Ségur jeune, Desfaucheret, and Despres. Produced for the first time April 23rd, 1800.

BIBLIOGRAPHICAL NOTES

II General Sources

[Only original works and a choice of works of proved utility are here cited.]

(a) BIOGRAPHY OF FIELDING

ARTHUR MURPHY, *Essay on the Life and Genius of Henry Fielding, Esq.* (Introduction to the edition of Fielding's works published by Millar in 1762)

W. M. THACKERAY, in his *English Humourists of the Eighteenth Century* (1853).

FREDERICK LAWRENCE, *The Life of Henry Fielding; with notices of his writings, his times, and his contemporaries* (1855).

THOMAS KEIGHTLEY, *On the Life and Writings of Henry Fielding,* in *Fraser's Magazine,* January and February, 1858.

AUSTIN DOBSON, *Fielding* (English Men of Letters series), 1883 ; 2nd edit. 1907).

G. M. GODDEN, *Henry Fielding : a Memoir, including newly discovered letters and records with illustrations from contemporary prints* (1910).

WILBUR L. CROSS, *The History of Henry Fielding,* 3 vols., Yale University Press (1918).

(b) LITERARY HISTORY AND CRITICISM

Among innumerable essays in literary criticism those by Gosse, W. E Henley, G. Saintsbury, and Leslie Stephen, are particularly noteworthy. Several articles by Dobson, scattered among his numerous collections, are excellent. Henley's article is reprinted in his *Essays,* Vol. I. (1908).

THE NOVELS OF FIELDING

For the literary history of the period we must, of course, refer to the classical works of Mr Wilbur L. Cross, and of Sir Walter Raleigh on *The History of the Novel*. The following may also be consulted with advantage :

J. G. AMES, *The English Periodical of Men and Manners*.

JOHN M. CLAPP, *A Bibliography of English Fiction in the Eighteenth Century* (Bibliographical Society of America. Papers, vol. VI, 1911)

W. DIBELIUS, *Englische Romankunst* : *Die Technik des englischen Romans im achzehnten und zu Anfang des neunzehnten Jahrhunderts* (*Palaestra*, XCII, Berlin, 1910).

R. DUEBER, *Beiträge zu Henry Fieldings Romantechnik*, (Inaug. dissert ; Halle, 1910).

A. ESDAILE, *A List of English Tales and Prose Romances printed before* 1740 (1912).

WILLIAM FORSYTH, in his *Novels and Novelists of the XVIIIth Century in illustration of the age.* (1871. A somewhat old book, but very fully documented).

T. H. GREEN, *An Estimate of the Value and Influence of Works of Fiction in Modern Times*. This essay of T. H. Green, the Oxford philosopher, is to be found in his *Complete Works*, but it has been reprinted separately by Fred. Newton Scott (George Wahr, Ann Arbor Press, Michigan, 1911). It was written in 1862.

C. F. HORNE, *The Technique of the Novel* (New York, 1908)

C. E. MORGAN, *The Rise of the Novel of Manners* : 1600-1740 (New York, 1911)

W. L. PHELPS, *The Beginnings of the English Romantic Movement* (Boston, 1902)

G. SAINTSBURY, *The English Novel* (1913)

G. SAINTSBURY, *A History of English Prose Rhythm* (1912)

S. L. WHITCOMB, *The Study of a Novel* (1906). A very good bibliography of the history of the novel and of novelistic criticism.

BIBLIOGRAPHICAL NOTES

ON PSYCHOLOGICAL AND INTELLECTUAL EVOLUTION

L. CAZAMIAN, *L'evolution psychologique et la litterature en Angleterre* : 1660-1914 (Paris, 1920)

LESLIE STEPHEN, *The History of English Thought in the Eighteenth Century* (1876-81)

(c) SOCIAL AND LITERARY ASPECTS OF THE EIGHTEENTH CENTURY

Here again the sources are innumerable. It would be impossible to give even an abridged list of the journals, periodicals, correspondence, and memoirs which might be worth consulting. Methodical research is only possible through the medium of the British Museum catalogue. Certain works are invaluable as guides to the period, e.g., those of *Andrews, Doran,* and *Sydney,* all three of which are old but of considerable worth. The collections of more or less authentic anecdotes are particularly untrustworthy.

A. ANDREWS, *A History of British Journalism* (1859)

A. ANDREWS, *The Eighteenth Century,* 2 vols. (1856)

A. BARBEAU, *Une ville d'eaux anglaise au XVIII siècle : la société elegante et littéraire à Bath sous la reine Anne et les Georges* (Paris, 1904)

G. T. BURROWS, *Some Old English Inns* (1907)

E. B. CHANCELLOR, *The Annals of Fleet Street* (1912)

A. DOBSON, *Eighteenth Century Vignettes* (1892-6) ; *Side Walk Studies* (1902) ; *At Prior Park and other papers* (1912) ; etc.

DORAN, London in the Jacobite Times, 2 vols. (1877)

AUGUSTIN FILON, *La caricature en Angleterre* (Paris, 1902)

C. G. HARPER, *The Bath Road* (1899)

253

THE NOVELS OF FIELDING

C. G. HARPER, *The Old Inns of Old England* ; 2 vols. (1906)

L. MELVILLE, *Bath under Beau Nash* (1907)

R. E. M. PEACH, *Life and Times of Ralph Allen ; introduced by account of Lyncombe and Widcombe, with notices of his contemporaries* (1895)

R. E. M. PEACH, *Bath, Old and New* (1888)

J. W. PERONNE, *Ueber englische Zustaende im 18 ten Jahrhundert nach den Romanen von Fielding u. Smollett* (Berlin, 1890)

W. C. SYDNEY, *England and the English in the Eighteenth Century*, 2 vols. (1891)

H. B. WHEATLEY, *Hogarth's London : pictures of manners of the eighteenth century* (1909)

C. A. WHITTUCK, *The Good Man of the Eighteenth Century : a monograph on XVIIIth Century didactic literature* (1901)

H. T. WOOD, *Industrial England in the Middle of the Eighteenth Century* (1910)

(d) QUESTIONS RELATING TO THE NOVELS

(1) *Joseph Andrews :*

E. BOSDORF, *Enstehungsgeschichte von Fieldings Joseph Andrews* (Weimar, 1908)

H. R. SCHACHT, *Der gute Pfarrer in der englischen Literatur bis zu Goldsmiths Vicar of Wakefield* (Inaug. dissert., Berlin, 1904)

C. L. THOMSON, *Samuel Richardson : a critical study* (1900)

(2) *Jonathan Wild :*

F. W. CHANDLER, *The Literature of Roguery*, 2 vols. (1907)
Eighteenth Century Literature : an Oxford miscellany (1909)

(3)   *Tom Jones and Amelia :*

R. LE BOSSU, *Traité du Poëme Epique* (Paris, 1714)
Monsieur Bossu's Treatise of the Epick Poem, 2 vols. (1719)
JOHN BROWN, *Essay on the Characteristics* (1751)
P. CLEMENT, *Les cinq années littéraires* (1748-1752), 4 vols.,
   (La Haye, 1754)
A. A. COOPER, *A Vindication of my Lord Shaftesbury*, etc.
   (1751)
MORVAN DE BELLEGARDE, *Reflections upon Ridicule*
   (1739)
W. WHITEHEAD, *An Essay on Ridicule* (1753)